Educating Deaf Students

EDUCATING DEAF STUDENTS

From Research to Practice

Marc Marschark

Harry G. Lang

John A. Albertini

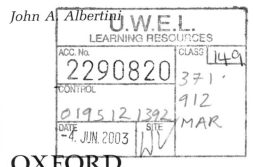

OXFORD
UNIVERSITY PRESS

2002

OXFORD
UNIVERSITY PRESS

Oxford   New York
Athens   Auckland   Bangkok   Bogotá   Buenos Aires   Cape Town
Chennai   Dar es Salaam   Delhi   Florence   Hong Kong   Istanbul   Karachi
Kolkata   Kuala Lumpur   Madrid   Melbourne   Mexico City   Mumbai   Nairobi
Paris   São Paulo   Shanghai   Singapore   Taipei   Tokyo   Toronto   Warsaw

and associated companies in
Berlin   Ibadan

Copyright © 2002 by Oxford University Press, Inc.

Published by Oxford University Press, Inc.
198 Madison Avenue, New York, New York 10016
http://www.oup-usa.org

Oxford is a registered trademark of Oxford University Press.

Library of Congress Cataloging-in-Publication Data
Marschark, Marc.
Educating deaf students : from research to practice / Marc Marschark,
Harry G. Lang, John A. Albertini
      p.   cm.
Includes bibliographical reference and index.
ISBN 0-19-512139-2
1. Deaf—Education.   2. Deaf children—Education.   3. Deaf children—Language.
4. Deaf children—Means of communication.   I. Lang, Harry G.
II. Albertini, John A. (John Anthony), 1945–   III. Title.
HV2437 .M27 2001
371.91'2—dc21   00-140070

9 8 7 6 5 4 3 2 1

Printed in the United States of America
on acid-free paper

To

Janie, Bonnie, & Kathi

for their patience, support, and perspective.

Preface

The field known as *deaf education* has undergone considerable change over the past decades. In part, this situation reflects the evolution of understanding concerning deaf people and American Sign Language. The magnitude of this change, however, owes much to progress in pedagogy, developmental psychology, psycholinguistics (including language acquisition), and other related fields. Together with dramatic changes in technology, scientific progress has provided new options and new perspectives for parents, students, and teachers.

We also have to acknowledge the fact that this book was written early in the new millennium. Perhaps caught up in the excitement of it all, but also with genuine commitment, we felt the need to share our optimistic, but realistic, view of what the future holds for parents and educators of deaf children, as well as for the children themselves. Given the progress of the past few decades and the sense of new beginnings, we thought that it was important to consider the education of deaf students from the perspective of *what we know* rather than *what we want*. In deciding to provide a research-based framework for educating deaf students, we sought to set aside as much as possible the politics, rhetoric, and confusion that often accompany such discussions. In the chapters that follow, we therefore consider the educational and research literature with an eye toward systematic inquiry and generality of findings. As far as the current state of the art allows, we summarize what we know about educating deaf students and draw implications for parents, teachers, and other interested parties.

Approaching the topic in this way, it became clear to us that some of the common assumptions that have driven deaf education for many years were based on methods, conclusions, or interpretations for which the validity is less than certain. For example, we will discuss how a variety of early (i.e., 1950s–1970s) studies concerning cognitive abilities of deaf children were based on the assumption that the findings reflected functioning *in the absence of language*. The failure to recognize American Sign Language (ASL) as a true language (it took some time for that revolutionary awareness to reach cognitive and developmental psychology) resulted in a rather skewed and inaccurate depiction of deaf individuals. The purported lack of linguistic and cognitive creativity of deaf children was based on tests involving English comprehension, and reports of shorter memory spans among deaf individuals (included on most intelligence tests) failed to take into account the fact that languages which take more time to articulate (such as ASL) take up more space in working memory. Deaf students were commonly assumed to be "deficient" or "intellectually inferior" often because investigators and teachers did not know how to communicate with them in the way that elicited optimal performance.

Beginning in the 1970s, there was a move by many hearing people— all with their hearts in the right place—to treat deaf individuals more fairly. But, as Paolo Freire (1970) noted, revolution for the people is revolution against the people; true change has to be *with*, not *for*, those who are oppressed. As commonly happens when a pendulum has been far to one side, it came back equally far in the other direction. Years of empty bias against deaf children were replaced with a seemingly uncritical acceptance of the assumption that there are no differences between deaf and hearing learners except for their hearing (an assumption that we will show to be wrong and potentially detrimental to the education of deaf children).

For example, intelligence tests that previously were far from culturally fair with regard to deaf children were replaced by tests designed using the criterion that deaf and hearing children are essentially identical, and subsequent studies using those tests concluded (circularly) that the assumption was true. It still remains unclear, however, whether the finding of similar distributions of deaf and hearing children's scores on nonverbal IQ tests really indicates that the two populations have comparable intelligence or is a consequence of the way in which the tests were constructed. If verbal (i.e., language-based) IQ is not important for deaf children, why do we continue to use it with hearing children?

Similarly, the lackluster results of English-based signing and Simultaneous Communication in supporting literacy development in deaf learners led to a fervent embrace of ASL and bilingual ASL-English programs as the solution to the *English* challenges of deaf learners. While the potential importance of sign language for most young deaf children seems beyond reasonable doubt, the theoretical rationale and empirical evidence for ASL serving as a bridge to English literacy are slim, at best. More important, we have been remarkably lax in holding such approaches to the same standards that led to the rejection, in many quarters, of English-based signing. In short, it seems no more valid now to reject out of hand all things "oral" or "inclusive" than it used to be to reject all things "manual" or related to being Deaf.

The use of *Deaf* in the previous sentence puts the reader on notice that, throughout this book, we distinguish the characteristic of being deaf (that is, "without hearing") from having an identity of Deaf. In the latter case, references to Deaf people, the Deaf community, and Deaf culture all indicate a group of individuals who constitute linguistic and cultural minorities in many countries and who often see themselves as an international, cross-cultural community. This is not a usage for the purposes of political correctness, but one that we believe must be taken into consideration if one is to understand the full complexity of the population we are educating. At the same time, the use of terms such as *deaf students* rather than more cumbersome constructions like "students who are deaf" or "students with hearing loss" reflect both a desire for readability and recognition that for many deaf individuals, their deafness is not an audiological characteristic, but a personal and primary one.

Above all else, this book is intended as an objective assessment of what we know and do not know about the education and development of deaf learners, and we bring to its writing a number of beliefs that guide us as teachers and researchers. Surprisingly, for three individuals who come from rather different backgrounds, there has been considerable convergence. Although perhaps we would not all have used the terms before, we found that we shared a cognitive orientation on deaf children's development and a social constructivist view of their education. Our unabashedly cognitive orientation means that we see various aspects of linguistic, social, and academic growth as linked to various mental processes underlying learning and other behavior (e.g., social perspective, memory, problem solving, knowledge organization). The social constructivism in our approach reflects our belief that learning is shaped by the sociocultural contexts in which it occurs. We also include healthy doses of environmental and biological contributions to learning, but believe that as the basic processes and structures of development fall into place, cognitive control comes into play to make deaf learners active participants in shaping the course of their own futures.

Perhaps most centrally, our thinking about deaf learners clearly has been molded by our understanding of the roles of communication and language throughout development and education. Communication is the tie that binds children to parents and to society and that provides for social and academic education. There is no aspect of educating deaf learners— from infancy to adulthood—that does not depend on or benefit from clear and accessible communication.

To some readers, parts of this book at first may seem disheartening, suggesting that there are more questions than answers with regard to the educational progress of deaf children. There *always* will be more questions than answers, but that does not mean that we are lacking successes. More progress has been made in educating deaf students during the last 30 years than in the previous 300. We know a lot about what works and what does not work to promote learning, language development, and literacy, even if there is still a long way to go. And a variety of practices central to the academic achievement of deaf students have come about as a function of basic and applied research: the use of more visually oriented teaching strategies, hands-on learning activities, the early use of sign language to enhance language and cognitive development, emphasizing relations among concepts, and many others to be described later.

Our goal in the following chapters is to present such information in a way that will be useful to teachers, parents, and other professionals. We believe that it is essential to consider both formal and informal education in the context of development and with a full understanding of the real world in which both are embedded. It would not do much good to propose educational methods for an ideal classroom (*mention*, yes; *propose*, no), when teachers are limited in the resources and administrative patience that are available. Similarly, although we do not believe that parents should be consumed with making every minute of the day educationally relevant, we will describe a variety of ways in which everyday situations can be structured to provide deaf children with opportunities for learning. In some cases, these opportunities will offset challenges related to growing up deaf and will level the playing field. In other cases, we suggest activities that can enhance motivation for learning and academic outcomes for all children.

In bringing together our diverse backgrounds and what we believed to be (at least, originally) diverse perspectives, we have found an unexpected synergy—the whole really is greater than the sum of its parts! Each of us was educated by the other two, giving up old assumptions that were found to be without basis and accepting new ideas previously removed from our own experience. Observing such changes in ourselves, appreciating our diversity, and sharing (or trying to) our enthusiasm when day-to-day responsibilities seemed overwhelming only added to our belief in what we were writing. The very challenges that we encountered in producing this book reflected the challenges confronted by parents and teachers who seek to optimize learning by sifting through alternatives and accepting the frustration of trial-and-error efforts of trying different strategies to find something that works. Happily, having gone through this ourselves, we will be able to save others some of the effort.

Perhaps part of the synergy that we found in writing together involved a syzygy. Normally used to refer to an alignment of planets, in this case we found that our different perspectives lined up in a way that we would not have seen working independently. Indeed, we had never noticed it before and had seen ourselves as laboring in related but distinct areas. Actually, that is where another aspect of syzygy comes in. This book was an accident. The three of us were meeting together regularly as a writing club, a mutual support group for obtaining feedback and overcoming writer's block. As we were closing out the millennium, we realized that just as we were benefiting from the experience ourselves, a similar exercise might be useful for deaf students as a means of learning from others and gaining pride in their writing. This realization fit with what we knew from research concerning literacy, social-emotional development, and the teaching-learning process. Voilá! Syzygy, synergy, and this book was born.

Occasionally—nay, rarely—during our writing, one of us was forced to conform to the preferences of the others in either emphasizing or deemphasizing a particular point that was held dear. Overall, such occurrences were spread remarkably evenly, and each of us believes that the collective "voice" is both stronger and better tempered than any of us could have provided alone. At the same time, our hope is that the three perspectives blend together seamlessly here, and that we can continue to blend them in the future for the benefit of deaf children, their parents, their teachers, and all others involved in educating deaf students.

In reminding ourselves that there is wisdom in diverse perspectives, we also express our appreciation to those who have shared theirs with us. A number of people have provided us with opinions, information, material, and moral support for this book. Others have read earlier drafts and provided us with feedback or explained to us the errors of our ways. For all of this, we gratefully acknowledge the contributions of Camille Aidala, Mark Benjamin, Joseph Bochner, Tony DeCasper, Karen Emmorey, Rosemary Garrity, Doug MacKenzie, Heather Maltzen, Joy Markowitz, Kathryn P. Meadow-Orlans (from whom we also borrowed the title of the final chapter), Jonathan Millis, Lori Nieman, Louise Paatsch, Robert Q. Pollard, Shannon Patton, Barbara Raimando, Donald Rhoten, Lauren Salomon, Larry Scott, Nora Shannon, Patricia Spencer, Michael Stinson, Dean Woolever, and the Western Pennsylvania School for the Deaf, as well as the many parents and teachers who shared with us stories, challenges, and successes involving their children. Joan Bossert, Catharine Carlin, and Oxford University Press also deserve honorable mention here for their seemingly infinite patience as we struggled to write this book in our spare time (such as it is), and allowing us to draw on *Raising and Educating a Deaf Child* (1997) and *Psychological Development of Deaf Children*, Second Edition (forthcoming). Finally, we acknowledge and remember our friend and colleague, Bill Stokoe, for his wit, wisdom, and support. He will always be with us.

We are grateful for permission to reprint the following:
The schematic of a cochlear implant (figure 3.3, p. 52) is reproduced courtesy of Advanced Bionics.

The photograph of the baby with headphones (figure 4.1, p. 65) is reproduced courtesy of Anthony DeCasper.

The set of "handshapes that appear consistently across deaf infants learning ASL as a first language" (figure 5.1, p. 95) is reproduced with permission of Sugar Sign Press © 1988.

The sample from *Reading Milestones* (figure 8.1, p. 167) is reproduced courtesy of Pro-Ed.

The photograph of men working in a print shop (p. 16) and the photograph of students in a CAD lab (p. 227) appear courtesy of the National Technical Institute for the Deaf.

All other photographs appear courtesy of the Western Pennsylvania School for the Deaf.

September 2000   Marc Marschark
                                                   Harry G. Lang
                                                   John A. Albertini

Contents

PART I

Educational Basics

What factors are most important in the development and education of deaf students?

What role does research play in informing us of the best educational practices to follow in educating deaf students?

1

ONE

Educating Deaf Students: An Introduction

Consider this passage from a letter written by Robert H. Weitbrecht, a physicist who was born deaf and went on to change the lives of deaf people throughout the world:

> Perhaps I was more fortunate than the average deaf child. My family had upheavals during my teens— my father passed away and we had difficult circumstances. My mother had faith in me and saw to it that I was given the best possible chance during these times. (Weitbrecht to Srnka, 1966)

As a young boy, Weitbrecht had difficulties learning to speak. His parents and teachers were not sure about his potential to acquire a normal education. Weitbrecht was teased by his peers because of his deafness. He did not have very positive self-esteem, and he was not happy in school. Despite the doubts and challenges, he went on to earn several academic degrees. In 1964, Weitbrecht developed a modem ("acoustic coupler") which enabled deaf people to use the telephone via a teletypewriter (TTY). Weitbrecht's modem was a major breakthrough in the lives of deaf and hard-of-hearing people, who had waited more than 90 years since the invention of the voice telephone by Alexander Graham Bell. It brought to them both access and independence with regard to long-distance communication.

Weitbrecht's story is one of a young deaf child with questionable abilities who went on to be successful in his chosen field. It is also a story that has often been repeated (Lang & Meath-Lang, 1995). Despite all of the hurdles which have threatened to thwart their progress, deaf people have found ways to go over, under, and around the barriers of attitude and access to distinguish themselves in many fields of endeavor. Imagine how much more they could do if society did not make it so hard for them.

This book is about learning, teaching, and the education of children who are deaf or hard of hearing, but it is not intended solely for those who make

their living by teaching. Rather, it is intended for parents, service providers, policymakers, and lay readers as well as teachers—anyone interested in the education of deaf children, whether or not they have a formal educational role. Our primary goals are to highlight the relationship between the development and education of deaf children and, in so doing, provide the reader with a rich understanding of what it means to be deaf, the abilities and needs of young deaf learners, and a broad perspective on educating them. Parents are a child's first teachers, and they will continue their teaching role in one form or another throughout their lives.

Whether deaf or hearing, the course of development for each child is a complex mosaic of formal and informal teaching-learning, the acquisition of knowledge and skills, and opportunities to test what has been learned. In most cases, observing the consequences of such efforts feeds back into the teaching-learning process and development itself. For that reason, we begin this book with the premise that to understand either the development or education of deaf students, we need to understand both.

Learning and Development

In the most general sense, development is a lifelong process of maturation and growth, regardless of whether we are talking about cognitive, social, physical, psychological, or academic domains. Education, on the other hand, normally is thought of as including planned and unplanned activities that foster development, while also building on it. In this book we examine some of the relations between development and education, with particular regard to the education of deaf children. The various chapters, as well as other sources of information about deaf children or hearing children to which the reader is referred, make it clear that there are many perspectives and approaches to each of these domains. Understanding the complex linkage between education and development in deaf or hearing children is a daunting task, but the path has been forged by the pioneering work of people like Piaget and Montessori with hearing children and Meadow-Orlans and Furth with deaf children.

It would be nice if there were a single, *correct* approach to educating deaf children, one for which we could describe a "theory of instruction." Unfortunately, this is not the case, and to even suggest such a thing often is seen as insulting or is relegated to strawman status. Neither children nor education is that simple, and yet the search for unitary, simple solutions persists. When it comes to deaf students, the search for unitary answers seems to occur most frequently with regard to communication. Advocates of a single mode of communication, whether it be sign language, spoken language, or a created sign system, do not have any strong evidence indicating that one form of communication is sufficient for all aspects of education, especially when literacy is at issue. The view taken in this book is that these are empirical questions, best left to classroom and laboratory research, rather than something that can be resolved by discussion alone. Toward this end, this book is aimed at providing state-of-the-art information concerning the foundations, processes, and outcomes of educating deaf students as based on available research findings.

> **Despite all of the hurdles which have threatened to thwart their progress, deaf people have found ways to go over, under, and around the barriers of attitude and access to distinguish themselves in many fields of endeavor. Imagine how much more they could do if society did not make it so hard for them.**

As will become clear, we believe that education is an eclectic endeavor, one in which parents and teachers constantly need to increase their knowledge and can always improve their methods. Simply put, we do whatever works, and what works in one context with one child may not work in another context with another. Armed with this orientation, we would like to think that we are not bound by any particular theoretical perspective or a priori biases. But there are two caveats.

First, we come to the educational enterprise with a *social constructivist* perspective. By that, we mean that the world as we know it—or will learn about it—is structured largely by the culture and the experiences from which we view it. Whether we are discussing language, science, or history, our understanding of objects and events around us is influenced by the knowledge and experience that we bring to the situation, as well as by the sharing of knowledge and experience with others.

A social constructivist approach to education places the teacher in the strategic role of encouraging learning and development as a social and cultural activity. Knowledge is not viewed as a commodity to be transferred from teacher to student. Rather, the teacher establishes meaningful contexts to help the students construct understanding. The emphasis in social constructivism applied to the classroom thus is on the primary role of communication and social life in meaning formation and in cognition. The educator approaching instruction from a social constructivist perspective guides the student in identifying existing concepts stored in long-term memory and in building new concepts and relationships. Thus, learning is both an active and a *dialogical*, two-way, process.

The second caveat is, in a sense, a product of the social constructivist perspective. As teachers and researchers ourselves, we have used our collective experience to synthesize existing research in several domains and arrive at some conclusions about ways to optimize the educational success of deaf students. It is because of this accumulated knowledge that we have come to believe that a book on the education of deaf students must speak to parents as well as to classroom teachers, policymakers, and school principals. Also on the basis of our review of educational and developmental research, we provide throughout the book objective explanations and suggestions for real-life educational situations. If biases emerge from careful research and even more careful consideration of results and their generalizability, so be it. Our goal, however, is not to further a particular educational approach but rather to ensure that any educational approach adopted has the best chance of success given what we know about child development, learning, and teaching.

Unifying Educational Themes

Although most of us involved in the education of deaf students believe that both our specific activities and general approaches to the teaching-learning process are all aimed at enhancing the academic pursuits of our wards, neither our methods nor our underlying assumptions are necessarily the same. We often are influenced by our own educational backgrounds, both in terms of our own school experiences and any formal training we might have had in education or related fields. In our quest for objectivity and consideration of available research, we do not intend to argue that coming to the educational context with a particular theoretical or pedagogical orientation is necessarily a bad thing. While we all might try to do whatever works in a particular educational setting, a focus only on the practicalities of getting across a particular concept or a particular subject matter runs the risk of teaching isolated facts or skills, rather than providing students with the knowledge necessary to be flexible in the face of novel situations and new information. An underlying understanding of the nature of learning and development is an essential component to teaching children how to learn, regardless of whether they are deaf or hearing. If we truly want deaf students to succeed, we must confront environmental and methodological barriers to education and to appropriate educational assessment. *If there is a problem, it is much more likely to be found in the way that we teach and what we expect from deaf students than in the students themselves.*

Throughout the various topics covered in this book, we will regularly come back to three factors that have preeminent importance in understanding and optimizing deaf children's educational and psychological interactions with the world: (1) early access to language, (2) social interactions, and (3) diversity in both object- and person-oriented experience. In addition to this developmental-educational triumvirate, four other themes have emerged from our study of the assumptions and outcomes in educating deaf students:

- The importance of parent advocacy and involvement in their children's education
- The need for diversity and flexibility in learning styles, teaching styles, and educational tools
- The importance of teaching to children's strengths, building on what is known
- The need to understand "the whole child" in order to best match educational methods with student characteristics.

Because they will emerge as major themes throughout the following chapters, it is not necessary for us to consider these four topics in any detail at this point. It is nonetheless important to remember that our understanding of the educational process for deaf children (and teachers' abilities to foster their learning) are made more difficult by the fact that, as a group, deaf children are likely to be more heterogeneous than hearing children. Deaf children generally are affected by the same factors influencing hearing children: their social environments, their families, and so on. Deaf children frequently also have additional challenges not experienced by hearing children, however, such as medical conditions related to the cause of their hearing loss,

An underlying understanding of the nature of learning and development is an essential component to teaching children how to learn, regardless of whether they are deaf or hearing.

parents' difficulties in accepting disability, and barriers to access in the home, school, and community.

Schooling for deaf students is evolving at a fairly rapid rate due to educational, scientific, and legal changes in many countries. In most cases, these changes have contributed to a much better understanding of the needs of deaf students and to greater educational opportunities, even if they have created ambiguity with regard to some practical issues. We now know, for example, that deaf children whose deaf parents expose them to sign language as their first language acquire that language at the same rate and with the same milestones as hearing children acquire spoken language from hearing parents (Meier & Newport, 1990; see Siple, 1997, for a review). Deaf children of deaf parents also frequently exhibit academic skills beyond those of same-age deaf peers with hearing parents (for reviews, see Marschark, 1993; Moores & Meadows-Orlans, 1990). Findings like these support the viability (but not the necessity) of academic instruction for deaf children through sign language, while contributing significantly to our larger understanding of interactions between learning and language development. Perhaps most important, such results indicate that one cannot ascribe observed educational challenges among deaf students to their hearing losses or to their lack of spoken language skills. Clearly, other factors are involved, and a significant body of research has focused on differences between deaf children from deaf families and those from hearing families, as well as comparisons of both to hearing children from hearing families.

A relatively recent change in the education of deaf children has been the broad establishment of early intervention programs for young deaf children and their families. As we will see, early intervention programs vary in their communication orientations and the range of services they offer, but early enrollment appears to be one of the single best predictors of deaf children's optimal development and academic success, as it is for other children with special needs (Calderon & Greenberg, 1997; Carney & Moeller, 1988).

Education and the Research Enterprise

Both the development of our own teaching styles and, more specifically, the content of this book have been shaped by our understanding of research in education, child development, language learning, and other fields. As research continues to inform us about how human cognition works and how it changes over time, theories and methods of teaching and learning will continue to evolve. Every teacher constructs (implicitly if not explicitly) a personal conception of effective instruction, and that understanding will change over time with personal experience, aided by systematic inquiry. Parents also construct an understanding of their role in their deaf child's development and education. This internal model undergoes constant revision that also can be aided by timely information. As evidenced by the themes of this book, we believe that all those involved in the education of deaf students should welcome such evolution. Further, the more informed we are by research, the fewer debates we will engage in fueled by emotion rather than by reason, and the better we will use our valuable time to enhance educational opportunities for deaf students.

The topics described in the following chapters, as well as the specific situations and examples we use, are intended to support the development and evolution of personal models, attitudes, and knowledge about educating deaf students. To accomplish this, we provide the results of recent research in a context that makes them clear and personally meaningful rather than seeming academic and remote. Knowing what others have found through various investigations and their own experience with deaf students is an efficient way of gaining knowledge on the subject. Research is, simply speaking, planned, systematic inquiry. It may be in the form of controlled empirical studies, interviews with parents, action research in the classroom, in-depth analyses of what deaf and hearing children tell us about how they learn, or numerous other approaches. With a minimum of research jargon, we summarize and, where necessary, interpret the existing research so as to inform parents, teachers, and other educational gatekeepers of their potential to positively influence the education of deaf students.

Some of the findings and conclusions described in this book may seem counterintuitive, and others may seem incomplete. Certainly, most research is incomplete insofar as it raises additional questions. This does not mean that the original questions were trivial or easily resolved. It means that we, like our students, are always constructing and refining our knowledge. Readers therefore should not assume that any of the specific conclusions described will apply to all students in all contexts. Those findings that are both *valid* (truly reflecting the states of affairs they are purported to reflect) and *reliable* (able to be duplicated in various settings with different participants) will stand on their own as representing our current knowledge in the field. The research synthesis and the consistent threads that have emerged should be self-evident with regard to their implications for policy and practice.

It is important to acknowledge at the outset that a variety of investigations have indicated that relative to hearing peers of the same age, many deaf children demonstrate lags in several academic domains. As we shall see, those lags often disappear over time or can be avoided entirely when children are provided with early access to the full range of language and other experiences of their hearing peers. In many cases, this will involve exposure to sign language in addition to, or instead of, spoken language. Although it is clear that a signed language can provide all of the content and linguistically relevant information of a spoken language, it may well be that there are areas in which signing provides deaf children with both advantages and disadvantages. Many parents and educators, for example, are concerned about the effectiveness of sign language in providing a bridge to reading and writing, an issue that we will consider later. Although there is strong sentiment to assume that signed and spoken languages are fully equivalent in their academic consequences and other domains, the question is one worthy of discussion. The following chapters, therefore, will provide an overview of the course of language development among children as well as careful consideration of the ways in which it influences other academic and nonacademic spheres of development.

Teachers and researchers, just like their students, always need to be constructing and refining their knowledge.

Even beyond the language issue, any attempt to integrate the diverse body of related research touched on in this book is sure to raise a number of social and political issues concerning the education of deaf children. Despite the recognition of Deaf people as a linguistic and cultural minority group in this country, there has been a move away from residential schools and educational methods that long served as an important source of cultural information for this group. The change certainly is related to the long-running debate about the best methods for educating deaf children, but the primary impetus for it came from elsewhere (see chapter 7). Additional perspectives have blended into the discussion, and social constructions have been added to educational theory in explorations of what works for whom and when (Gregory & Hindley, 1996).

Avoiding Some Pitfalls

In providing an integration of the evidence relevant to education and development among deaf children, we should warn readers that what might seem like dichotomies in this field often really represent two ends of a continuum. For example, it might already have been noticed that we typically refer to "deaf children" rather than "deaf and hard-of-hearing children." Indeed, implicit throughout this book is an apparent dichotomy between "deaf" and "hearing," with "hard-of-hearing" left somewhere in between.

The distinction between deaf and hearing may seem clear in the case of normally hearing children and profoundly deaf children. However, a hearing aid, cochlear implant, or use of residual hearing may provide auditory information to a profoundly deaf child *in support of* language development and learning, even if they do not provide for the full perception of language (see chapter 2). Auditory signals may indicate that an event is happening, call attention to relations between events and language in the environment, or communicate social information such as turn taking demands or the emotions of others.

For both practical and theoretical reasons, most research concerning the education of deaf children, as well as a number of other domains, has focused primarily on those who have the earliest and most severe hearing losses. This situation largely results from the fact that as the age of onset and amount of residual hearing increase, spoken language and interactions with hearing individuals become increasingly available and part of a young child's language repertoire. There often will be less explicit intervention than is the case for children with greater hearing losses (as well as perhaps less need for such intervention).

Methodologically, the relative influences on educational progress of hearing loss, language experience, and the quality and frequency of social or other experiences become more blurred, and the experimental control needed for many kinds of research is lost. It also becomes more difficult to confidently ascribe observed differences among deaf children or between deaf and hearing children to any particular factor, deafness related or not. The fact that deaf children tend to be more heterogeneous than hearing children only makes this situation more complex. None of this should cause the reader any hesitation with regard to the remainder of this book, because we have taken care to hedge where hedging is necessary and be definitive where that is possible. It may be disappointing, however, to find that some particularly interesting questions have not yet been answered.

For the present purposes, the terms *deaf* and *hard of hearing* refer to children with severe to profound and mild to moderate hearing losses, respectively. At the same time, it will be helpful to keep in mind that the acquisition of sign language by most deaf children is supported by spoken language, which brings us to a second dichotomy.

The distinction between "spoken language" and "sign language," while a theoretically important one for linguists and other investigators, is clearly an oversimplification. It is rare that deaf children are exposed only to spoken language or only to sign language, even if that is the intention of their parents or their teachers. The realities of the world are such that even while spoken language predominates in the environment, most deaf children are still exposed to sign language either formally or informally. Usually, therefore, it is more helpful to focus on which language modality is *primary* for a particular child, a circumstance often determined by the hearing status of the parents (Calderon & Greenberg, 1997; Mayberry & Eichen, 1991). But even the designation of primary mode of communication is not entirely clear. Particular deaf parents or children with some residual hearing might benefit from spoken language while still using sign language in particular contexts. Similarly, even when deaf children are educated in spoken-language environments, systems of gestural communication may develop between parents and children. Such variability will play an important role in the language models available to deaf children. The mixing of spoken and sign languages also will be considered in assessing the influence of early sign language on the development of spoken and written English skills and the implications of bilingual educational settings.

Problems of interpretation also may arise in attempts to compare the academic success of deaf children who are educated using sign language and deaf children who are educated using spoken language. Such comparisons represent one of the most popular and potentially informative areas in research relating to language development and education among children with hearing loss, but they are also one of the most intractable. Educational programs emphasizing spoken or sign language often have different educational philosophies and curricula as well as different communication philosophies. They may have admissions policies that give preference to children with particular histories of early intervention or hearing profiles, and parents will be drawn to different programs for a variety of reasons. Thus, differences observed between students in any two educational programs might be the result of any of a number of variables, and we have no way of knowing whether the children were equivalent at the outset.

> **The distinction between *spoken language* and *sign language*, while a theoretically important one for linguists and other investigators, is clearly an oversimplification.**

Seeking Relationships and Regularities

The issue of the relative differences between groups of deaf students in different educational settings will be of particular importance in chapter 7, when we compare deaf children in local schools (*mainstream* educational programs) with those in special schools or programs designed for deaf students. In that context, we also will be confronted with several issues concerning the interaction of both teaching and learning with students' language fluencies. Developmental and educational achievement of deaf children clearly will be affected by an interaction between degree of hearing loss and the communication fluency of adults around them who serve as informal and formal teachers. Young deaf children of hearing parents frequently do not have any truly accessible and competent language models, either for sign language or for spoken language. To the extent that language acquisition is positively related to the diversity of adult models available and social reinforcement from those models, deaf children clearly will be at some disadvantage in a variety of educational settings. It will not always be apparent when the difficulty is one of communication versus what is to be communicated. In both of these domains, it will be important to distinguish superficial differences due to the modalities of language used from underlying abilities (including language) that have far-reaching implications for the ever-increasing scope of academic tasks.

The use of the term *superficial* here is not intended to subtly bias readers with regard to a particular perspective on either language or education for deaf children. Rather, it is intended to start the discussion with a neutral stance, recognizing the equal potentials of alternative approaches to education. Nevertheless, it is important to recognize that observed differences between children acquiring a spoken language and those acquiring a signed language as their first language may or may not have long-term implications for development or academic success. Apparent differences between the two modes of communication may result from either the specific behavior under consideration or from the context in which it occurs. For example, the language used by a deaf preschooler may not affect social relations with peers significantly because many such interactions depend primarily on nonverbal communication. Language modality may have significant impact on social functioning during the school years, however, depending on whether the child's peers are hearing or deaf (i.e., whether the school is a mainstream setting or a residential school). Similarly, we need to be aware of possible interactions of hearing loss, language, and other aspects of development.

Discussions concerning deaf children's educational progress frequently focus on the nature of observed or hypothesized relationships between hearing status and specific domains (e.g., peer relations, problem solving, literacy). Beyond any direct effects of hearing loss (i.e., those relating to hearing and to speech), there are other consequences of children's hearing loss that are likely to affect academic achievement. These factors, in turn, may influence other aspects of development, resulting in differences among children which vary according to the environment.

In summary, there are several obstacles to conducting and interpreting research on language development in deaf children, due to both *nature* and *nurture* factors. If some of these issues appear minor from the perspective of a competent adult language user, they certainly are not trivial in the context of language and other domains of development. The challenge is to discover the mix of experiences that have real impact on development and, in a research context, to distinguish them from factors that are irrelevant (Nelson, Loncke, & Camarata, 1993).

Looking Ahead

If the following chapters are grounded in research and practice, they also are carefully measured so as not to overgeneralize or underestimate the challenge of teaching deaf students in any context. This approach to the teaching-learning process is a reflection of the way in which we teach our own students. By providing our students with both the work of others and in-depth discussions of the key issues, they come to understand the content of our courses as well as why things are the way they are.

One of our goals is to dispel some long-standing myths and misunderstandings in deaf education (as well as in education at large). We also will explain some of the dangers of establishing educational methods on the basis of investigations that may or may not have been shown to be of general utility. At the same time, summarizing relevant research will clarify how we arrived at this point and provide information that will be immediately and directly useful for those interested in optimizing home, school, and community learning environments for deaf learners.

At the beginning of this chapter, we introduced Robert Weitbrecht, one of the inventors of the modem that gave deaf people access to the telephone. Weitbrecht's mother, Winifred M. Weitbrecht (1887–1973) once reflected on the kinds of issues we have raised in a personal essay about her son entitled *Making the Grade*. At the end of her unpublished essay, she added a handwritten note:

> It is my hope that some part in this simple story of my son's success may help a worried parent, as the experience of others has helped me. By living one day at a time, with hope and patience and the firm faith that in God, all things work together for good; misery and despair cannot prevail—and by unflinching courageous effort, a beneficial climate can be created, in which the deaf child will prosper and overcome his handicap, and grow to be a happy, useful member of society. (W. Weitbrecht, n.d.)

As the Weitbrechts knew, parents can make a difference in their children's education. Indeed, as we will see, parental involvement in curricular and extracurricular activities is one of the best predictors of children's academic success. In addition to the usual kinds of questions that all parents have about their children in school, however, parents of deaf children also want answers to some unique questions: What kind of language experience is best for my child, speech or sign language? Will my child ever learn to speak normally? What kind of school is best? These questions are not as simple as they might appear, but there is sufficient information available to allow parents to make informed decisions. This book is intended to bring some balance to that discussion and provide both the content and context necessary for them as well as for teachers, other school officials, and service providers.

Each of us can make a difference.

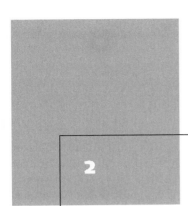

How has schooling for deaf children been viewed at different points in history?

What have been some of the key historical influences on educational policy?

2

TWO

Lessons from History

The adage "those who do not learn from history are doomed to repeat it" is a powerful one for parents and teachers of deaf students. Myths that have grown from ignorance have dogged us in this field as far back as we can see, and faulty assumptions and overgeneralizations have been sustained through time. A study of history also reveals what at first might seem like a series of random events, but which actually manifest patterns that have influenced today's educational policy (see Fischer & Lane, 1993; Van Cleve, 1993). These patterns are related to several themes critical to the emphases of this book. One such theme is the importance of parental involvement in the education of deaf children. History provides us with factual accounts and anecdotes that enrich our understanding of the advocacy roles parents have played, especially with regard to the establishment of school programs. As we shall see, research clearly supports the role of parental involvement in both formal and informal education, as evidenced in studies demonstrating the long-term influence of mother–child relationships and early communication and the need for providing deaf children with a variety of experiences during the early years.

Another theme that emerges from a historical perspective relates to how deaf people have taken an increasingly greater role in influencing their own education. Histories have been published that describe how deafness was perceived in ancient times, how various societies changed with regard to their attitudes toward deaf people, and that highlight the turning points in the education and acceptance of people who are deaf. In most published histories of deaf education, we see the long-standing conflicts through the centuries pertaining to sign language and spoken communication philosophies and the contributions of the individuals who founded school programs or attempted to teach deaf children. Often, however, writers have neglected to examine how deaf people themselves have overcome barriers in many periods of history and under a wide variety of conditions to make important contributions in education and other fields. A

history of the education of deaf individuals thus should be more than just a study of changes in educational practices. It also can serve as a study of self-empowerment by deaf people and help to describe the shaping of Deaf communities around the world.

There are also some patterns we find while studying history that have not yet influenced educational policy to the extent we believe they should. These include, for example, recognizing the need for a diverse approach to language learning, and realizing that technology can be both a boon and a bane in the education of deaf children. With regard to diversity in language learning, subsequent chapters will describe the need for educational policy that recognizes individual differences and individual needs with regard to learning environments. On the issue of technology, regardless of the seeming wonders, whether the technological advances be "magic lantern" slides of a century ago or today's hearing aids, the Internet, or cochlear implants, these are *tools*, not elixirs. Their use requires thorough understanding of their appropriate roles in the teaching/learning processes.

Along with these lessons, the study of history shows that many of the contemporary emphases in deaf education are not new and that many good practices have been lost or neglected over time. In history we find valuable techniques for instruction, such as providing metacognitive skills to enhance reading, or using writing as a process to assist learning the curriculum—emphases promoted by teachers of deaf children a century ago, but not applied extensively in today's classrooms.

There is indeed much to learn from history, and we have only begun to explore its potential as a teaching-learning tool. This chapter therefore will not only describe some of the milestones in the history of the education of deaf students, but it also will offer some of these lessons from the past which will help us to find the best approaches for educating deaf students in the twenty-first century.

The Deaf Experience in Early Times

In the context of majority cultures and societies in history, the reality of deaf people's lives has often been summarized in general terms such as "isolation," "invisibility," or "oppression." There are so few reports about deaf people before the sixteenth century that we can only hypothesize about the way they lived and how they may have been educated, if at all. In examining the few records from classical and ancient times handed down to us, however, we see that throughout history, deaf people faced a gamut of perceptions and attitudes held by community and family members.

From the time of the ancients we have only a few pieces of the puzzle, and it is not an easy task to see the picture clearly. We have records pertaining to the role of signs and gestures in the daily lives of deaf people, leading to consideration of the extent to which deaf people were seen as able to reason and communicate thousands of years ago. In Plato's *Cratylus* (360 B.C.), for example, Socrates poses a rhetorical question related to the use of signs, implying that such a form of communication was used by deaf people. There is also brief mention of deafness in the writings of Aristotle. In the fifth century B.C., Herodotus authored a history of the Greco-Persian wars, a work for which he earned the title "father of history." In one story, King Croesus says to his son Atys: "For you are the one and only son that I possess, the other, whose hearing is destroyed, I regard as if he were not" (Herodotus, 1947, p. 22). Croesus appears to disown his deaf son in this report; the deaf boy's name is never even mentioned. But we may also find a kernel of parental support in this story by looking further. As Herodotus explained, "in the days of his prosperity Croesus had done the utmost that he could for [his deaf son], and among other plans which he had devised, had sent to Delphi to consult the oracle on his behalf" (p. 47). Thus, like many contemporary parents, Croesus struggled personally with the acceptance of a deaf child and searched far and wide for advice.

In the first century A.D., we find another story of an influential parent seeking assistance for a deaf child. In *Natural History*, Pliny the Elder briefly mentions Quintus Pedius, the deaf son of a Roman consul. The father's efforts apparently paid off. Permission was granted from the emperor Augustus to allow Quintus Pedius to become an artist, and the boy became a talented painter. Occurring hundreds of years apart, these early cases reflect a role for parent advocacy in seeking educational opportunities for deaf children.

Theological literature has added some pieces to the puzzle. The Talmud, the rabbinical teachings and Jewish oral law begun in the fifth century A.D., raised the possibility of instructing deaf children. In the Mishnah of the Talmud, the writers described people with disabilities as children of God who might be capable of reasoning despite their handicaps. Christianity also brought new views on the injustice of neglecting deaf people.

Saint Jerome's translation of the Vulgate, in the fourth century A.D., discussed deafness and the possibility of salvation through signed as well as written communication. He viewed "the speaking gesture of the whole body" as serving to communicate the word of God as well as speech and hearing.

Saint Jerome's contemporary, Saint Augustine, wrote *De Quantitate Animae* and *De Magistro*, in which he specifically discussed gestures and signs as an alternative to spoken language in the communication of ideas and in learning the Gospel. He asked: "Have you never noticed how men converse, as it were, with deaf people by gestures and how the deaf themselves in turn use gestures to ask and answer questions, to teach and to make known either all their wishes or, at least, a good many of them?" (quoted in King, 1996, p. 133). While some may take a skeptical view of such references as "thought experiments" not representing real-life observations, others may see them as evidence that forms of manual communication existed in this period of history. Saint Augustine's description of a conversation between hearing and deaf persons suggests that such communication was commonplace. This may indicate that conversation among deaf people in late ancient Roman society was not only familiar, but that deaf people were not as isolated as some have surmised.[1]

Over the next 10 centuries we find little biographical information that might help us understand how deaf people lived. It seems likely, however, that the Dark Ages were especially dark for deaf persons. Mystical and magical cures for deafness were prevalent, illustrating the range of beliefs people held about hearing loss.

Some stories of cures for deafness were documented with enough detail that we might surmise something about the times. Among such reports was one by the Saxon monk Bæda, known as "the Venerable Bede" and the first historian of the English people. In *The Ecclesiastical History of the English Nation*, written around 700 A.D. and still an important source of knowledge of the early Anglo-Saxon period, Bede tells of Saint John of Beverley's cure of a young deaf boy. The Venerable Bede's writing has been carefully examined with regard to his use of the terms for "deaf" and "mute," and

---

Saint Hildegard of Bingen (1098–1179)

"Deafness may be remedied by cutting off a lion's right ear and holding it over the patient's ear just long enough to warm it and to say, 'Hear *adimacus* by the living God and the keen virtue of a lion's hearing.'" [This process was to be repeated many times.]

there seems little doubt that the boy was deaf. (King, 1996). More important, the story reveals the continued view of spoken language as a theological, rather than a physiological function.

The Venerable Bede's writing was one of the chief texts of Anglo-Saxons until the twelfth century. In the thirteenth century, Bartholomaeus Anglicus, a member of the Minorite Order and Professor of Theology in Paris, developed *De Proprietatibus Rerum* (*Of the Properties of Things*), which included three chapters on hearing, the ear, and deafness. That work reflected the prevailing ideas of the time. The opening sentence in the chapter on deafness, "Deafnesse is privation and let [hindrance] of hearing, that is the gate of the inwit [knowledge]" (Farrar, 1926, p. 390), did little to encourage teaching of deaf children; the popular work was translated into English in 1398 and printed several times over the next two centuries.[2]

In the early fourteenth century, a miracle was carefully documented in an affidavit in support of the canonization of Saint Louis. A young man, also named Louis, had been deaf for many years, and his deafness was well documented. Using signs, he was able to communicate with the Smith of Orgelet (County of Burgundy), who took him in for 12 years, and was reported to have conversed with members of the court of King Philip of France. The detailed account of his using signs both before and after Louis regained his hearing hints at a general acceptance of the deaf man, despite his inability to speak and hear (Fay, 1923).

The Renaissance

The Renaissance was defined by the revival of classical art, literature, and learning after the Dark Ages. To praise art or poetry in the fifteenth century was to compare it favorably with that of the ancients. We can find no such comparison in the art of teaching deaf children. Some indication of the attitudes about deaf people during the Renaissance may be found in the writings of the Dutch humanist Rudolphus Agricola and the Italian mathematician and physician Girolamo Cardano. Both are now recognized for opening the minds of others to the potential of deaf persons to learn.

In the late 1400s, Agricola described a deaf person who had been taught to read and write. When Agricola's work was published 43 years after his death, it came into the hands of Cardano, who elaborated on the uniqueness of deaf people being able to "speak by writing" and "hear by reading." Cardano described how a deaf person may conceive such a word as "bread," for example, and associate the written word directly with ideas. Cardano himself apparently never attempted to teach a deaf person, and it is unclear whether he was speaking about instruction.

It was unusual during this period to find deaf persons who were able to read and write, but many were leading productive lives. Before Cardano's book came out in 1575, for example, there were distinguished deaf artists in Italy such as Bernardino di Betto Biagi, born in 1454, who painted Frescoes of the life of Moses in the Sistine Chapel, and Cristoforo de Predis, a successful illuminist, whose hearing son was a student of Leonardo da Vinci. In Madrid, the deaf artist Jaime Lopez decorated the sixteenth-century Hermitage of Notre Dame. Juan Fernándes de Navarette, a painter for Philip II of Spain, was best known for his exquisite coloring and experimentation with light. Deafened in 1529, at the age of three, he earned the honor of being called the "Spanish Titian," after the Italian master. He communicated in signs with the curate of the parish of Santo Vincente, who found them "as intelligible as speech." Navarrete died in 1579, three years after Cardano's book was published. On his death bed, with pen and paper, he wrote out his own will and appointed an executor (Lang & Meath-Lang, 1995).

Navarrete had studied history and the Scriptures in a monastery of La Estrella of the Order of St. Jerome in Logroño more than a decade before the work of the great Spanish Benedictine monk Pedro Ponce de Leon. It was in 1578 that Ponce de Leon described how he had taught the congenitally deaf sons of great lords and other notables to read and write, attain a knowledge of Latin and Greek, study natural philosophy (science) and history, and to pray. Ponce de Leon's students included the deaf brothers Pedro and Francisco de Velasco, and the congenitally deaf Fray Gaspar, who later became a priest.

Abandoned in historical anonymity are the teachers before Ponce de Leon. The success of these and other deaf individuals in Cardano's time attests to the fact that deaf people had found ways to communicate in Renaissance Europe. These appear to be the first indications of the empowerment of deaf people through education. The fruits of these labors were immediately observable in lasting works of art and other contributions to the world. The promise was there.

In a sense, the theme represented by the Cardano story repeats itself in contemporary society when professionals or parents new to the field make generalizations about what deaf people can or cannot do. Given the rich biographical resources available today, familiarization with the wide range of accomplishments of deaf people should be an expectation in orientation and teacher preparation programs.

The Age of Reason

As word of Ponce de Leon's methods of instructing deaf students spread through the writings of Juan Pablo Bonet and, later, Sir Kenelm Digby, the education of deaf children in Europe slowly took root. Bonet's book, *The Reduction of Letters and the Art of Teaching the Mute to Speak*, was published in 1620, apparently the first treatise on the education of deaf people.

A critical assumption in his writing was that thought precedes language (Moores, 1996). Bonet also stressed the importance of activity and multi-sensory learning. In comparing and contrasting objects, for example, he wrote that "some of them are so similar as to demand feeling rather than sight to distinguish them, and these [the deaf child] must weigh in his head, so as to reorganize differences in things that need some consideration" (quoted in Deland, 1931, p. 33). Thus, in this first book ever published on educating deaf children, we find the roots of a theory of learning as an active construction of meaning.

The experiment of instructing deaf children began to spread throughout Europe. In 1670, William Holder, a priest, and John Wallis, a mathematician, publicly argued in the *Philosophical Transactions of the Royal Society* their respective claims of being the first to teach deaf students to speak and speechread in Great Britain. Other writers influenced by Ponce de Leon's work included England's George Sibscota (*Deaf and Dumb Man's Discourse*, 1670); his countryman John Bulwer, who published a study of manual language (*Philocophus; or, the Deaf and Dumbe Man's Friend*, 1648); the Scot George Dalgarno (*Didascalocophus; or, the Deaf and Dumb Man's Tutor*, 1661); and the Dutch physician Johan Konrad Amman (*The Speaking Deaf*, 1692; *A Dissertation on Speech*, 1700). As this base of literature was being established, the groundwork was also being laid for one of the most disheartening philosophical conflicts in the history of the education of deaf learners: the controversy over the use of signed and spoken communication methods.

One myth, perpetuated even into modern times, was the belief that abstractions could not be conveyed through sign language. Yet, the anecdotes of this early period reveal that the signs used by deaf people contradicted this view. In Cardano's time, we find a report in 1576 of a wedding of a "naturally deafe, and also dumbe" couple, Thomas Tilsye and Ursula Russel, at St. Martin's Parish, Leicester. Tilsye was described as having used signs "for the expression of his minde instead of words [on] his owne accorde." (Hay, 1996, p. 7). The use of signs to convey the abstraction inherent in marital vows was apparently accepted as equivalent to spoken or written language by the minister and the families of the betrothed. Similarly, in *The History of the Worthies of England* (1662), Thomas Fuller described the exchange between the congenitally deaf Edward Bone and his friend Kemple, who communicated effectively "with passionate gestures, that their want of a tongue seemed rather an hindrance to others conceiving them, than to their conceiving one another" (*American Annals of the Deaf*, 1870, p. 189).

Another relevant anecdote, from 1636, involved Dr. William Harvey, known for his work on the circulation of blood in the human body. Harvey kept a journal during his continental journey with the Earl of Arundel. In it, he documented a sibling interpreting sign language for "a poore Boy

The Worthies of England (1662)

"With passionate gestures," the congenitally deaf Edward Bone and his friend Kemple, communicated so effectively "that their want of a tongue seemed rather an hindrance to others conceiving them, than to their conceiving one another."

standing among other poore people begging for reliefe, who looked very strangely and could neither speake nore heare." As Harvey wrote, "there was with him his sister, a pretty girle, who when one spake to him, made him understand by signes" (quoted in Keynes, 1966, p. 239).

Public schools were not yet established, and we do not know much about how deaf children were taught, but we do know there were communicative exchanges between hearing persons and intelligent, if not fully educated, deaf people. The diary of Samuel Pepys, for example, is considered of historical value in the way it documented daily life, and it offers at least some insight. One evening in 1666, as Pepys dined with Sir George Downing and other friends, a young deaf boy entered the room. Pepys reported that Downing conversed with him in signs and interpreted for Pepys as they talked about the Great Fire of London, how the King was abroad, and other matters. When Pepys inquired about the signs, Downing responded, "Why, it is only a little use, and you will understand him and make him understand you, with as much ease as may be" (quoted in Grant, 1988, p. 14). There is a possibility that Downing's fluency with signs was a result of his having grown up in the woodlands of Kent, where a semirestrictive gene pool may have helped to form a small community of deaf individuals (Groce, 1985).

In September 1677, John Evelyn, a founding member of the Royal Society who also chronicled contemporary events, wrote of having dinner with Sir John Gaudy. Gaudy was described as a deaf artist who communicated with his family in signs (Evelyn, 1955). The fact that he had been knighted suggests that Gaudy was a highly respected member of the community.

The lesson we learn from these accounts provided by people well recognized for their scientific and literary skills is that there is a growing body of literature revealing that in the sixteenth and seventeenth centuries, prior to formal public schooling, the self-determination of deaf people may have been bolstered by their use of sign language.

Deaf Education and the Growth of Science

The establishment of scientific societies in the seventeenth century helped to bring legitimacy to the instruction of deaf students. The lineage of these societies has been traced back to Plato, and, as described earlier, the literary records associated with Plato's famous academy offer a Socratic discussion of deaf persons and their ability to communicate with gestures. As scientific societies spread through Europe in the sixteenth and seventeenth centuries, particularly in Naples, Rome, Leipzig, and Florence, they became centers of experimentation. In the early reports of these academies, we find studies on the anatomy of the ear and the use of tubes and trumpets for improving hearing.

In 1662, the London Royal Society was established, closely followed in 1666 by the Royal Academy of Sciences in France. The early interest in acoustics in these organizations may have led to discussions of hearing loss. Deafness, deaf people, and their instruction would become focal points of debate. Although few in number, there were also deaf and hard-of-hearing scientists fully accepted as contributing members of these societies. Guillaume Amontons, for example, born in 1663, was an active member of the French Academy. The profoundly deaf physicist is recognized both as a pioneer in optical telegraphy and for laying the foundation for the study of heat and temperature (Lang & Meath-Lang, 1995).

Yet, generally speaking, it was still only the deaf sons of the privileged nobles, royals, and other wealthy people who reached even a modicum of visibility. In the seventeenth century, few were able to find and afford instructors for deaf children or to find opportunities for them to apprentice in suitable trades. History has been unkind to deaf children of the poor, those unable to speak or write their own names, or those living in small towns or in the countryside. In the absence of antibiotics, there was certainly a larger percentage of such deaf people than exists today. Unfortunately, they remain nameless and invisible. How did they live? Were they educated enough to communicate their needs? If so, who educated them?

Deaf education in the seventeenth century, although in its infancy, provided insights that have influenced practices today. In the 1660s, for example, the mathematician John Wallis wrote of the challenge of teaching a first language to deaf children, emphasizing that "we find by experience that the most advantageous way of teaching a child his first language, is that of perpetual discourse." Wallis recognized that deaf children are perfectly capable of developing the ability to use language: "why should it be thought impossible, that the eye, (though with some disadvantage), might as well apply such complications of letters or other characters, to represent the various conceptions of the mind, as the ear a like complication of sounds?" (Wallis, 1851, pp. 228–229).

Another early thinker, George Dalgarno, expressed similar optimism:

Deaf people are equal, in the faculties of apprehension, and memory, not only to the Blind; but even to those that have all their senses: and having formerly shewn that these faculties can

> as easily receive and retain, the Images of things, by the
> conveiance of Figures, thro the Eye, as Sounds thro the Ear: It
> will follow, That the Deaf man is, not only, as capable, but also,
> as soon capable of Instruction in Letters, as the blind man.
> (Dalgarno, 1680, p. 8).

Dalgarno offered another provocative comment about the use of signs with deaf infants. There might be "successful addresses made to a Dumb child, even in his cradle," he wrote, if parents had "but as nimble a hand, as commonly they have a Tongue" (Dalgarno, 1680, p. 9). This observation of the critical nature of visual communication with deaf children during infancy shows that Dalgarno was far ahead of his time.

As the scientific societies grew in Europe, the scientists and philosophers expanded their interests. Jean-Jacques Rousseau, an instigator of the French Revolution; his compatriot Denis Diderot; and the naturalist Georges Louis Leclerc, Comte de Buffon, keeper of the Jardin du Roi and author of the 44-volume *Natural History*, were among those who examined the potential of deaf youth to learn. Rousseau was among the early influential proponents of "learning by doing." In his book *Émile*, Rousseau expressed views which became the basis for reform in France after the Revolution. In redirecting attention to learning through the senses and the importance of the child's interaction with the environment, he challenged the prevalent emphasis on memorization of the classics. As a member of the French Academy of Sciences, he took a special interest in examining deaf children who were instructed by the teacher Jacobo Pereire. Through the efforts of Rousseau and others, the instruction of deaf pupils gained increasing respect as a profession. In the 1740s, they invited Pereire to demonstrate his instructional techniques. Pereire had successfully taught several deaf youth, using pronunciation, signs, fingerspelling, and speechreading.

Slowly, the isolated attempts to instruct deaf youths gave way to observable gains. By the 1760s, under the guidance of Charles Michel Abbé de l'Epée, France had established the world's first government-sponsored school for deaf children. L'Epée saw sign language as a natural way for deaf people to communicate. He and his successor, Abbé Roch Ambroise Sicard, emphasized its use in the school's curriculum. Their method, however, was soon assailed by Samuel Heinicke, who established a school in Leipzig in 1778 based on the practice of teaching deaf pupils to speak. Heinicke was one of the first to try to link speech to higher mental processes, arguing that articulation and vocal language was necessary for abstract thought (Lane, 1984).

The European founders of manualism (l'Epée) and of oralism (Heinicke) exchanged letters expressing their irreconcilable differences in views on educating deaf students. Thus began the war of methods between the proponents of the systematic use of sign language in educating deaf children and those who stressed the use of speech, speechreading, and residual hearing without signs as an all-encompassing solution. Throughout the following centuries, equally bold and emotionally laden judgments regarding methods of communicating with deaf pupils have done little to bring the opposing camps together.

The eighteenth century was a period when Deaf communities began to emerge in Europe, particularly in Paris where the status of deaf people was rapidly changing. We use the term "community" in the most basic sense of a group of people who share common interests and a language. The school established by L'Epée, the acceptance of sign language as a true language, and the growing success of deaf artists, teachers, and writers were elements of the community. Among those who distinguished themselves in the latter part of the eighteenth century were Pierre Desloges, a deaf bookbinder, who published a defense of sign language in the education of deaf pupils, and Ferdinand Berthier, the born-deaf graduate of the Paris Institution who established the first social organization for deaf people (Bézagu-Deluy, 1993).

Meanwhile, in Great Britain, the Royal Society members continued to examine hearing and deafness and the abilities of deaf pupils to communicate and to learn. But it was a concerned parent whose efforts led to the first school. Nearly a century after John Wallis provided an account of his work with deaf pupils, his writings fell into the hands of a merchant in Leith, Scotland. Charles Shirreff was the father of a deaf boy and determined to find someone who would establish a school in which his son might be educated. Shirreff encouraged Thomas Braidwood to open an academy in Edinburgh in 1760. The school's success may be seen in both anecdotal reports and by researching the lives of some students. In 1773, for example, the writer Samuel Johnson visited the Braidwood Academy and described how he had found a group of deaf children waiting for their master, "whom they are said to receive, at his entrance, with smiling countenances and sparkling eyes delighted with the hope of new ideas" (quoted in Johnson, 1912 p. 323). Johnson took special note of how the pupils were learning arithmetic. Among the children attending the Braidwood Academy during his visit was John Goodricke, a nine-year-old boy, born deaf, whose work would one day lay the foundation for the study of binary stars. That Great Britain's first school for deaf children was a direct result of the parental advocacy of Charles Shirreff is worthy of emphasis. It would be a story often repeated in the New World.

Deaf Education Begins in America

Despite the progressive thinking of some Europeans, colonists in the New World were struggling to come to terms with views about deaf children and learning. In 1679, only a year before Dalgarno's book was published,

Philip Nelson of Rowley, Massachusetts, endeavored to "cure" a deaf child, probably meaning that he had tried to teach the child to speak. Nelson faced the wrath of the people of Rowley, who viewed deafness as predestined. Attempts to teach deaf children were seen by some in the colonies as sorcery or witchcraft.

Yet, not far away in the Massachusetts town of Scituate, the second oldest town in Plymouth Colony, settlers had come from Kent and appear to have had both a higher proportion of deaf people among them and a wider acceptance of the use of signs (Groce, 1985). Families from Scituate moved to Martha's Vineyard, along with families from other towns in Massachusetts. Intermarriage on the island led to an extremely high rate of deafness. Through time, both hearing and deaf people used signs on such a common basis that it seemed natural to everyone. At least as far back as the 1690s, there were literate deaf people at Martha's Vineyard, including Jonathan Lambert, the first case of deafness recorded on the island (Groce, 1985). We do know that there were partially educated deaf people on Martha's Vineyard at least a century before the first formal school was established in America.

A few scholars in the New World closely followed the work of European scientists, but translating observations on the education of deaf children to useful practices in the colonies was no easy task. There was doubtless still much to learn about teaching deaf children.

The first members of the American Philosophical Society (founded by Benjamin Franklin in 1743) gathered to discuss natural philosophy, history, and politics and conducted studies in botany, medicine, chemistry, and other scientific areas. But, unlike their European counterparts, there was no concerted effort to study the educational needs of deaf pupils. In the colonies, there were few opportunities for deaf children to receive any formal schooling. One exception is found in John Harrower, a teacher in Virginia who had arrived in 1774 from Scotland. According to Harrower's diary, shortly after his arrival, he took on the instruction of John Edge, about 14 years old, for twice the fee he charged for hearing students. Little is known about how he taught the boy, although Edge learned to read and write, and it is reported that he performed "tolerably well" in mathematics (*Association Review*, 1900).

A few American deaf children were sent to Europe to receive their education. A deaf nephew of President James Monroe was sent to Paris for his education at the school established by L'Epée. Major Thomas Bolling, a descendant of Pocahontas, sent several of his children to the Braidwood Academy, and Francis Green sent his son there. These children were among the earliest deaf Americans to be formally educated. In 1783, Green published *Vox Oculis Subjecta* (*Voice Made Subject to the Eyes*). The title of this report was the motto of the Braidwood Academy and reflected Green's appreciation for the school that had succeeded so well in instructing his son.

We also know that several deaf folk artists at this time received private instruction from skilled painters or apprenticed to other artists and craftsmen. William Mercer, born in 1765 in Virginia, and John Brewster, born in 1766 in Connecticut, became freelance artists and distinguished themselves before formal schooling was established in America. They were educated enough to be able to handle their own business dealings and are highly respected today for their contributions to early folk art (Lang & Meath-Lang, 1995). Most deaf children of this era were not so fortunate, receiving neither academic nor vocational instruction through apprenticeships. But a spark of interest had been kindled in America.

The American Philosophical Society holds the distinction of having been the first scientific society in the colonies to publish a report on teaching deaf children. In 1793, William Thornton, head of the U. S. Patent Office, published a treatise on elements of teaching speech and language to deaf children in the *Transactions of the American Philosophical Society*. The essay, which earned him a Magallenic Gold Medal, was titled "On the Mode of Teaching the Deaf, or Surd, and consequently Dumb, to speak," and appeared as an appendix to the work, "CADMUS, or a Treatise on the Elements of written language, illustrating, by a Philosophical Division of Speech, the Power of each character, thereby mutually fixing the Orthography and Orhoepy" (Thornton, 1793).

Thornton had probably observed the work of the followers of the Braidwoods and L'Epée during his own studies in Edinburgh and Paris, respectively. He was one of the first scholars in America to provide salient perceptions on deaf education, writing on the phonological basis for reading, the importance of vocabulary building, and the varied ways to communicate with deaf people, including speech, fingerspelling, and signs. Nearly a quarter of a century before the first school for deaf children was established in the United States, Thornton wrote, "A deaf person not perfectly skilled in reading words from the lips, or who should ask anything in the dark would be able to procure common information by putting various questions, and by telling the person that, as he is deaf, he requests answers by signs, which he will direct him to change according to circumstances" (Thornton, 1793, reprinted in *Association Review*, 1903, p. 414).

The Nineteenth Century

After the turn of the century, momentum in educating deaf children increased. In 1803, Francis Green, still active in the developing field of deaf education even after the accidental drowning of his deaf son, published a request in a Boston newspaper to the clergy in Massachusetts to obtain information on the number of deaf children residing in the state. It was his intention to determine whether the number warranted the establishment of a special school. In the following year, the Reverend John Stanford found several deaf children in an almshouse in New York City and began to teach them. The movement was slowly gaining advocates, including an anonymous parent who published a letter in the Hartford, Connecticut *Courant* on May 26, 1812 p. 135:

> Deaf children are the most assiduous scholars in the world, when they have an instructor who is able clearly to communicate ideas to them; they receive every new idea with peculiar pleasure, and where they have been favoured with an appropriate school, very many have become useful and respectable members of society. What a pity that this class of citizens, capable of great improvement in many arts and some of the sciences, should be wholly overlooked at home, in this time of great and laudable zeal for sending instruction abroad.

In 1812, Thomas Hopkins Gallaudet began teaching Alice Cogswell, the deaf daughter of his neighbor, Mason Fitch Cogswell, a New England physician. Cogswell eventually gathered enough financial support to send Gallaudet to Europe to study the methods employed in the well-known schools begun by Braidwood and l'Epée. Meanwhile, Braidwood's grandson, John Braidwood, had come to America in search of a teaching position. In March 1815 he opened Braidwood's Institution for the Education of the Deaf and Dumb at Colonel William Bolling's mansion in Chesterfield County, Virginia. Bolling, a hearing man whose father had earlier sent three deaf children to the Braidwood Academy, had a deaf son himself. Bolling had earlier hired John Braidwood to experiment with a similar school, but Braidwood fell into debt and Colonel Bolling had to rescue him.

Braidwood's problems continued despite the fact that he showed evidence of being a capable instructor. He left the school in Virginia by the fall of 1816 and never returned to the field of instructing deaf children. In Great Britain, Gallaudet was unable to reach an agreement with the Braidwood Academy with regard to his learning their methods of instruction. He had better luck after attending a lecture given in London by Abbé Sicard. Impressed by Sicard's demonstration involving two successful deaf pupils from France, Jean Massieu and Laurent Clerc, Gallaudet spent several months at the National Institution for Deaf-Mutes in Paris. There, he was able to convince Clerc, a thirty-year-old assistant teacher, to accompany him to Hartford, Connecticut. Back in America, after a 52-day voyage, they obtained funds to establish the Connecticut Asylum for the Deaf and Dumb (now named the American School for the Deaf) in 1817. Gallaudet was its director, and Clerc became the first deaf teacher in America. Alice Cogswell was enrolled as one of the first seven pupils.

Again, we see the role of parents in this history. The efforts of Bolling, Green, the anonymous Hartford parent, and Cogswell firmly established parental leadership in the early movement toward quality education for deaf children in the United States. Like their European counterparts, these parents deserve more recognition for providing the necessary impetus for establishing schools.

Self-empowerment of deaf people also can be seen in how they served as important pioneers in establishing schools over the next few decades. After Laurent Clerc, about 25 other deaf people played instrumental roles in the founding of educational institutions. Some became superintendents. Many were among the schools' first instructors. Schools soon opened in Philadelphia (1820), Kentucky (1823), New York (1818 and 1825), and Ohio (1827). Numerous smaller schools which did not remain open long were also started. In Palmyra, New York, in 1822, for example, Franklin Scovel, who had studied at the Hartford school, started a one-room school in the wilderness outside of Rochester. By 1850 there were more than 15 residential schools serving deaf pupils, with nearly 4 out of every 10 teachers in these schools deaf themselves. With the attendance of deaf male and female students at these residential schools and the increased use of sign language to teach them, the Deaf community in the United States also began to grow.

It was not long before proposals for "high schools" and "high classes" for deaf pupils in America were presented at national conventions and published in journals for educators. The New York Institution for the Instruction of the Deaf and Dumb was a leader in the implementation of such a program. In 1851, two weeks before the death of Thomas Hopkins Gallaudet, W. W. Turner made a plea: "What [the deaf pupil] needs is a school expressly provided for him and for others in his circumstances, a High School for the Deaf. . . . [If it were] suitably endowed and judiciously managed, we might expect such a development of deaf-mute intellect as has not hitherto been witnessed in this or any other country" (Turner, 1851, p. 45).

Support for providing deaf individuals with greater educational opportunities was bolstered by the increasing visibility of deaf scientists, artists, and writers emerging around the United States. Some were born deaf and others were adventitiously deafened; some were immigrants and many more were Americans by birth. These talented individuals had begun to command authority in their respective fields. H. Humphrey Moore became a distinguished artist, as did August Fuller and John Carlin. James Nack excelled in poetry. Leo Lesquereux, a paleobiologist, became the first member of the National Academy of Sciences.

Frederick Augustus Porter Barnard, progressively deafened by hereditary otosclerosis, was a nineteenth-century Renaissance man with expertise and accomplishments as a mathematician, physicist, and chemist. He was also an educator who studied the effects of deafness on language development. Barnard, who taught at the Hartford school alongside Gallaudet

A Deaf Student, after Learning about Deaf Scientists and Their Accomplishments

"I am now more aware of how we (deaf) have to work twice as hard to get where we want to be, to get what we need, to get support and equal rights. By doing this we will make it easier for our next generations to have more equal access to life as did the past generations made it easier for us today."

and Clerc, later took a half dozen deaf pupils with him from the New York Institution to Virginia for demonstration and, as a result, induced the legislature to appropriate funds to open a new school at Staunton (now the Virginia School for the Deaf and the Blind). Barnard was a clear thinker who published in detail his perspectives on the education of deaf children only two decades after the first school for deaf students was established in Hartford, writing of the need for bilingualism and studying sign language scientifically (Lang & Stokoe, 2000). He saw the child's mental construction of the world as a series of inductions, from which understanding grows.

While at the New York Institution, Barnard's fellow Yale alumnus, David Bartlett, had become dissatisfied with the fact that deaf children were unable to enroll in a school before the age of seven for additional help. He opened an early version of a mainstream program in 1852, integrating hearing and deaf students and using both sign language and communication through speech and speechreading to optimize learning. The private school founded by Bartlett was shortlived, but it may claim some credit for preparing a young boy who studied there to become the first deaf American to earn a Ph.D. Gideon E. Moore (1842–1895) attended the Bartlett School with his deaf brother, H. Humphrey Moore, who was two years younger. Later, the elder Moore entered Yale College, from which he graduated with honors in chemistry in 1861. In addition to chemistry, Moore studied German, and after graduating from Yale he traveled to the University of Heidelberg, where he earned his Ph.D. summa cum laude in 1869 (Lang & Meath-Lang, 1995).

These are but a few of the many deaf people who, with access to schooling, empowered themselves to become leaders in the community, in education, and in many fields of endeavor. Their life stories are important lessons for our children today.

Higher Education for Deaf Students

Among the gifted deaf graduates of residential schools was the visionary artist John Carlin. In 1854, observing "prodigious strides" of deaf pupils in subjects like astronomy, chemistry, and algebra, he published an article entitled "The National College for Mutes" in the *American Annals of the Deaf and Dumb*. In that article, he proposed the establishment of a college which would offer a course of instruction corresponding to that of American colleges for hearing students.

Three years later, in 1857, Amos Kendall, the business manager for Samuel F. B. Morse and his telegraph business, met with Edward Miner Gallaudet, the son of Thomas Hopkins Gallaudet, and encouraged him to accept responsibility as the superintendent of a school for deaf and blind children which Kendall had established the previous year in the District of Columbia. The Columbia Institution for the Deaf, Dumb and Blind, incorporated by Congress in 1857, was authorized by President Lincoln in 1864 to grant college degrees in the liberal arts and sciences. The first freshman class was admitted to the collegiate program, the National Deaf-Mutes' College, in September of that year. Years later, the college would become Gallaudet College and later Gallaudet University (Gallaudet, 1983).

The establishment of the schools, and now a college, was a significant step toward empowering deaf people, but there was a long way to go. During the 1870s, the educational empowerment of deaf women also grew. In 1875, Laura C. Sheridan presented a passionate plea for higher education for deaf women: "The world has lost immensely by being so long in awaking to the importance of equal education for woman [*sic*]," she wrote. Sheridan was a deaf teacher at the Indiana School for the Deaf. She enrolled in a correspondence program of the Chatauqua Literary and Scientific Circle and received a diploma. In her effort to bring the plight of deaf women to the attention of authorities, she wrote: "So there has been much agitation of the question of the higher education of woman within the last few years, the result of which is that the doors of colleges and universities are opening to her everywhere. But what have we heard of the question in the silent world? Nothing" (Sheridan, 1875, p. 248).

Indeed, nothing happened for another six years until January 11, 1881, when the issue of admitting deaf women to the National Deaf-Mutes' College was discussed at a faculty meeting. "The Faculty," observed Edward Miner Gallaudet, "showed no disposition to change the policy of the College which declines to admit ladies" (quoted in Boatner, 1959, p. 114). In the course of working hard against one form of discrimination, Gallaudet and his colleagues were actively defending another equally obvious form. The accomplished deaf poet and feminist Angeline Fuller Fischer even called for a separate college for deaf women, but Gallaudet did not change his opinion. Three years later he again expressed this opposition while visiting a school for deaf pupils in Council Bluffs, Iowa.

The faculty did not drop its resistance until 1887, when it opened the college doors to women as an "experiment." In that year, the first deaf women students were admitted on the same terms as the men. The college admitted six women in the fall of 1888. Self-advocacy and empowerment again paid off for deaf people.

The Oralist Movement Comes to America

The German oralist movement had thrived in the early nineteenth century, let by John Baptist Graser and Frederick Moritz Hill. Their influence soon spread throughout Europe. Heinicke had died in 1784, and with no one to carry on his work, l'Epée's influence had grown. But this influence was short lived as nationalism led the Germans to renew and intensify their emphasis on articulation and experiment with integration of deaf children in the 1820s.

In the United States, the bitter debate among oralists, manualists, and combinists (those who mixed the methods in various degrees) raged between Alexander Graham Bell and Edward Miner Gallaudet. Thomas H. Gallaudet had died in 1851. His wife, Edward's mother, was deaf and signed. Bell's mother was hard of hearing and his wife was deaf; but neither used signs. Thus, Bell and Gallaudet had personal as well as professional attachments to their philosophical views and fought bitterly in public as they defended them (Winefield, 1987). Bell was also prominent in the eugenics movement, intended to keep the human race healthy by reducing hereditary deficiencies, and this added fuel to the fire generated by the oral–manual controversy.

At the 1880 Congress of Milan, there was an explicit denial of the emerging deaf empowerment. Congress participants, overwhelmingly hearing educators, voted to proclaim that the German oral method should be the official method used in schools of many nations: "The congress, considering the incontestable superiority of speech over signs, for restoring deaf-mutes to social life and for giving them greater facility in language, declares that the method of articulation should have preference over that of signs in the instruction and education of the deaf and dumb" (quoted in Lane, 1984, p. 394). Many of the proponents of sign language communication were unable to attend, and deaf people themselves were excluded from the vote. Deaf communities around the world were infuriated by the oppressive strategies of the hearing authorities in the schools. Partly as a result of the Milan vote, the National Association of the Deaf (NAD) was established in the United States to strengthen the political clout of deaf persons, who wished to have control over their own destiny. The choice of communication methods was a human rights issue, in reality, and one that remains volatile today. The emotions involved in this conflict are intense. The controversy has blindsided far too many educators and has pushed the goals of research into the background.

Gallaudet and Bell continued to argue over this issue of communication for many years. Gallaudet, the champion of deaf people, fought to have the combined system of spoken and sign language communication in instruction continued in the schools and to preserve sign language. Bell disagreed and broke away from the Convention of American Instructors of the Deaf to form his own group to advocate for teaching speech to deaf children and against the use of sign language. That organization, later renamed the Alexander Graham Bell Association for the Deaf, is still active today.

Despite intense controversy, educators of the late nineteenth and early twentieth centuries in America established a rich knowledge base, publishing their perspectives on teaching in the *American Annals of the Deaf and Dumb*, which began in 1847. The early issues of the *Annals*, as well as other nineteenth century literature, provide a fascinating storehouse of lessons for us today. In 1888, for example, J. Scott Hutton, the principal at the institution for deaf students in Nova Scotia, presented a paper at the Sixth National Conference of Superintendents and Principals of Institutions for Deaf Mutes in Jackson, Mississippi, describing "action-writing" as an essential part of the curriculum:

> [Action-Writing should be] I might say the chief characteristic, of the Natural Method, and for the first two or three years should be constantly, if not exclusively followed. Nothing interests the child so much as a lesson which is visible and tangible, or an exercise in which he is himself a principle performer. His active instincts lead him to delight in the *doing* of things, in being called on to act his part in the little dramatic exercises which are to be embodied in verbal forms. The constant association of words, and phrases, and sentences, with the objects and actions they represent, gives a reality and an interest to them which cannot be secured in any other way. Action-writing, in fact, is the nearest approach possible to the way in which hearing children learn their mother tongue. (Hutton, 1888, p. 98)

Similarly, astute educators touched on such relevant topics as reading, time on task, use of illustrations with instructional materials, motivation, memory, and the importance of hands-on activities and drawing connections to cognitive development. One of the most influential educators in regard to the latter issue was Adolphe Ferrière, the deaf Swiss "father of the activity school" who laid the foundation for new kind of public education in the early twentieth century. Ferrière argued that the school that offers nothing but information (i.e., lectures and reading) must disappear: "In its place must come the school which teaches the child how to use the lever which has ever raised the world above itself—purposeful activity" (quoted in Halberstam, 1938, p. 758).

Founding the International League for New Education in 1921, Ferrière and his colleagues incorporated the theoretical work of Rousseau in France, Johann Pestalozzi in Switzerland (who worked with poor children), Friedrich

Froebel in Germany (founder of the kindergarten system), and John Dewey and his progressive education movement in America. They developed a pedagogical theory that valued the child's initiative and used concrete objects to foster powers of observation and reasoning. These views still have considerable power today, particularly with regard to deaf children. They clearly point to the need to avoid "chalk and talk" teaching and the need to link new information to what students already know. Interestingly, such methods also led to an increased focus on educating students in more practical matters relating to employment.

Technical and Vocational Education in the United States

On the heels of the Industrial Revolution, industrial education was a priority issue for the Deaf community, and it was the opening topic on the agenda for the first convention of the NAD on August 25, 1880. Later, at the Conference of Principals and Superintendents of the American Schools for the Deaf held in Colorado Springs in August 1892, a proposal for the establishment of a national technical training school for the deaf was presented for discussion by Francis D. Clarke from the Arkansas School for the Deaf. In September 1892, the Deaf community's periodical *The Silent Worker* published a brief but provocative editorial comment: "By all means let us have a technical school. It is just as important as [Gallaudet] College at Washington. We should say that it is more important" (p. 3).

Proposals for a technical college proliferated as years went by with no satisfactory progress. Meanwhile, largely a result of the Milan Conference edict of 1880, the number of deaf teachers in American school programs dropped to about 1 in 10 by the 1920s—a number that has not changed significantly since. Because they could not teach speech, qualified deaf men and women who might have capably taught in technical education classes (as well as in general education) were left to find other means of employment.

When the United States entered into World War I, President Woodrow Wilson implemented plans to increase agricultural and industrial production to meet the demands. World War I was an important factor in bringing business managers to realize the value of deaf laborers and professionals as the inventive talents of many hearing and deaf people were applied. As hearing men went to war, more industrial positions were offered to deaf people. During this period, the Deaf community saw the promise of rehabilitation assistance begin, first with the federally funded efforts in the form of the Smith-Fess Act in 1920 and then with private organizations such as the National Rehabilitation Association.

The Deaf community's attempts to gain a technical college for deaf students continued for more than a century (Lang & Conner, 2001); equitable technical education opportunities would provide another means

of empowerment. In the latter half of the twentieth century, federal legislation began to help out. Public Law 88-565, the Vocational Rehabilitation
Act passed by Congress in 1954, provided many services to people with
disabilities. For deaf people, the law included funding for continuing education in university or technical training programs, but opportunities for
technical education remained inadequate. Public Law 89-36, signed by
President Lyndon B. Johnson in 1965, was a critical turning point. The
legislation addressed this need through the establishment of the National
Technical Institute for the Deaf (NTID) at the Rochester Institute of Technology (RIT). NTID admitted its first students in the fall of 1968 and now
enrolls more than 1100 deaf college students in various scientific and technical career programs, roughly the same number enrolled in liberal arts
studies at Gallaudet University. Along with NTID, regional programs for
deaf students have been established at the Technical Vocational Institute
in St. Paul, Minnesota; the Seattle Community College, Washington; the
Delgado Vocational Technical Junior College in New Orleans, Louisiana;
and the California State University at Northridge.

The Modern Era: 1950–2000

The decades following World War II were a period of continued struggle for
deaf people. In the face of prejudice and discrimination, much more was
needed to change attitudes. With the impetus of the civil rights movement
and federal legislation in vocational rehabilitation and education, the 1960s
and 1970s were particularly exciting, if not revolutionary, years for the Deaf
community in America. The scientific recognition of American Sign Language (ASL) as a true language in the early 1960s led to its receiving more
respect and attention in school environments. Greater public awareness and
acceptance of ASL was accompanied by a growing political voice among
people who were deaf and hard of hearing. The social and political transformations that took place led to wholly new lifestyles for many deaf people
as well as improved attitudes about deafness in general.

As noted earlier, the Vocational Rehabilitation Act of 1954 provided
much-needed federal support for Americans with disabilities, particularly
in allowing states to develop rehabilitation centers. Inspired by the great
gains experienced as a result of the Civil Rights Act of 1964, people with
disabilities pressed further for their legal rights. Changes in vocational
rehabilitation and other legislation soon followed. Section 504 of the Rehabilitation Act of 1973, which prohibits discrimination against qualified
people with disabilities on the basis of handicap, was a major step for the
legal rights movement for persons with disabilities in the United States.

Another major turning point was Public Law 94-142, enacted in 1975,
the Education of All Handicapped Children Act. Signed by President Gerald

Ford, it guaranteed free, appropriate public education for all children with disabilities. Since then, PL 94-142 has been a catalyst for educational research, curriculum development, and the promotion of active involvement and change in professional organizations concerned with education.

Deaf education in the modern era has been characterized by dramatic changes in its content, orientation, and the number of children it reaches. From 1850 to 1950, enrollment in special schools or classes for the deaf had risen from about 1100 to more than 20,000. When special classes in regular schools were included, figures reached close to 82,000 (Craig & Craig, 1986). Enrollment in residential schools, especially for children of elementary school age, decreased after the passage of PL 94-142, the result of a clause requiring education in the "least restrictive environment" for all handicapped children. According to the Center of Assessment and Demographic Studies Center of Assessment and Demographic Studies Center of Assessment and Demographic Studies report of 1985, enrollment in public residential schools dropped 18.3 percent from 1974 to 1984, and enrollment in private residential schools dropped 69 percent. During the same period, enrollment in public day-school programs increased more than 30 percent, and fully 40 percent of the children attending programs as residential schools were actually day students (Calderon & Greenberg, 1993). By 1986, approximately 29 percent of deaf children in the U.S. still attended state-run residential schools for the deaf, while 68 percent attended public schools either in special classes for deaf students or in regular classes with an interpreter or special resource teacher (Craig & Craig, 1986). For the most part, those children who remained in residential schools tended to be those with congenital or early onset, severe to profound deafness (Schildroth, 1986).

Although a full consideration of the virtues and criticisms of PL 94-142 are beyond the scope of the present discussion, there is no doubt that this law has affected the philosophical underpinnings of deaf education in the United States (see Calderon & Greenberg, 1993; Vernon & Andrews, 1990). Whether those changes are seen as improvements or setbacks depends largely on the hearing status and knowledge of the individual making the judgment. It is clear, however, that while the U.S. Congress placed the obligation of deaf education squarely on parents and local school systems, it has never appropriated sufficient funds to implement the law fully (Lowenbraun & Thompson, 1987). The result has been that most hearing parents of deaf children have taken on more responsibility for their children's education, but without added external support. In many cases, this situation has forced parents into greater dependence on relatives, inconsistent child-rearing practices, and the cumbersome shuffling of work schedules and residences (Calderon & Greenberg, 1993; Luterman, 1987).

Public Law 94-142 was amended by the Education of the Handicapped Amendments of 1986 (Public Law 99-457) and the Individuals with Disabilities Education Act or IDEA (Public Law 101-476). One of the emphases of the original act, and indeed the whole legislative package, is the greater involvement of families in educational decision-making relevant to their children, through the establishment of Individualized Education Programs (IEPs). Together with the move toward educating deaf children in more inclusive settings, the opportunity for broader family participation in educational planning has affected several factors contributing to language development, including children's exposure to adult language models, interactions with multiple deaf and hearing peers, issues of self-esteem and locus of control, and the level of parent and teacher expectations for deaf children.

In the absence of full implementation of PL 94-142, it is difficult to determine its potential impact on deaf education and the Deaf community. Meanwhile, many schools for the deaf are finding it difficult to maintain minimum enrollments, and it remains to be determined whether regular public schools really represent less restrictive environments for deaf children than do residential schools.

The education of deaf students in the modern era is also being significantly influenced by recent advances in medicine and technology. Most obvious with regard to medicine is the elimination of some formerly common etiologies of hearing loss in children (e.g., maternal rubella) and the relatively greater occurrence of others (e.g., premature birth). Of growing significance, however, is the rapidly increasing number of deaf children who are receiving cochlear implants. Research concerning effects of implants on aspects of development other than hearing is just beginning, and so the long-term implications for language, social, and cognitive growth remain unclear (see chapter 3).

The Americans with Disabilities Act (ADA) of 1990 has been the most important civil rights legislation for people with disabilities in the history of the United States. Much stronger than earlier legislation, the ADA provides employees with disabilities with legal protection against discrimination in public and private areas. For deaf people, this means greater access through interpreters and telecommunication devices.

Public service announcements produced by the federal government now must be closed captioned. Through the ADA, the responsibility for reasonable accommodation is clearly on the shoulders of employers and service providers. Known as the "Emancipation Proclamation of the Disabled," the ADA provides more than 43 million people with disabilities the same civil rights protection that previous legislation provided on the basis of sex, race, religion, and national origin. Access to mass transportation, public accommodation services, and state and local government are key issues in the act. To respond to the growing demand for information about the ADA, the President's Committee on Employment of People with Disabilities expanded the Job Accommodation Network established in

1984. Building on the substantive framework of Section 504 of the Rehabilitation Act of 1973, the ADA renewed attention to issues of access and programs on college campuses as well.

Inroads made by legislative acts of the modern era led to a much more encompassing and politically sophisticated social movement that has significantly affected the lives of deaf people in the United States. In addition to the general disability rights movement and the enhanced educational opportunities for children with disabilities that resulted from self-advocacy and activism, there were several major movements in the modern period that were unique to deaf people. Both were critical turning points in their empowerment. The first was the telecommunications access movement, which began with the development of the acoustical telephone coupler in 1964.

Deaf people first came to be able to use the telephone in a practical way by connecting it to a Teletype machine via an acoustic coupler. Three deaf men, a physicist, a dentist, and an engineer, patented and marketed the ingenious device. It is a compelling story of an insurrection by deaf people against corporate America as they sought independence and access to long-distance communication. Realizing that assistance from corporate America was not forthcoming, deaf people took into their own hands the design, implementation, and marketing of an assistive device technology. The marriage of a new technology (the modem) with an old technology (the teletypewriter, or TTY) provided a means for long-distance communication. Until this technology was developed, deaf people were totally dependent on hearing family members or friends to communicate by telephone. Massive volunteerism for many years slowly resulted in the growth of a TTY network across the country, but this process was arduous due to the lack of cooperation by major telecommunications corporations. In the 1970s, following the Vocational Rehabilitation Act, the Deaf community used this technology to increase its activism and pursue legal channels for enhanced equity and access.

The telephone access movement is a human interest story that shows how diverse groups within the Deaf community (the National Association of the Deaf, which advocates the use of sign language, and the Alexander Graham Bell Association for the Deaf and Hard of Hearing, which emphasizes oral/aural communication) can work together to advance the quality of living conditions for people who are deaf, their education, and opportunities for employment (Lang, 2000).

The implementation of closed-captioning technology also required persistence on the part of the deaf individuals and the Deaf community, who wanted access to "talking" movies. In 1958, President Eisenhower signed Public Law 85-905 creating the Captioned Films for the Deaf Program, with Malcolm J. Norwood as the chief of Media Services and Captioned Films for the Deaf Department of the Bureau of Education of the Handicapped, the first deaf person to hold a professional position in the

Department of Education. In 1971, the first closed-captioning demonstration took place in Knoxville, Tennessee. With support from the U.S. Office of Education, the caption decoder was developed, but its use grew slowly. In 1976, the Federal Communications Commission agreed to reserve line 21 of the television signal for captions, and captioned television was on its way. But the struggle for telecommunications access is an ongoing one, now led by the national organization TDI (formerly Telecommunications for the Deaf, Inc.).

The stories of deaf people gaining access to the telephone and to captioning are important for deaf children to learn. Technology will continue to advance rapidly, and today's deaf children will be tomorrow's community leaders and advocates for access to equitable educational and employment opportunities.

The second sociopolitical movement, which began in March 1988 at Gallaudet University, propelled political momentum further. When Elisabeth Zinser, a hearing university administrator, but a person with no experience in the Deaf community, was selected as the university's new president over two capable deaf finalists, the campus exploded in outrage. Deaf students demanded a deaf president at Gallaudet University. The news spread quickly around the world as the students organized the "Deaf President Now" protest, barricaded the entrances to the university, and emotionally called for resignation of Zinser. The protest closed down Gallaudet University for a week. The demands that Zinser resign and that 51 percent of the board at Gallaudet University be made up of deaf persons were met. I. King Jordan became the first deaf president of Gallaudet University. The message behind this protest soon became clear. Ripples of reform have since been observed across the country, with more and more qualified deaf professionals being appointed to leadership positions. The empowerment of deaf people in their own education has dramatically gained a foothold as a result of this experience.

The need for empowerment of deaf people is seen in their individual efforts in the eighteenth and nineteenth centuries to contribute meaningfully to the arts, sciences, and humanities despite the attitudes and prejudice they encountered. It grew with the establishment of the NAD, and became most effective in the insurrection for telecommunications access and the Gallaudet University protest. The message that deaf people should control their own destiny is one that needs to be remembered as new educational programs are established.

Summary

This chapter has woven historical events and some lessons which should help us as we seek to enhance the education of deaf students in the twenty-first century. We see from this brief glimpse at history the need to foster self-actualization in deaf learners, the importance of parental involvement as advocates and in the teaching-learning process, and the roles of technology and government support in effecting positive change. We also learn the value of sharing life histories of deaf people in teaching deaf children today that with quality education they can aspire to do anything.

Probably the most poignant lesson we have learned from history is that controversy grows from ignorance. We began this chapter with the adage, "those who do not learn from history are doomed to repeat it." This lesson emerges most obviously with regard to our failure to recognize heterogeneity in the students we teach, particularly in terms of their communication skills and needs. The issue also has been unnecessarily politicized in the inclusion controversy. History is replete with examples of schools adopting a predominant method of communication, making little allowance for students who may not benefit from the approach selected. In the controversies that have raged for centuries and in the more recent ones ongoing today, the tendency is to polarize educators, parents, and other gatekeepers whose philosophical views rarely or adequately recognize the universal truth that no one method or educational environment is suitable for all students.

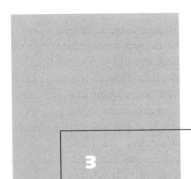

How common is hearing loss in children, and what are the most frequent causes?

What characteristics of deaf children should be considered in planning their educations?

Characteristics of Deaf Learners

In the interests of equality, sensitivity, and political correctness, it is often claimed that deaf and hearing individuals are exactly the same, except for their hearing losses. To some extent, this attitude may reflect an understandable swing of the pendulum after years of society's treating deaf individuals as though they are deficient. At the same time, we believe that there is now considerable evidence to indicate that the experiences, knowledge, and strategies of deaf individuals often differ in some ways from those of hearing individuals, and that such differences are likely to influence learning.

At one level, the question of differences between deaf and hearing learners is a statistical, descriptive one. This chapter provides some basic information in that regard, including demographics, types and causes of hearing loss, and issues relating to educational placement. We discuss populations and their characteristics. At another level, however, the question of differences between deaf and hearing learners is about individuals. There, the relevant issues are more empirical than descriptive, and an interdisciplinary perspective becomes important. If deaf and hearing students were the same except for their hearing losses, then we would not have to worry about special educational methods, issues of social integration, or whether a local public school or special school program would be better for a deaf child. If deaf and hearing children were the same except for their hearing losses, we could put them in the same classrooms and assume the same background knowledge, social skills, and educational futures.

The problem is that life is rarely so simple. By virtue of their hearing losses, many deaf children (and particularly those with hearing parents) have somewhat different early environments than hearing children. Frequently, those children do not have access to the language of their families, and their parents are not fully prepared for handling the special needs of a child who cannot hear. With differences in communication, early social interactions, and ways of acquiring new information, it seems likely that deaf children will have some characteristics that distinguish them from hearing children. This is not to claim that deaf children will be in any way deficient, only that they may have different backgrounds, different knowledge, and different ways of dealing with the world. In this and following chapters, we argue that educators need to be cognizant of such variability if they are to provide deaf learners with academic content and contexts that allow them full educational equality. To do otherwise would be to ignore reality and deny deaf learners opportunities to which they are legally and morally entitled.

In describing similarities and differences between deaf children and hearing children, we give special consideration to ways in which deaf children of hearing parents might compare with deaf children of deaf parents. Beyond their hearing losses and having sign language as a first language, deaf children of deaf parents might be expected to have somewhat differently structured social environments, but we now have enough information from studies to know that the cultural variation is not really greater than those of other cultural minorities existing within the larger society. Where deaf learners, as a cultural and linguistic minority, diverge from other such groups is in the fact that more than 90 percent of them have parents who are not already members of that minority, meaning that they are not deaf themselves. From an anthropological and sociological perspective, this fact provides an interesting situation in which it is often the children who introduce the parents to the cultural group and community rather than the other way around. From a psychological and educational perspective, this situation means that hearing parents and teachers frequently will need information or training that goes beyond any experience they might have had with hearing children. This book provides some resources in that regard and indicates directions and locations useful for seeking additional information. First, it will be helpful to have some understanding of the size and nature of the population.

Definitions and Demographics

In 1999, Congress passed the Newborn and Infant Hearing Screening and Intervention Act. That law authorized federal agencies, including the

Health Resource and Services Administration and the Department of Health and Human Services, to help states voluntarily set up newborn hearing screening and intervention systems. By mid-2001, 35 states and the District of Columbia already had established hearing screening programs for newborns and legislation was pending in 5 more states. Once universally implemented, hearing losses in young children will be identified much earlier than the two to three years that previously was common, and parents will be able to take appropriate steps to optimize their children's environments for developmental and educational success. Screening programs also will provide a clearer picture of the demographics of hearing loss, as many families report "unknown" causes and age of onsets of childhood deafness.

Where deaf learners, as a cultural and linguistic minority, diverge from other such groups is in the fact that more than 90 percent of them have parents who are not already members of that minority.

As in other populations, deaf and hard-of-hearing individuals vary widely, and statistics cannot capture the true character of the group. In some ways, deaf individuals would be expected to vary more widely than hearing individuals. Beyond whatever other characteristics one might want to use to describe a group of people, deaf individuals also vary in the degree of their hearing losses, age of hearing loss onset, and the etiologies or causes of the losses. There may be factors related to their hearing losses, regardless of whether they are hereditary or adventitious deafness (e.g., accompanying genetic syndromes, physical injury), and several investigators have obtained results suggesting that hereditary deafness may even carry with it some advantages (Kusché et al., 1983; Zweibel, 1987; cf. Ulissi et al., 1990). Then, of course, there are issues of whether deaf children were born into deaf or hearing families, the extent of their early exposure to language, and the quality of interactions with adults and peers during childhood. These variables make for a more diverse population and, at the very least, will affect the utility of one-size-fits-all approaches to education.

At this point, we should be more specific about what we mean by *deaf* and *hard-of-hearing* learners. Superficially, people are often described as deaf if they use sign language rather than spoken language. But there are many deaf people who use spoken language rather than sign language, hard-of-hearing people who prefer to sign rather than speak, and hearing people who sign exclusively in some settings. Similarly, there are people who are members of the Deaf community even though they are hearing, either by virtue of having deaf family members and growing up in that context or having joined that community and having been accepted. For the purposes of this book, we usually refer to individuals or groups of individuals as being *deaf* or not in terms of hearing and hearing loss, the latter primarily with regard to whether or not they are able to hear spoken language (with or without amplification).

Because of the physics and biology of speech and hearing, speech perception will be most affected when sounds at the frequencies of 500 Hertz (Hz), 1000 Hz, and 2000 Hz are not heard. In age-related hearing losses, or *presbycusis,* which will be of lesser interest to us here, perception of the higher frequencies typically is lost before perception of lower frequencies. In congenital and early-onset hearing losses, in contrast, the particular frequencies involved vary widely, and attention must be given to which frequencies are affected as well as how much hearing is lost. Quantitative descriptions of hearing loss are typically given in terms of decibel (dB) loss in the better ear. People with hearing losses up to 25 dB are still considered to have normal hearing. Although definitions sometimes vary slightly, hearing losses from 26 to 40 dB are most often categorized as *mild*, those from 41 to 55 dB as *moderate*, from 56 to 70 dB as *moderately severe*, from 71 to 90 dB as *severe*, and losses greater than 90 dB in the better ear are categorized as *profound.*

Hearing losses also are categorized as *conductive*, involving the middle ear; *sensorineural,* involving the inner ear and auditory nerve; or *central*, involving auditory centers of the brain. In all three cases, the measurement of practical interest is the *loss of pure tone receptivity*, specifying the limit of potential hearing for simple tones. Being able to detect a sound ("I hear something") is very different from being able to identify it ("It's a voice") and far less demanding than the understanding of speech ("It's a man saying 'hello'").

Depending on how broadly one defines hearing loss, the number of people who can be considered deaf or hard-of-hearing will vary widely. Our primary focus will be on individuals of school age, but because hearing loss is so common in older individuals, it might be helpful to get a broad perspective first. For example, the U.S. Bureau of the Census and the National Center for Health Statistics (NCHS) report that there are approximately 23 million people in the United States with chronic, significant hearing losses, or just under 10 percent of the population. Approximately 1.5 million of those individuals are classified as deaf in both ears (NCHS, 1999). However, there is no legal definition of deafness comparable to the federal definition for blindness, so estimates of the number of people who are deaf vary considerably. Thus, whereas the NCHS reports more than 210,000 deaf individuals under 18 years of age (and does not count children under age 3), the Bureau of the Census reports that approximately 61,500 children and youth between the ages of 6 and 21 years have hearing losses and are being served under the Individuals with Disabilities Education Act (IDEA; see chapter 2), and unpublished data from the Center for Assessment and Demographic Studies at Gallaudet University puts the number of deaf youngsters between the ages of 3 and 17 years at just over 50,000.

Overall, the NCHS data indicate that males are about 30 percent more likely to be deaf than females, whites are about twice as likely as African Americans to be deaf, and non-Hispanics are about twice as likely as Hispanics to be deaf. Figures for school-age children are more difficult to come by because the federal data do not meet standards of reliability or precision, but it appears that deaf males outnumber deaf females by about 5:4 during the school years. Approximately 20 percent of individuals who are categorized as having significant hearing loss in the United States experienced the onset of those losses before 18 years of age, and about 5.5 percent of those before age 3.

Etiologies of hearing loss in children vary widely, although accurate numbers are difficult to find. For example, etiology information is available for only about half of the children included in the most inclusive annual survey of children with hearing loss, conducted by Gallaudet University's Center for Assessment and Demographic Studies, and that survey includes only about 60 percent of the deaf and hard-of-hearing children in United States. Generally, though, almost half of the children in the 1999 survey had significant hearing losses at birth, and another 23 percent had onsets after birth (approximately 30 percent are unknown or not reported). Among those children for whom the causes of their hearing losses were reported, 13 percent were linked to hereditary factors. Other frequently reported etiologies include pregnancy or birth complications such as prematurity and Rh incompatibility (8.7 percent), meningitis (8.1 percent), and infections/fevers including measles and mumps (4.0 percent). Maternal rubella was once the leading cause of deafness in younger children, accounting for 24 percent of cases as recently as 1984, but it now accounts for only about 2 percent of the cases.

The variety of causes of congenital or early-onset deafness also may contribute to diversity in the development of those children. Most notably, hearing losses associated with illness or accidents may carry the possibility of damage to other sensory systems or of related neurological effects (Konigsmark, 1972). This relationship means that reports of psychological or behavioral differences between deaf and hearing children need to be considered with care and caution. Differences that might be described as due to deafness may well be the result of other factors. It also is important to note that statistics concerning the academic success of deaf children, literacy rates, intelligence, and so on will include a variety of children and do not only reflect implications of hearing loss.

For most readers, *hard of hearing* is a broad category that includes people with mild to moderate hearing losses—an interpretation that generally will be appropriate throughout this book. Other authors have described hard-of-hearing people not in terms of the hearing loss, but as people who use spoken language regardless of the amount of hearing they might have. This definition seems to follow from the fact that such individuals might have residual hearing across a fairly wide range (in decibels and frequencies) and be able to process and acquire spoken language. It seems odd, however, to use a term descriptive of hearing loss that is based on spoken language ability, particularly when the difference between deaf and hard-of-hearing learners might end up being one of social orientation or a question of whose parents placed a priority on speech therapy.[1]

The age at which an acute or progressive hearing loss begins also might have important implications for a child's education. Children who have been exposed to sound, even if they lose their hearing before learning language, appear to have greater success with cochlear implants and may generally be advantaged in linguistic, visuospatial, and other domains (see Marschark, 2001b, for a review). When hearing losses occur after spoken language has been acquired and education begun, we also can take advantage of the fact that children already have an understanding of reference (what words or signs stand for), learning strategies, and social experience. Whether or not they continue to use spoken language into adulthood, it is often easier for such children to communicate with others, even if others cannot communicate easily with them. As we shall see in chapter 4, acquiring a spoken language without auditory access to speech, or acquiring a signed language when parents are not skilled users of it, represents a significant challenge. Hearing aids and cochlear implants can compensate for a considerable amount of hearing loss, allowing those with later-acquired losses make use of learned speech-processing skills and comprehension strategies. Learning language for the first time using either of these technologies may be different matter, and we now turn to their consideration.

Hearing and Hearing Aids

To help understand how hearing aids work, first consider how hearing works. Sounds are normally heard when some force (including air being forced across the human vocal cords) sets up vibrations in a medium like air or water, which conducts the vibrations to a receiver that decodes the acoustic vibrations into an auditory event. The magnitude of the vibrations ("sound waves") determines the perceived loudness of the sound (in decibels). For example, the loudness of normal speech, without background noise, is about 60–65 dB. A live rock band begins at about 85–90 dB and may be as loud as 115 dB, about 10 percent louder than a jackhammer.

Loudness is not the only factor affecting whether we can hear speech, because the human ear (really the brain) can only perceive certain frequencies, corresponding to the number of sound waves reaching the ear per second. Normal hearing for humans is in the range of 20–20,000 Hz. Dogs can hear sounds greater than 30,000 Hz, so that "silent" dog whistles are simply designed to produce high-pitched (i.e., high-frequency) sounds between 20,000 and 30,000 Hz. When it comes to human speech, losses that affect hearing in the range of 500–2000 Hz are most troublesome, because, as we have noted, those are the frequencies at which the important features of spoken language are expressed. Vowels tend to fall in the lower frequency range; fricative consonants like /th/, /s/, and /f/ are in the higher frequency range. Vowels also tend to be louder than consonants, but they are not as important for distinguishing one word from another.

The variety of causes of congenital or early-onset deafness may contribute to diversity in the development of those children.

To give some idea of how hearing is visualized, we have provided copies of the audiograms for the three authors, one of whom has very acute hearing, one of whom has a mild hearing loss in one ear, and one of whom is profoundly deaf (fig. 3.1). Although the audiograms do not provide complete information concerning the qualitative or quantitative aspects of hearing/hearing loss, they are sufficient in this case to distinguish among the three of us and to suggest in which cases some kind of accommodation might be necessary. The situation is not necessarily obvious, however, and none of us wears hearing aids.

When sounds reach the outer ear, the vibrations in the air are funneled into the ear canal to the eardrum, which vibrates in response to the changing pressure. These vibrations correspond to the frequency or pitch of the sound and cause small movements in the hammer, anvil, and stirrup, the three small bones of the middle ear (and the smallest bones in the human body). The linked movement of the three bones transmits the vibrations through its connection to the oval window, a soft piece of tissue on the cochlea. That vibration of the oval window causes vibrations in the fluids on its other side, in the cochlea proper. Higher frequencies have shorter distances between waves and therefore make for faster vibrations that are passed along this chain.

The spiral of the cochlea contains a soft tube that holds the hair cells that receive the sound. When the fluid in the inner ear moves, the hair cells wave like seaweed on the floor of the ocean, creating nerve impulses that normally are carried to the auditory centers of the brain by the auditory nerve.[2] Hearing loss occurs when there is damage or blockage somewhere along this sequence, from the outer ear to the brain. Usually, problems in the middle ear are less severe or less difficult to correct, whereas problems in the cochlea or the auditory nerve tend to result in more severe hearing losses.

A common cause of hearing loss in children, although one that usually is only temporary, is otitis media—frequently referred to simply as

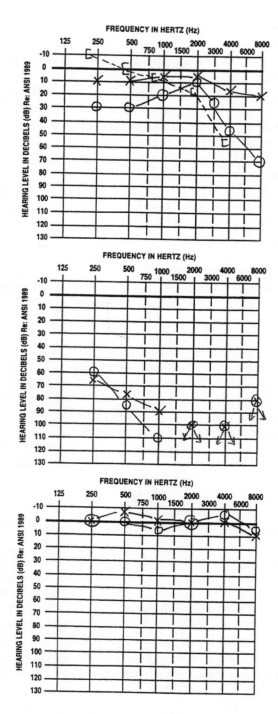

Figure 3.1. Audiograms of the three authors.

"ear infections." Otitis media occurs when the eustachian tube leading from the throat to the ear becomes blocked and fluid builds up in the middle ear. The hammer, anvil, and stirrup are designed to work in air, not in fluid, so that when an infection fills the area, movement along the chain is reduced and sounds are muffled. Antibiotics usually clear up ear infections, although the insertion of drainage tubes may be necessary in chronic or more severe cases. In remote geographical areas where antibiotics are not readily available, chronic otitis media can lead to permanent hearing loss. Even in less severe cases, occurring commonly in the United States, recurring bouts of otitis media may result in delays in reading ability and lower performance on verbal intelligence tests (Kindig & Richards, 2000; see also Johnson et al., 2000). It should not be surprising, then, that more severe, permanent hearing losses in deaf children can influence such abilities.

When hearing losses result from causes that are not readily cured or corrected, some degree of artificial correction might be provided by assistive listening devices, most notably hearing aids. Hearing aids amplify sound across a broad spectrum. Regardless of whether they fit behind the ear, in the ear, or are carried in a pocket, hearing aids are all much the same inside (fig. 3.2). Sound is picked up by a microphone, amplified, and sent via a speaker into a small tube. The tube is connected to a custom-made, plastic earmold that ensures a snug fit. The high-pitched "eeeeee" sound sometimes heard from hearing aids usually means that they are not tightly in place, so that there is feedback from the speaker to the microphone, much

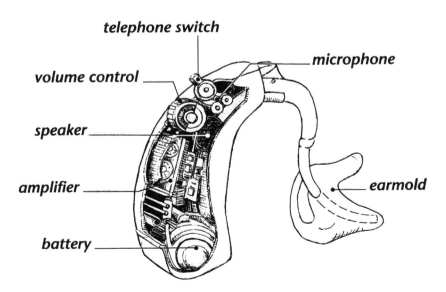

Figure 3.2. Schematic diagram of a hearing aid.

as would occur if a hand-held microphone were passed in front of a public-address speaker.

Most hearing aids are not specifically tuned to speech sounds the way that fully functioning human ears are. They amplify all sounds equally, so that background noise is increased just as much as the important sounds. These *analog* aids directly amplify sound picked up by the microphone. Sometimes background noise with such aids can become so loud that it impedes the perception of speech and desired environmental sounds. Newer hearing aids, both analog and digital, can be programmed to particular frequency patterns, matching the hearing losses of their users and blocking out other noise. Digital hearing aids, or *digital signal processing instruments*, are at the cutting-edge of this technology, as they can be matched precisely to the hearing losses of the user in terms of both decibels and frequency. Digital aids are now being produced by most hearing aid companies, but, like analog programmable aids, they are still quite expensive. Data for 1998 indicated that digital hearing aids represented only about 8 percent of total hearing aid sales, while programmable aids, overall, represented about 17 percent of sales in the United States. As development continues and prices decline, they should become increasingly popular, and user satisfaction should increase. This user satisfaction issue is not a trivial one. The hearing aid industry has a problem with consumers being disappointed with hearing aids, and approximately 20 percent of all aids sold, analog and digital, are returned to the manufacturer for credit (Kirkwood, 1999).

For children with some residual hearing, the use of hearing aids can be very important. Not only do hearing aids provide access to the spoken language of hearing parents and siblings, but in cases of progressive hearing loss, they can facilitate those children learning sign language and/or receiving speech therapy to maintain their spoken language skills. When there is more severe hearing loss, hearing aids, a cochlear implant, or the use of residual hearing may provide information to a deaf child in support of language development, even if they do not provide sufficient information for comprehension of language. Even a degraded auditory signal can indicate that a language event is happening, call attention to possible relations between prior events and language, and communicate social information such as turn-taking demands and emotional responses of others. Indeed, acquisition of sign language by most deaf children is assisted by spoken language received either by using residual hearing or speechreading, and hearing aids often provide an important support during the school years, even if they later are worn less frequently as an adult. Most audiologists recommend starting children with hearing aids immediately after diagnosis of hearing loss, or as early as possible, so that they become used to them and are exposed to auditory information as early as possible. Early use of hearing aids also typically is associated with better language development in children, although research is less clear on this issue when children have congenital hearing losses (see Marchark, 2001b, for a review).

Hearing aids also allow access to *loop systems*, which involve closed-circuit wiring that sends FM signals from an audio system directly to an electronic coil in the hearing aid. The receiver picks up the signals much like a remote control sends infrared signals to a television. There are also infrared loop systems that work exactly the same way. These systems are especially useful in large classrooms and lecture halls, situations where sound quality normally would suffer. Since 1988, federal law in the United States has required that all new telephones include loop-type circuitry that is consistent with hearing aid coils, making them more useful for many people with partial hearing losses.

Cochlear Implants

By 1997, more than 9000 adults and 700 children worldwide had received cochlear implants, and they have rapidly become one of the most important issues for teachers, school administrators, and educational researchers (Marschark, 2001a). We therefore will try to at least touch on the major issues concerning cochlear implants in children.

Perhaps the best summary of the functioning of cochlear implants was provided by the National Institutes of Health (1995):

> The cochlear implant is an electronic device that, under the appropriate conditions, provides a sense of sound to persons who are profoundly hearing impaired or deaf. It does not restore normal hearing, but it can help the user understand speech and perceive sounds from the environment. The vast majority of adults who are deaf and have cochlear implants derive substantial benefit from them when they are used in conjunction with speech reading, and a considerable number of implanted individuals can understand speech without visual cues. Benefits also have been observed in children, including those who were born deaf or lost their hearing before learning spoken language. (p.4)

Whereas hearing aids amplify sound, cochlear implants provide a direct connection between sound in the environment and the nerves that normally carry that information to the brain. Implantation involves surgically inserting a set of electrodes directly into the cochlea. Like a hearing aid, the user has one of several models of the external device that includes a microphone and a receiver which converts sound to electrical energy. (The external mechanism is attached magnetically to the internal part of the unit; there are no wires sticking out of the head.) The cochlear implant system includes a micro-processor which generates electrical signals corresponding to sounds varying in loudness and frequency and sends them directly to nerve fibers in the cochlea (fig. 3.3)

One does not frequently encounter opposition to hearing aids, even if some deaf people prefer not to wear them. Cochlear implants are a more sensitive issue, for several reasons. First, implantation involves invasive surgery (with attendant risks) that destroys any residual hearing in the implanted ear, although complications appear to be rare. Second, implantation is not a simple, "one-shot" affair. The initial implantation surgery costs $40,000–$50,000, expenses now being paid by most health insurers, and requires minimal hospital stay. Following implantation, however, support for speech and hearing rehabilitation involves a team of individuals including doctors, speech therapists, and others working with a child for years and, according to recent figures, this follow-up can cost another $20,000 or so a year.

Beyond practical matters, a third issue with regard to implantation comes from the social-cultural perspective, held by some Deaf and hear-

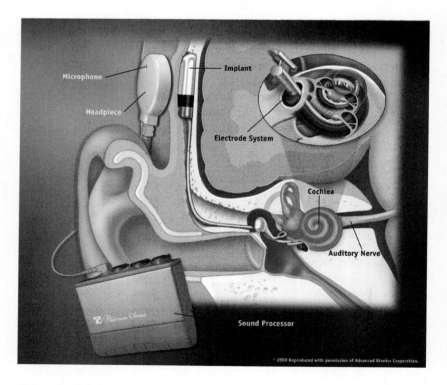

Figure 3.3. Schematic of a cochlear implant. (Courtesy of Advanced Bionics.)

ing individuals, that performing surgery to try to restore hearing implicitly tells children that being deaf is bad and that they have to be medically repaired. There is some concern that such children will lack self-esteem and may find themselves stuck between Deaf and hearing cultures, not a member of either. There is also an underlying, less-frequently stated fear that the increasing number of cochlear implantations might lead to the demise of the Deaf community. In chapter 2, we described the history of deaf people seeking to be recognized as individuals, and the emergence of Deaf communities as a linguistic and cultural minority group. Throughout that history, the long-running debate about the best methods for communication has blurred with other issues, and social opinions always have been added to the argument of what works for whom and when. With increasing visibility now being given to the Deaf community and to the roles of deaf people in all walks of life, cochlear implants do seem threatening—and apparently with good cause.[3] An eminent physiologist whose research contributed significantly to the development of the cochlear implants currently in use has argued that deafness is a medical condition that needs to be cured. "The simple fact is," he noted, "that if the culture could be reliably wiped out, it would be a good thing to wipe out" (Clay, 1997, p. 28). Nevertheless, some Deaf adults have chosen to get implants and stay in the Deaf community. Others have made different decisions.

While social-cultural concerns are important to some individuals, they are likely to be of only secondary importance for hearing parents who are more interested in trying to have their children be as "normal" as possible. In the end, it will be the decision of parents—hopefully an informed decision—as to whether a child receives a cochlear implant. Motivation and enthusiasm for a cochlear implant on the part of the recipient generally is the best predictor of its success, providing perseverance through the operation and the extensive "mapping" (tuning of the device) and training periods that follow. When parents decide on a cochlear implant for their young children, or when adults are pressured into implantation by family members, the outlook is less certain. Yet, parents often appear to value cochlear implants more than the children do, hoping to give their child "a normal life." Not surprisingly, the lowest usage rates among individuals with cochlear implants are found in teenagers, who typically have already established sign communication skills, are less likely to acquire strong speech skills, and are likely to be influenced by identity and psychosocial implications of using the device (i.e., peer pressure; O'Donoghue, 1996; Pollard, 1996).

Setting aside opinions about cochlear implants, the most important issue for educators and parents is the extent to which the implants contribute to language development, social development, cognitive development, and educational success. This means balancing risks, benefits, and the alternative of not having the implantation. Many parents are under-

standably concerned about possible isolation, depression, academic difficulties, and future employment challenges for their children. Support from
the Deaf community and others notwithstanding, these are certainly risks
to be considered, and many deaf adults report having experienced such
obsstacles, even if they ultimately were successful in overcoming them.
Not being familiar with either deafness or the Deaf community, the promise of making their child able to function in a hearing world is very attractive to hearing parents.

At the same time, hearing parents cannot really understand what it
means—and does not mean—to be deaf. We have already noted that deaf
life is different from just life without hearing, and there is nothing that will
turn a deaf child into a hearing child. Even with a cochlear implant, there
is no guarantee that a particular child will be able to understand spoken
language—even if the implant's microprocessor is commonly referred to
as a "speech processor" by manufacturers. It therefore is worth considering the language issue a bit more thoroughly.

As can be seen in the schematic of a cochlear implant (fig. 3.3), the
business end of the device is the wire inserted into the cochlea. The wire
contains multiple "channels," each consisting of an electrode sending a
different frequency. Early single-channel cochlear implants, first implanted
in adults in 1957, were rarely successful in allowing deaf children to understand speech and did not significantly improve their speech intelligibility
(Carney & Moeller, 1988). With the development of more sophisticated,
multiple-channel implants transmitting 22–26 separate frequencies, studies have demonstrated that deaf children's speech perception and production ability continue to increase 4–5 years after implantation. In 1995 the
National Institutes of Health (NIH) stated that "speech produced by children
with implants is more accurate than speech produced by children with comparable hearing losses using vibrotactile devices or hearing aids. . . . just one
year after implantation, speech intelligibility is twice that typically reported
for children with profound hearing impairment and continues to improve."
It is important to note the reference to profound hearing losses, because
children with hearing losses up to around 90 dB have been found to have as
good or better speech perception and production with hearing aids as children with cochlear implants, and children with losses less than 90 dB typically are not considered candidates for cochlear implants.

On the basis of advertising of implant manufacturers and seeing "cochlear implant stars" on television, many parents believe that implantation will improve deaf children's auditory perception and speech production sufficiently to make them fully able to communicate through spoken
language alone. Those expectations frequently are not met, sometimes with
significant negative emotional consequences for all concerned (Kampfe
et al., 1993; Pollard, 1996). The outcome of receiving a cochlear implant
can range from the success of those perhaps infrequent stars to acceptable

levels of functioning to no benefit at all to the occasional catastrophic failure, in which an implant must be removed. At present, we are unable to find any statistics concerning the frequency of the two extremes in this continuum, although they are both infrequent.

Based on a thorough review of the literature, it is evident that there are many more positive outcomes of cochlear implantation than negative outcomes (Spencer, in press). The "average" outcome is one in which sounds are detected 90 percent of the time, but spoken language is correctly identified less than 50 percent of the time. Although the "success stories" are described as being able to talk fluently on the telephone, the average recipient of an implant has only limited use of the telephone for short and contextually well-defined utterances. Unfortunately for both users and investigators, outcome variability is so great that it is difficult to make any good generalizations at this point.

Descriptions of particular studies concerning the speech and hearing abilities of children who have received cochlear implants are beyond the scope of the present discussion and invariably will capture only part of the bigger picture. More important for present purposes, research concerning language development (see chapter 5) in deaf children with cochlear implants is just beginning, and we do not yet know how implants will impact school achievement and socialization. In fact, few studies have addressed either academic or social functioning.

In one study, described as a follow-up of all of the children who had received cochlear implants at a particular center, among eight children who had received implants and were in mainstream educational settings, all but two were performing in the top half of their classes (Nevins & Chute, 1995). Five of the children were rated by their teachers as academically and socially successful in the classroom, two as socially but not academically successful, and one not successful in mainstream. Unfortunately, the investigators did not follow-up the other eight children, who were not enrolled in mainstream programs, so it is difficult to draw any firm conclusions. Taken together, however, the published research indicates that cochlear implants improve speech perception at frequencies that might contribute to language processing and language acquisition. They also suggest that language development may be enhanced by cochlear implants relative to preimplantation levels for many children, particularly those who lost their hearing after some exposure to auditory stimulation (Tait & Lutman, 1994; Vermeulen et al., 1995; see Spencer, in press, for review).

One often encounters claims by manufacturers and individuals that implanted children in spoken-language environments do better in language development than children in environments that include sign language (e.g., Tait & Lutman, 1994). Such claims are difficult to evaluate because most children who receive implants were previously educated in spoken-language environments and continue in those programs after they receive their implants. Several published and unpublished studies suggest that children enrolled in total communication settings have shown the greatest advances in language development (e.g., Preisler & Ahlstroem, 1997).

Length of time with the implant has been reported to be an important predictor of speech and language success in some studies, but not in others (Dawson et al., 1995). Unlike adults deafened later in life, who show the greatest benefits from cochlear implants within the first year or two of implantation, children tend to show smaller gains during the first 18 months after implantation. One recent investigation (claiming strong support for implantation), however, found that the length of time with an implant accounted for only 1 percent of the variability in whether children attended mainstream programs rather than special programs for deaf children (Francis et al., 1999). In contrast to the view of many medical researchers, the consensus among investigators of the development of deaf children appears to be that most children who receive implants are ill-prepared for full-time placement in mainstream programs without additional support (Patricia Spencer, personal communication, March 2, 2000).

Clearly, there are many questions to be answered. Most important, perhaps, is the issue of who will benefit from implants and who will not. As the implantation of young children continues, it is essential that we conduct more research on the linguistic, cognitive, and social impact of cochlear implantation, coupled with ongoing research concerning speech perception and production. In the meantime, as long as it appears that sign language might support the development of spoken language by children with implants, total communication environments appear to offer the broadest possible support for language and social development. Even if children with cochlear implants eventually come to depend more on spoken language than on sign language, early access to language is essential for deaf children's cognitive development and literacy skills in their ability to benefit from school experiences, and sign language may be helpful for many children with implants (Preisler & Ahlstroem, 1997; Tomblin et al., 1999). Because understanding that different school settings can support and emphasize different aspects of development in education, let us briefly consider the issue of alternative school placements.

Experiences in School Environments

Beyond audiological differences, one of the most academically significant characteristics of deaf learners, and a characteristic by which many deaf and hard-of-hearing individuals identify themselves, is the kind of school they attended. Differences in school experience have been linked to understanding language, social, and personality development of deaf children, as well as academic preparation and educational performance.

As described more fully in chapter 7, the three primary categories of educational programming at issue here are schools for the deaf, special programs for deaf students, and mainstreaming, or enrollment in regular classes in local public schools. Schools for the deaf frequently draw from relatively large geographical areas and are commonly referred to as "residential schools" even though children who live within commuting distance typically do not reside there. Special programs for deaf children outside of residential schools can be entirely separate (private or public) or can be housed in public schools.

In either case, special programs provide deaf children with the opportunity to interact with other deaf children and to have both deaf adults and older deaf children as role models in all areas of work and play. Residential schools thus have long been seen by the Deaf community as the center of Deaf culture and are the preferred educational system for most deaf children of deaf parents as well as being a desirable place to work for deaf teachers. The Deaf community points out that without such programs, few deaf children would have fluent knowledge of American Sign Language (ASL) or Deaf culture (Padden & Humphries, 1988). Only the small proportion of deaf children with deaf parents would have the opportunity to identify with deaf role models. While early intervention programs provide some such stimulation, the concern is with maintaining a social, cultural, and academic context that provides older deaf children with a supportive learning environment.

It should not be surprising that there are social and personality differences among deaf children who attend residential schools only with other deaf children, those who attend local public schools only with hearing children, or other alternatives in between. The importance of social functioning to educational success and normal development notwithstanding, parents are particularly concerned with how the education that deaf children receive in schools for the deaf compare to those they would receive in their local public schools. The issue is not whether the educational programs themselves are the same, but what the students learn and take away from those programs. At the extremes, neither an inaccessible but high-quality program nor accessible but low-quality program will be to a child's advantage. Therefore, the question at issue concerns the extent to which alternative programs contribute to the child's growth in academic and other domains (see chapter 6).

In chapter 2, we described the signing of Public Law 94–142, the Education of All Handicapped Children Act, in 1975. The law that guaranteed free, appropriate public education for all children with disabilities also indicated that they should be educated with non-disabled children to the maximum extent possible, generally referred to as mainstreaming.[4] Mainstreaming can take several different forms. In full inclusion settings, children are included in all aspects of the public school with only the minimum of supplementary support services, all of which are provided in the classroom. Fully mainstreamed students, who attend classes with hearing students, and partially mainstreamed students, who attend some classes with hearing peers and some with only deaf peers, typically also have a resource room and/or personnel outside of the classroom dedicated to their special needs. Mainstreaming would seem to ensure equal educational rigor for deaf and hearing students, but this assumes that teachers treat both groups exactly the same and that both deaf and hearing students have equivalent access to information in the classroom. This appears not to be the case, at least with regard to the frequency with which teachers direct language to deaf and hearing children (Cawthon, 2001).

One potential difficulty of mainstreaming is that the dispersal of deaf children throughout local school systems means that often there is only one deaf child in a class. Beyond the significant social-emotional consequences of being different and often unable to communicate with peers during the school years, teachers may be unfamiliar with the needs of deaf students and ill-prepared to ensure that they are able to fully participate equally with hearing students of the same age (see chapter 7).

The success of deaf children in public schools, while an admirable goal in many ways, requires considerably more study. At present, it appears that deaf children who are alone in mainstream settings tend to be less well-adjusted and exhibit lower emotional maturity than those enrolled in residential schools, although the evidence is not unequivocal (Lowenbraun & Thompson, 1987; Stinson & Lang 1994). A host of variables related to school placement make any general conclusions about the utility of one kind of program or another difficult. Mainstreaming may be an excellent alternative for children with greater residual hearing or who benefit more from hearing aids or cochlear implants. The option may be less successful for children with greater hearing losses or less spoken language skill. Throughout this book, we present several domains in which alternative school programs appear to have a differential impact on development and education for students with different characteristics. Looking ahead, the only safe conclusion is that there needs to be a broad array of alternative school placements for students with different strengths and needs.

Family Status

Deafness not only affects the child, it affects the whole family. Certainly, having a deaf child influences everyone in the family and influences families in different ways. But families with deaf parents or deaf children also might differ from hearing families, and this makes it even more difficult to sort out the impact of hearing loss on the development and education of deaf children. The level of a mother's education is one such factor, as mothers with more education are more likely to have better sign language skills, and their deaf children show better academic achievement. Parents with more education also tend to be more involved in their children's school activities.

Family socioeconomic status (SES) appears to be another factor that might differentiate families with deaf children. It has been argued that hearing loss is distributed evenly over various social strata (Rodda & Grove, 1987). That assertion is at odds with the fact that deaf adults tend to be overrepresented in the lower SES groups in most countries, although cause and effect are somewhat difficult to separate. In the United States, for example, deaf individuals are more likely to have lower family incomes than hearing individuals (NCHS, 1994; Schein & Delk, 1974). This may be related, in part, to the fact that some hearing losses may result from factors frequently associated with lower SES, including proximity to environmental noise, poor nutrition, and occupations in heavy industry. Still, deaf individuals tend to be disproportionally employed in the service and clerical sectors, overqualified for their jobs, and earn less than their hearing peers (MacLeod-Gallinger, 1992). Individuals with congenital or early-onset hearing losses appear to be the most disadvantaged in terms of SES, whereas those who become deaf after age 11 are best positioned (Schein & Delk, 1974). Of course, cause and effect are also unclear in this situation, as hearing loss, education, literacy, and employer selection biases are intertwined. Deaf individuals who have graduated from college earn closer to what their hearing peers earn, but they still are in the minority.

Family SES also appears to be related to the characteristics of students attending different school programs. Children who attend residential schools tend to be from households with lower average incomes, although it is unclear exactly why this is the case (but see Schildroth, 1986). Deaf children from more affluent families are more likely to attend specialized, privately run programs at which they receive more individualized attention and academic tutoring, and their parents may be more financially and psychologically able to support them. The link between academic achievement and parents' involvement in their children's school activities might be an effect of SES: Higher SES parents may be more involved and may have children with higher achievement for different reasons. Residential schools also tend to be near cities and may either draw from a different population of parents or may be less demanding on them in terms of encouraging their involvement in school activities (especially when parents live at some distance from the school).

Finally, in considering acquired (nonhereditary) hearing losses, one would expect that higher SES families are likely to have better medical insurance and that mothers in those families would have better prenatal and postnatal care. Those parents also seem likely to be better educated with regard to medical issues, and thus they might be more likely to recognize symptoms of illness in their children that might lead to hearing loss. Parents without medical insurance would be less likely to seek medical help in general, even if their child's hearing loss has already been identified. Consistent with such expectations, approximately half of the deaf children from families with the lowest incomes became deaf after birth, compared to only 17 percent of children from families with the highest incomes (Rawlings & Jensema, 1977). In short, both deaf adults and deaf children of hearing parents, on average, live in families at or below the middle-class level, and deafness may not be as socioeconomically unbiased as is sometimes suggested.

Emotional and Mental Health

Another factor that may differ across families with and without deaf members is emotional stability or mental health. With only 1 in 10 deaf children having even one deaf parent, few are raised in close contact with the Deaf community. Upon their entry into residential schools or other programs, some deaf children will encounter that community for the first time, including its values, customs, and rules. Most young deaf children, however, reside almost entirely in the hearing world. Developing a sense of identity and self-esteem, therefore, may be all the more challenging.

During the early school years, children normally identify with their parents and siblings, who are similar to them in a variety of ways. This identification process facilitates the development of healthy sex roles, moral values, and social behaviors. When children do not have such models, they can become less confident and more prone to inappropriate behavior (see Vaccari & Marschark, 1997, for a review). Hearing parents and other hearing adults can serve as excellent examples for young children if they can communicate effectively with them, but having deaf role models appears to be important for deaf children, even if it represents a challenge for many parents and teachers. Effective communication is an important ingredient of healthy psychological functioning.

Studies conducted during the 1960s and 1970s concerning the emotional and mental health of deaf individuals reported that deaf adults, on average, were more emotionally and behaviorally fragile than hearing adults. We now know that such characterizations were overblown, deriving largely from communication barriers between deaf individuals and the medical community, inappropriate use of diagnostic tools, and concerns about competency on the part of professionals when dealing with deaf individuals (Pollard, 1998). Nevertheless, the challenges confronted by deaf individuals as either primary and secondary effects of their hearing losses might increase their risk for psychological distress, including depression, frustration, and lack of self-esteem.

Evidence indicates that less than 10 percent of deaf individuals in need of mental health services actually receive them. Few psychologists or psychiatrists can use sign language with sufficient fluency to evaluate the mental health of deaf individuals, and the involvement of a sign language interpreter is a sensitive issue and a difficult concept for many professionals to accept (Pollard, 1998). Accessibility of social services for the deaf continues to be poor, despite the availability of interpreters. Psychological needs of deaf individuals also are often misdiagnosed, largely because of communication barriers. Perhaps most common in this regard is the misdiagnosis of deaf children as mentally retarded, seemingly a catch-all classification made by hearing professionals who are unable to elicit appropriate re-

Effective communication is an important ingredient of healthy psychological functioning.

sponses from deaf children and who are unfamiliar with deafness and deaf people. Mental disorders actually appear to occur with equal frequency and severity in deaf and hearing populations, although some forms of hearing loss may be linked to neurological disorders that have related psychological effects. Lack of treatment also may lead to the exacerbation of some psychological conditions, and impoverished early environments for deaf children may later give the appearance of cognitive limitations. As one clinical researcher noted: "In the deaf *patient* population, it is common to find individuals who suffered such environmentally induced deficits, including severe cases of early and prolonged neglect by families or institutions that left them with serious and permanent cognitive deficits that were otherwise entirely preventable" (Pollard, 1998, p. 183; see also Marschark, 2000).

Precise information about the frequency of psychological problems in deaf individuals, and especially children, is difficult to obtain for a variety of reasons. Obviously, most personality and social-adjustment tests are normed on hearing individuals. Just as in the case of intelligence and achievement tests, there might well be cultural biases in such tests that give a distorted view of a particular deaf individual (Marschark & Lukomski, 2001). A second problem for both validity (whether the test measures what it purports to measure) and reliability (whether a test gives the same results at different times and with different individuals) is the fact that most of these tests are given in written format and require some facility with English. In research conducted with children and adults with lower English literacy skills, even apparently simple standardized tests and demographic questionnaires can be misinterpreted (see Braden, 2001). Changing such tests or interpreting them for deaf individuals is helpful, but generalization from original norms again creates problems of validity. As a result, when relationships are found between hearing loss and emotional self-report measures, investigators are unsure whether they indicate test bias or real emotional difficulty. The greater variability of deaf individuals, relative to hearing individuals, also creates a challenge for test interpretation as well as planning therapeutic interventions.

Summary

A variety of factors can influence the social and academic success of children. It is during the school years that language, social, and cognitive development are fine tuned through a variety of experiences. Peers and teachers become as important as parents in many ways, both from the perspective of children's desire to please them and the degree to which they influence development and learning. Hearing loss can affect the amount of information that a child receives, thus influencing growth in almost any domain. Hearing loss also can affect the way in which a child is perceived and received by others, thus creating cascading consequences in these areas. Although hearing aids or cochlear implants help compensate for hearing loss, they do not make deaf children into hearing children. Aside from the amount  of support they provide for interactions with the environment, such devices may produce their own effects on self-esteem, self-image, and social comfort.

Overall, it appears that the incidence of psychological disorders is essentially the same in deaf and hearing populations, even if communication barriers between deaf individuals and mental health professionals are notoriously problematic. Nevertheless, almost a third of all deaf children have additional medical conditions that place them at risk for developmental or educational difficulties. Being at risk need not entail negative consequences for development or education. It does, however, emphasize the need for parents, teachers, and researchers to work together to understand the complex interaction of variables in deaf students and structure children's learning environments appropriately.

Educational success also demands that children are supported by adults they respect and with whom they identify. The value placed on academic activities by parents and teachers is internalized by children, and lowered expectations will most certainly be met with lower achievement. Greater parental support and involvement in school activities typically lead to greater academic achievement in both deaf and hearing children. We now turn to education and the teaching-learning process, first as it begins informally in the home and then in more structured school settings.

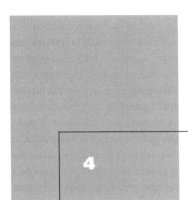

What special efforts should parents make for their deaf babies and children?

How can we make sure that young deaf children will be ready for school?

4

Education Begins at Home

Parents, siblings, and others provide young children with a context in which development occurs and supports and promotes early learning. In this chapter, we consider the roles of various individuals and early interventions in social, language, and cognitive development before children enter school. Because most deaf children are born to nonsigning, hearing parents, communication in the home is given special consideration, particularly with regard to the kinds of information and experience that contribute to those domains. We also consider the importance of implicit instruction in relation to fostering educational readiness and the potential effects on long-term academic achievement and personal growth.[1] Parents will encounter both opportunities and challenges in raising a deaf child, and research has demonstrated a variety of ways in which they can optimize their child's development. Therefore, we devote some space to describing the field on which early development takes place. Most important, we will see the importance of deaf children having early access to language, social interaction, and experiential diversity.

In the Beginning

Because most cases of deafness are not hereditary, many deaf children will have congenital or early-onset hearing losses that are totally unexpected (and usually unrecognized for some time) by their parents. Some of those children will be considered at risk at birth because of the maternal, fetal, or neonatal medical problems that contributed to their hearing losses. Beyond the consequences of initial medical difficulties, factors related to prenatal or postnatal hearing loss may well influence the quantity or quality of interactions the infant has with others in the environment during the first few months. These earliest influences, and their effects, can have ever-widening consequences for development over the first months and years of life.

Even before birth, sounds perceived from within the womb can influence the course of development. Early in the last trimester of pregnancy, a fetus will rotate and adopt a new position with the head against the mother's pelvis. Most fetuses already have considerable responsiveness to sound at this point and can perceive the mother's voice and heartbeat through bone conduction (Als et al., 1979).[2] This earliest experience can influence postnatal learning and perception in humans, just as it does in many animals (both live-born and hatched). In a pioneering study involving human infants, babies less than three days old learned to suck on a nipple in a particular pattern (faster or slower than their baseline average) in order to listen to sound of their mothers' voices (DeCasper & Fifer, 1980). Similar results were found with babies who could control their access to the sound of maternal, intrauterine heartbeats (DeCasper & Sigafoos, 1983) (see Working Newborns—How Do They Do It? p. 65).

The ability of a newborn to discriminate its mother's voice from that of other females and orient to it means that, at some level, babies recognize their mothers. Indirectly, this ability also will influence both social and language development. That is, human babies who can hear will turn their heads in the direction of "interesting" and familiar sounds, in this case, the mother's voice. This behavior will help to initiate the first social interactions, support the fine-tuning of perceptual and motor skills, and help to promote mother–child bonding.

Although vocalizing and hearing play a central role in early bonding for humans and many animals, they are not essential. Other factors contribute to bonding between deaf babies and hearing mothers or hearing babies and deaf mothers, including visual, physical, and olfactory cues. There are biologically based mechanisms in all children that influence and are influenced by development as an interdependent relationship with the environment is formed. To the extent that hearing mothers with deaf infants or deaf mothers with hearing infants interact differently from hearing mothers with hearing infants or deaf mothers with deaf infants, early social and communication strategies may look different in some subtle or not-so-subtle ways. Such differences should not be viewed negatively, any more than differences in parent–child interactions across different countries should be viewed negatively. The hearing parents of a deaf baby may need to do some things differently or do some things more often than they would if they had a hearing baby, but the substance of development is all

Working Newborns—How Do They Do It?

DeCasper and Fifer (1980) studied the ability of newborns, only one to three days old, to recognize their mothers' voices. DeCasper and Fifer fitted the babies with stereo headphones and a non-nutritive nipple attached to a pair of tape recorders. After establishing the baseline for spontaneous sucking in each infant, they presented infants with a two-choice task in which they could select one of two tape recordings by sucking at a rate faster or slower (alternating across babies) than their baseline sucking rates. One recording for each baby contained its mother's voice, whereas the other contained the voice of an unfamiliar woman; both women were reading the same book. The results were clear: DeCasper and Fifer's babies, who had less than 12 hours postnatal experience with their mothers, were willing and able to work to hear their mothers' voices. In fact, DeCasper and Spence (1986) showed that when mothers read a particular passage aloud, daily, during the last 6 weeks of pregnancy, their newborns showed a preference for the familiar passage over a novel one two to three days after birth. Fathers' voices, which are not typically available to the fetus until after birth, do not show any sign of being reinforcing for the newborn (DeCasper & Prescott, 1984).

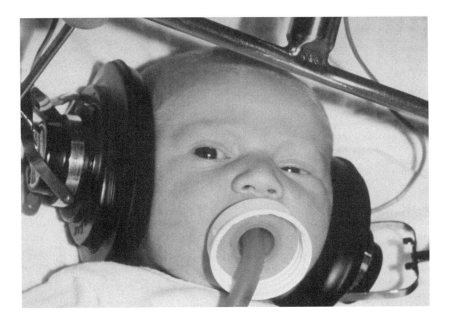

Figure 4.1. One of DeCasper and Fifer's working newborns. (Courtesy of Anthony DeCasper.)

pretty much the same regardless of whether or not a child can hear. Let us now consider several aspects of early environments, inside and outside the home, that play key roles in development.

Infancy: A Critical Period

During the first months of life, mothers and infants develop ways of interacting with each other through a variety of shared experiences, from diaper changing to dancing. Eventually, their actions become intertwined in a way that teaches children simple interpersonal routines and provides information about successful and unsuccessful social interactions. Those actions also contribute to the emotional bonding between parents and children. For example, when an infant cries, an adult is likely to pick him up. The infant temporarily ceases to fuss and looks at the adult—often the mother—who often speaks or smiles in return. The baby then makes some noise or smiles and is again answered by the mother with more talking, more handling, and so on. It is important to notice that the infant is playing a vital role in this two-way interaction by giving the mother cues that help to determine her behavior, including passing other cues back to the infant. Over time, both mother and child will become more adept in these interactions, developing routines that will increase in smoothness and complexity (Bateson, 1975; Bell & Ainsworth, 1972). Hearing parents of hearing infants also spend considerable time talking to their babies and delighting in their responses. They notice their hearing babies' attention to dogs barking, television, and other noises and often comment on them. Two-way language conversations may be a long way off, but the child is learning to communicate through behavior and is learning about being part of a complex social unit.

The situation will be different in some ways when an infant is deaf and, as in most cases, the hearing parents initially do not realize it.[3] The fussing baby will not stop crying when mother enters the room, and soothing words will have no impact. Parents do not realize that they have to be within the child's line of sight for interactions to occur, and they often seem to be ignored. Eventually, parents see that their infant's behavior is different from what they and their friends have experienced with hearing infants, and the child is not meeting the expected language milestones. Many parents come to feel rejected or anxious about the perceived lack of their child's reciprocity, but they are assured by pediatricians and family members that the child will catch up eventually (Harris, 1978). In the absence of hearing screening for newborns, however, most hearing losses in young children are not diagnosed until the second or third year, by which time the lags behind other children already have become pronounced (see chapter 3). At this point, diagnosis of "only" a hearing loss may come as a relief.

The above scenario notwithstanding, a variety of studies have indicated that the earliest interactions between hearing mothers and their deaf infants are also similar in many ways to those seen in hearing mothers and their hearing children. Perhaps without even recognizing it, for example, mothers come to use much more nonvocal behavior such as waving, smiling, and touching. Intuitively, they develop other strategies for interacting with their deaf babies, and the mother–child bond appears to be just as strong as it is when mothers and babies have the same hearing status. Some caution should be taken in interpreting such findings because the studies necessarily involved situations in which the mothers were aware of their children's hearing losses. Research of this sort also generally includes only healthy babies, and it is difficult to extrapolate to situations where there are multiple handicaps or other birth-related complications relating to mother or infant. As a result, we cannot know about the nature and quality of mothers' interactions with their deaf infants before hearing losses are identified (see Calderon & Greenberg, 1993).

Implications of Early Interactions

The visible characteristics of early interactions of parents and infants, as well as related emotional factors, may influence the development of *attachment*. In humans, the first phases of attachment are seen in early infancy, as infants seem to respond more to their parents and other caregivers than to others. By eight months of age, the infant attempts to stay near the mother in unfamiliar contexts. At this point, attachment can be assessed using the "strange situation." In this paradigm, an 8- to 18-month-old child is occupied in a play room, accompanied by the mother and a stranger. At several points, one of the adults leaves the room and returns after a brief absence. Children who greet their mothers positively when she comes back or who go to them for comfort if they have shown signs of distress are classified as *securely attached*. Children who ignore the mother's return or start to greet her but turn away are classified as *avoidant*; and those who have temper tantrums, react negatively toward the mother, or approach her but cannot or will not be comforted are classified as *resistant* in their attachment (Ainsworth, 1973).

In the case of deaf babies, any differences observed in attachment may or may not have consequences for later parent–child relationships or on social development. Deaf infants and toddlers, for example, sometimes demonstrate what appears to be more separation anxiety than hearing children, but this may result from their not noticing when someone leaves (thus being surprised later when they realize a parent is gone) or not understanding that the person will be back. These are both hearing-related difficulties, and such behavior does not appear to occur in deaf children of deaf parents any more frequently than it does in hearing children of hearing parents. In fact, contrary to some early observations in this area, the weight of evidence now suggests that deaf children are just as securely attached to their mothers as hearing children, regardless of whether their mothers are deaf or hearing (e.g., Lederberg & Mobley, 1990). This finding can be taken as a reflection of the flexibility of both parents and children as well as an indicator that observed differences between deaf and hearing children early on need not have any long-term implications. Once again, however, studies in this area typically involve a limited pool of participants, and we hesitate to generalize too far.

Another area of development that appears to be influenced by hearing losses during infancy is *visual attention*. Hearing infants learn to connect sounds and the producers of sounds as well as to triangulate themselves with speakers and with objects that are designated by naming and pointing. There do not appear to be any global differences in visual attention as a function of infant hearing status only. Both deaf and hearing infants whose mothers use more visual communication spend more time watching their mothers. Hearing infants who receive auditory communication during play from their hearing mothers, however, spend more time attending to objects than either deaf or hearing children whose mothers use only visual communication (Spencer, 2000). Such findings indicate that, like development in other domains, visual attention is the product of a complex interaction of learning and maturation. Auditory experience and coordination between auditory and visual modalities may not be necessary for the development of visual attention, but they do support it.

Visual attention differences also have been observed in tasks involving deaf children and young adults. Findings indicating significant improvement in visual attention (measured in terms of being able to maintain attention) after nine months with a cochlear implant clearly indicate the role of hearing in its development (Quittner et al., 1994). Still to be determined is whether such differences influence later academic performance. One could imagine that children who are more easily distracted during visual tasks would have more difficulty in learning to read, for example, and this may account in part for the relatively poor reading scores observed among deaf children (discussed in chapter 8). More generally, it is clear that early experience—or lack thereof—can influence later learning and performance in both direct and indirect ways. We have to be able to identify such relations if we are to facilitate development appropriately.

Optimizing Early Communicative Interactions

During early childhood, both deaf and hearing infants learn much about things and people in the environment as well as about how to learn and interact with others. Many deaf children exhibit delayed language acquisition, however, and the frequency with which we see educational underachievement suggests that delayed language acquisition and educational underachievment both have early roots (Marschark, 1993; Moores & Meadows-Orlans 1990). It is sometimes erroneously assumed that such delays are somehow caused by deafness per se or by deaf children not using spoken language. But deaf children of deaf parents typically do not exhibit those difficulties, and thus there cannot be anything specific to deafness or sign language that would directly account for these outcomes. Rather, available research suggests that such delays in learning or development are more likely to be the result of a lack of effective communication between parents and children (Harris & Mohay, 1997; Hart & Risley, 1995; Meadow-Orlans & Steinberg, 1993).

Deaf parents have a variety of visual and tactile strategies for communicating effectively with their young children, but hearing parents are unlikely to discover such techniques spontaneously (Koester, 1994; Mohay et al., 1998; Swisher, 1984). When we see these strategies produced by deaf parents, in context, they appear relatively straightforward and natural, but using them consistently is a real challenge for most hearing parents. Consider the following 10 examples, all of which would be helpful for teachers as well as parents.[4]

Using facial expression and body language. Facial expression, body language, and gesture are important components of communication and are used much more frequently by deaf parents than by hearing parents. Deaf mothers, for example, frequently smile as a means of providing positive feedback and use facial expression to convey feelings and attitudes much more often than do hearing mothers (Meadow-Orlans et al., 1987).These kinds of nonverbal communication encourage children to look at their parents, thus fostering the development of looking patterns that enhance communication in the visual modality.

Gaining attention using hand and body movements. Gaining, holding, and directing the attention of a young deaf child is a challenge for any parent, but especially so for many hearing parents of deaf children. Deaf parents achieve these by waving a hand or an object in front of a child or moving their heads from side to side in the child's visual field and providing positive feedback when the child's attention has been gained (e.g., through smiling or clapping) (Kyle et al., 1989). These techniques are used most frequently with very young deaf children and are replaced by signs as visual attention skills improve.

Using touch to gain attention. Touch is another strategy used by deaf parents to gain (and train) their children's attention (Koester et al., 2000b). Maternal touch can have powerful effects on newborns and young children, both deaf and hearing, and deaf mothers generally touch their infants more than hearing mothers. Deaf parents also are much more persistent and insistent than hearing parents in gaining their child's attention when they think it is important (Harris & Mohay, 1997; Rea et al., 1988). Once they have succeeded, touch can be used to provide positive feedback to children and to reassure them of the parent's presence when they are outside of the child's visual field. Although this may seem obvious, hearing parents have been found to use this strategy much less frequently than deaf parents (Meadow-Orlans & Steinberg, 1993).

Using pointing to direct attention and permit language input. Hearing parents typically direct a hearing child's attention to an object or event by pointing to it and talking about it. This strategy does not work well with deaf children, who are usually unable to see both the object and the parent at the same time. Deaf parents first gain children's attention, then tell them what they are going to see and direct their attention to the relevant object or event (Kyle et al., 1987). Sometimes they then displace their signs to a location between the child and the object so that both sign(s) and object can be seen simultaneously. It is essential that hearing parents learn to use pointing in such a way that their deaf children are not excluded from valuable language learning opportunities.

Reducing communication so the child recognizes it as important. To perceive language, deaf children must divide attention between their activities and the person with whom they are communicating. The constant switching of attention can be disruptive and interfere with what children are doing. It is therefore important to ensure that communication is meaningful and worth watching, or children will not direct their visual attention to the communicative partner (a feature frequently observed in the interactions of deaf children with their hearing parents). Several studies have shown that deaf parents actually communicate with their children less frequently than do hearing parents and often wait for children to look at them before communicating (Gregory & Barlow, 1989; Mohay et al., 1998; Spencer et al., 1992). Communication by deaf parents is visually accessible, occurs when a child is likely to be receptive, and is only minimally disruptive. Children accordingly come to recognize the value of parental interruption as something worthy of attention.

Using short utterances. Having to switch attention between an activity and the language being produced by a parent disrupts both. It also places added cognitive demands on deaf children as they attempt to make sense of the language input (Wood et al., 1986).Unlike hearing children, who can simultaneously listen to language and attend to the object of attention, deaf children must retain information in memory as they shift from one source of information to the other. Deaf parents typically use short utterances when communicating with their young deaf children, thus minimizing disruptions to a child's activity and reducing the demands on memory.

Positioning self and objects in child's visual field. The need for a deaf child to divide attention can be significantly reduced if parents place themselves where both they and the object of interest to a child are within the child's visual field; it then is unnecessary for a child to make significant shifts of attention to see both language and the object of the language. Hearing parents usually attempt to achieve this by sitting opposite a deaf child. For close-up activities, deaf parents are more likely to sit beside or behind a child and curve their arms and bodies around so that they can be both seen and felt. This achieves the same results in a more subtle way, simultaneously providing a child with reassurance about parents' presence during periods when no communication occurs (Jamieson, 1994; Mohay et al., 1998).

Moving hands or face into a child's visual field. In addition to their initial positioning during an activity, deaf parents actively shift position and displace their signs during an interaction. A number of researchers have observed deaf parents making their signs within a child's signing space rather than their own or by making the sign on the child's body to connect the signs to the child's reality (see Koester & Trimm, 1991; Kyle et al., 1987). Both strategies allow signs to be perceived with minimal need to redirect attention from objects of interest.

Using bracketing to clarify meaning. Bracketing involves putting a sign, gesture, or phrase at both the beginning and end of an utterance ("See the dog over there? [Point] Yes, that's a dog!") (Ackerman et al., 1990; Kyle, 1990). Deaf parents frequently sign the name of an object, point to it, and then sign it again. They also sometimes ask a question by presenting a question sign followed by the content of the question and then repeating the question sign. This strategy helps to ensure comprehension and is likely to facilitate vocabulary learning.

Modifying signs/gestures by exaggeration, and repetition. This strategy includes three related techniques: (1) displacing signs and gestures so that they are made on or close to an object, thus clarifying the link between the two (Lederberg & Spencer, 2001), (2) prolonging signs and using repetition and exaggeration to ensure that a child attends to the signs (Koester & Trimm, 1991) and (3) promoting understanding by giving a child more time to assimilate messages (Erting et al., 1990). Frequently referred to as *motherese*, such strategies simultaneously make communication more perceptually interesting and signal a child that important information is coming. Parents who do not use sign language will benefit from using such modifications in communicative gestures.

Helping to Ensure Communication with Young Deaf Children

To get and keep a young deaf child's attention:
   Use facial expressions and body language to appear interesting to
      the child
   Use hand and body movements within their line of sight (to break
      their gaze)
   Touch the child gently to interrupt other behaviors
   Point to interesting things (and look at them yourself)
To facilitate communication:
   Point to things and then say what they are (and perhaps point
      again)
   Wait until the child is looking before communicating
   Slow down the rate of communication
   Don't make the child continually have to shift attention away from
      something interesting
   Use short utterances
   Position yourself and objects within the child's visual field
   Ensure that your hands (if signing) or face (if speaking) is in the
      child's visual field
   Put important information (e.g., the topic) at the beginning and the
      end of utterances
   When referring to things, make signs or gestures with the hands on
      or near the objects
   Exaggerate, repeat, and prolong signs to make sure they are seen
      and recognized
   Allow more time for children to understand messages

In short, the earliest stages of mother–child interaction involve the development of interwoven parent–child routines that depend on and foster communication. Normally, the development of *behavioral reciprocity* in humans and animals involves vocalization by both parent and child, but in humans, at least, vocalization can be replaced by smiles, postures, and touch (Brazelton, 1982). The importance of rhythmic patterning is reflected in other research showing that many of the nonverbal features of communication with infants, such as touch and exaggerated facial expressions, are synchronized with language input (Koester et al., 2000).[5] However, such findings say little about the majority of deaf infants whose hearing parents initially are not aware of their children's hearing losses and thus do not attempt to compensate with increased touching. The replacement of maternal vocal cues with nonlinguistic signals likely occurs naturally and intuitively for most hearing parents with deaf infants. In some cases, that adjustment may be more difficult, and early intervention programs or explicit tutorials that teach particular strategies can be helpful in supporting family members in their interactions with deaf children (see chapter 6).

From Communication to Language

For those children whose hearing losses are severe enough that they cannot master a spoken language, sign language provides an excellent alternative. Sign languages like American Sign Language (ASL), British Sign Language (BSL), or Italian Sign Language (LIS), are not just gestural communication. They are full languages just like English or Spanish (Stokoe, 1960). Some investigators have even argued that gesture and rudimentary sign languages may have pre-dated spoken languages in the human species (e.g., Armstrong et al., 1995; Stokoe & Marschark, 1999).

The question, *to sign or not to sign,* is just one of many issues facing the family of a deaf child. In some ways it is the most central one. For many parents, accepting their child's hearing loss is difficult enough, and deciding that sign language will be their child's first language seems a big step. Some parents therefore attempt to have their children acquire spoken language, something that is particularly difficult for very young deaf children. Unfortunately, the relative merits of spoken language versus sign language for young deaf children is clouded by disagreement, personal opinions, and contradictory findings. We will try to avoid this controversy in most contexts and focus on the need for successful communication regardless of its mode. Our own reading of the history of deaf education (see chapter 2) and the available research on language development has led us to conclude that sign language is an important ingredient of early communication for most young deaf children. Nevertheless, we need to recognize that different children will benefit from various communication alternatives.

Although the degree and quality of vocal–auditory interaction will vary, we have already seen that its absence can negatively influence the developing parent–child relationship. One would expect that these effects would be fewer and less pronounced when parents are aware of their infant's hearing loss (e.g., parents who are deaf or have other deaf children). If parents are familiar with deafness through friends or relatives, they are likely to be more aware of and more comfortable with strategies that enhance interactions in nonauditory domains. Knowing that a child is deaf at least provides parents with the opportunity to seek out information and resources, including other parents and teachers who have experience with deaf or hard-of-hearing children. Most such resources will emphasize the importance of communication, even if they differ in the mode of communication they advocate.

For deaf children with more profound hearing losses, the issue of communicating often translates into a signing versus speaking dichotomy, but this situation is far more complex than most popular arguments would suggest. Those deaf children who learn to sign at a young age tend to be better adjusted emotionally, on average. They also tend to do better in school and have better social relationships with their signing parents and peers in comparison to children with similar hearing losses raised only with spoken language. Certainly, there are exceptions in this regard, and many deaf children (although a minority) use only spoken language. One ongoing, large-scale study in Canada, for example, indicated that although 93 percent of the deaf children initially were enrolled in auditory/oral programs, that figure was down to 67 percent by the time they were in preschool. By elementary school, 58 percent were still in oral programs, with 31 percent remaining when they were in middle school (Akamatsu et al., 2000). Meanwhile, more than half of all deaf children in Canada and United States have been reported to have "unintelligible" speech (Cole & Paterson, 1984).

The situation is even more cloudy for hard-of-hearing children, who have less severe hearing losses and who thus may have better access to spoken language. Although there have been some studies concerning language development in children who are hard-of-hearing (see chapter 5), however, there does not appear to be any available research concerning the link of language and social development in hard-of-hearing children.

It is easy to understand the desire of most hearing parents to have a "normally" speaking and acting child. Few deaf children, however, will ever talk like their hearing brothers and sisters, and most will not be proficient at understanding the speech of others. Contrary to the popular myths, very few individuals with severe to profound hearing losses can read lips well enough for the purposes of everyday communication. Lip-reading or *speechreading* as it is now more commonly known, is difficult and error-prone, depending more on the characteristics of the speaker, linguistic context, and the physical environment (e.g., lighting) than the skills of the deaf person. Proficiency certainly is not something that should be expected from young deaf children. One of our friends who is profoundly deaf met someone on a recent vacation with whom he could comfortably converse only using spoken language (i.e., with speechreading). But that was only the second such occurrence in the 35 years he has been deaf (the other person is his barber), and he had the benefit of being able to hear speech until he was a young teenager.

Spoken language skills may be at a greater premium later in life, insofar as they would contribute to social interactions with a broader segment of society, and seem likely to influence employment conditions and opportunities (the Americans with Disabilities Act aside). A study involving employers of deaf individuals found that supervisors reported it easier to communicate with deaf employees who used speechreading and spoken language rather than sign language. In part, their preference in that regard related to saving time because they did not have to write messages back and forth. Employers also noted, however, that adjustments were necessary in spoken communication with deaf employees and there was a high frequency of miscommunication. Further, the availability of speechreading and speech was said to prevent the development or use of other communications strategies, such a sign language, even when speechreading and voice were relatively ineffective (Foster, 1995; see also Steinberg et al., 1999).

Some hearing parents mistakenly believe that learning to sign will interfere with the acquisition of spoken language in their deaf child and thus they may resist sign language as long as possible. If anything, sign language seems to support learning of spoken language in deaf children, including for those with cochlear implants, and there is no evidence to suggest any interference. Delaying the learning of sign language in the hope of better speaking skills in deaf children has not been shown to have any advantages. More commonly, such delays make matters more difficult for both children and their parents. The first years of life are when basic language skills develop, and the first two to three years are generally recognized as a critical period for language learning. There is no substitute for natural language learning, and language acquisition that begins at age three or four is not natural.

It should be apparent by this point that the early acquisition of language—any language—is a critical emphasis that guides most of our thinking about the normal development of both deaf and hearing children. Although it sometimes appears that language fluency is achieved easily and naturally, it frequently involves explicit instruction at home and in the classroom. At the same time, the majority of children's experience comes in the form of language or is accompanied by language. Our perceptions and conceptions of the world often thus are colored as much by the way something is described as by its reality (Stokoe & Marschark, 1999).

Regardless of whether parents are using English, Spanish, ASL, or another language, the content and effects of communication are always present. Most obvious, perhaps, are the many ways in which early social interactions and other diverse experiences depend on interpersonal communication and help foster the acquisition of language. We have touched on these areas already, and we need to consider them in more detail to gain a fuller understanding of their roles in establishing the psychological foundation for education. First, however, we briefly consider the communication alternatives available to young deaf children.

Sign Language and Forms of Manual Communication

Almost every country has its own sign language. Some countries, like Canada and South Africa, have more than one, corresponding to their multiple spoken languages. National boundaries are less important than cultural similarities, so that American Sign Language (ASL) has French roots, and these roots can still be seen in the grammar in some signs.[6] Despite this borrowing, ASL differs dramatically from both the sign language used in Quebec (La Langue des Signes Quebecoise) and England (British Sign Language). In fact, the manual alphabet used in the United States probably should not be called English because it bears little resemblance to the two-handed manual alphabet of British Sign Language (BSL), used in England.

Like spoken languages, signed languages vary. Sign languages have their own accents, dialects, and idiosyncratic vocabulary. Particular signs may be limited to particular regions, schools, or even families. *Home signs*, for example, are signs used in much the same way as some special words and names are used in hearing families. Both are most common in homes with small children, often originating from misarticulations or "portmanteau words" like one family's "Democraticle" referring to the local newspaper, *The Democrat and Chronicle*, and another family's "grabbers," referring to tongs and similar untensils.

Deaf children's exposure to a *natural language* is an important step beyond the establishment of parent–child communication. By "natural" language, we mean a formal, rule-governed, social communication system that has evolved in the real world to serve the personal, social, and political–economic needs of a particular community. Although debate continues, it appears that natural languages like English and ASL have some significant advantages for learning over artificially constructed, English-based sign systems designed to facilitate the development of reading and writing skills by deaf children. Artificial sign systems do not appear to lead deaf children to fluency in either sign language or in English (see chapter 8), and it appears that the link between language acquisition and literacy is not as straightforward as has been assumed (Supalla, 1991). Let us consider the alternatives more carefully.

Natural Sign Languages

Like a spoken language, a sign language consists of a large vocabulary of arbitrary signs, together with a set of rules, or *grammar*, that govern the formation of individual units, their modification, and their combination into phrases and sentences.[7] Signs are composed of several clearly defined characteristics: handshape, place of articulation, movement, and whether one or two hands are used. Changes in one on these characteristics normally will change the meaning of a sign, but signs can be modified or *inflected* to indicate number, tense, or mood, just as English words can be inflected by adding certain beginnings or endings to words (*dog* becomes *dogs, jump* becomes *jumped*, etc.). In ASL, DOGS may be signed by signing DOG more than once, and JUMPED can either be signed by adding the past tense marker, FINISH, to the sentence or by letting context specify the past. ASL has other ways of modifying signs to change meaning. A change in the movement of the sign COMPLAIN can communicate the concept COMPLAIN CONSTANTLY or COMPLAIN VEHEMENTLY, and a change in movement and position in space can change the meaning of the sign, CHAIR to COUCH or ROW OF CHAIRS. In addition, signs are inflected by the use on nonmanual markers, such as the raising or lowering of the eyebrows and shaking the head.[8] The ability to make such changes, in fact, represents one of the properties that distinguishes sign language from gesture. A true language must have a mechanism for modifications of this sort to be efficient and allow a full range of communication.

One feature of sign language not present in most spoken languages is the use of *classifiers*. Classifiers are particular handshapes that have general-purpose or categorical meanings. For example, an upright 1-hand (a raised index finger) may be used for representing an individual (human); and a 3-hand (made with the thumb up and the first two fingers pointing away from the signer) may be used to represent CAR or other vehicles, after it has been appropriately designated. Another type of classifier functions more like an adjective than a noun, indicating either the shape, size, or arrangement of objects. For example, F-hands or C-hands moved vertically or horizontally indicate the size and position of cylindrical objects, while I-hands indicate thin filaments or lines (the I-hand also is used for the signs STRING and SPAGHETTI). Although most classifiers make use of alphabetic and numerical handshapes, their meanings are not tied to the letter or number meanings of the handshapes.

Another unique feature of sign languages is their use of space to communicate time and location. A speaker of ASL uses positions to indicate PAST (behind the signer), present or NOW (beside or just in front of the signer) and FUTURE (farther out in front of the signer). The sign WEEK, made in front of the body, can be inflected to indicate LAST-WEEK by finishing the sign in an arc backwards, towards the right shoulder (for right-handed people). NEXT-WEEK is made by finishing the sign WEEK with an arc forward, out from the body. The signs for YEAR and MONTH are similarly inflected in ASL.

Signers also use space to establish locations for places, people, and objects for later use as pronouns. A signer might identify several individuals by name (by means of fingerspelling or name-signs), for example, and place them in different locations in the signing space, to the right, to the left or directly in front. To refer back to any individual, the signer need only point, nod, or look in the direction that the person was originally positioned in the sign space (like using *there*, *him*, or *that*).

Together with signs, facial expression, and body movement, sign languages also make use of a manual alphabet. The use of the alphabet, through *fingerspelling*, serves a somewhat different function in a signed language than in spoken language. We spell words in English when they are unfamiliar, but we normally do not use spelling in everyday conversation. Users of ASL, in contrast, use fingerspelling when there are no conventional signs for particular words, where the signs are obscure or unknown, and in a variety of cases where signs exist but are being replaced with *fingerspelled loan signs* (Metzger, 1998). Loan signs are often made with particular movements. The loan sign for SALE, for example, is made by producing each letter while the hand is moving in a clockwise circular motion (from the perspective of the signer), with the palm facing outward. The loan sign for EASY is made with the palm facing upward for the E and rotating it until it is downward for the Y, meanwhile passing through the letters "A" and "S." Fingerspelling normally does not replace signing, but supplements it, and its use varies in different regions.

Other Forms of Communication on the Hands

Fingerspelling, classifiers, and the ways in which signs are formed, modified, and combined illustrate the distinctive characteristics of sign languages. This is not to say, however, that they develop in isolation from spoken language. When hearing and deaf people come into contact, they often use a simplified form of signing that includes the grammar of the local spoken language. In the case of English-speaking North Americans, this hybrid is usually referred to as *Pidgin Signed English* (PSE) or *contact sign*.[9] Users of PSE employ a basic ASL sign vocabulary, but because their lexicons tend to be smaller, they rely more on context and mechanisms like initialization to figure out meaning. For example, to sign the concepts, *situation, context,* and *environment*, PSE speakers will use the same sign with a different fingerspelled letter on the dominant hand for each term (*S*-ITUATION, *C*-ONTEXT, *E*-NVIRONMENT). As in spoken pidgins, PSE uses minimal inflection (compared to English and ASL) and a basic subject-verb-object word order.

Existing side-by-side with such naturally occurring systems as PSE are several systems constructed by educators to teach English. These systems attempt to represent English by combining ASL signs, English word order, and some invented signs to represent grammatical markers in English. *Signed English*, for example, combines the signs of ASL with the grammatical structure of English. Beyond the use of initialized signs, Signed English includes a set of 14 invented markers to indicate plurals, possessives, tenses, adverbs, adjectives, and so on. The stated goal of including these markers is to support the acquisition of English structure necessary for reading, writing, and possibly speech.

Seeing Essential English, or *SEE1,* and *Signing Exact English,* or *SEE2,* similarly were developed as ways to represent English visually on the hands. In SEE1, for example, every English word has a basic ASL sign, and signs are produced in English word order. Additional signs are used to represent English grammatical structures, as in Signed English. SEE1 goes further than signed English in attempting to communicate English fully, using a different sign for each morpheme (meaningful unit) of English rather than for each concept. Thus, where ASL and Signed English have single signs for concepts like "butterfly" and "sweetheart," SEE1 uses two signs, one for each part of the compound word. "Butterfly" is signed by combining the signs BUTTER and FLY, and "sweetheart" is signed by combining the signs SWEET and HEART. Children acquiring English-based sign systems like SEE1 appear to have better literacy skills than children exposed to Pidgin Sign English; but they do not exceed the skills of children who have acquired ASL, despite the original arguments for constructing such systems (Luetke-Stahlman, 1990; Power & Hyde, 1997; Power & Leigh, 1997).

One alternative to natural sign languages and signed systems is *cued speech.* Cued speech is a supplement to spoken English intended to make important features of spoken language fully visible (Cornett & Daisey, 1992; LaSasso & Metzger, 1998). Many speech sounds look alike on the lips when they are pronounced, making speechreading difficult. For example, pronunciation of the letters c, e, g, and z, all look similar on the lips. English cued speech uses 36 different cues to clarify the 44 different sounds in English. Cues for vowel sounds are produced by placing the hand at one of seven different locations on the face in the area of the mouth. Cues for consonant sounds are provided by making one of eight alternative handshapes and combining them with the vowel locations. The handshapes of cued speech thus play a very different role from the handshapes of sign languages, which carry information about meaning rather than about sound.

Given the several alternative sign-based systems available for deaf children, it would seem that those systems that are likely to be most effective are those that combine as many sources of information as possible. That is the philosophy behind *total communication*, which includes *simultaneous communication* (sign language and spoken language together) and support for residual hearing through assistive listening devices. At present, however, it is unclear whether the limited benefits to deaf children's literacy or spoken language skills after learning a hybrid sign system are enough to offset their not being fluent in either a signed or a spoken language. Given the importance of early communication for young deaf children, it appears unlikely that this is the case. Nevertheless, it may be that some kind of manually coded English would be of benefit after a child has learned ASL as a first language, thus providing a bridge to written English. We consider this possibility in chapters 5 and 8, in the context of language development and literacy.

Early Access to Language

Language acquisition presumably begins at birth, with both passive expo-sure to language input and communication-based, dynamic interactions with parents and siblings. True *language production* will not occur until about the age of six months, but in the meantime, hearing babies learn a variety of things about *language use*. For example, pausing, often with a head-nod or raised eyebrows, indicates that it is baby's turn; rising into-nation indicates a question; and harsh or loud language tends to be pre-ceded or followed by something bad. Vocabulary and the structure of lan-guage start to become familiar, and young children learn that language typically accompanies interesting events in the environment.

The fundamentals of language acquisition are essentially in place by about the age of 3, while language-specific details such as grammar will continue to be acquired over time.[10] Given this very early language-learning scenario, it should be apparent that the language *environment* and language *accessibility* for children in the first few months are crucial. Language development in hearing children has been shown to vary considerably depending on how much language experience they have, but this is not about teaching language. Parents who just talk with their children to en-gage them and to be social, who use language to stay involved with their children even when they are doing other things, and who tell children more than they need to know all add to the quality of their interactions and fos-ter language development. Such language-based interactions also inform children about things that are worth noticing in the world and provide a model for social language behavior. Accordingly, up to 98 percent of the words found in hearing children's vocabularies are also found in their par-ents' vocabularies (Hart & Risley, 1995).

Such findings provide additional evidence of the importance of early language exposure to children's later language development and confirm the long-held intuition of many researchers that deaf children who do not have effective access to language in the family are at a decided disadvan-tage. That disadvantage will increase through the school years if not some-how remedied. However, the provision of interpreters or other support services within the school environment (see chapters 6 and 7) cannot over-come existing lags if children do not have the linguistic and cognitive tools to use them effectively (Mayer & Akamatsu, 1999; Winston, 1994). That would be like enrolling in a course taught in an unfamiliar language.

Children and parents who share an effective mode of communication, in contrast, have a means of interacting that serves cognitive, linguistic, and social functions from the outset. The advantage of this availability can be seen in findings from a variety of studies indicating that deaf children of deaf parents are more academically skilled and socially competent than peers who have hearing parents. Further, children of hearing parents who

become deaf after learning language generally demonstrate superior academic abilities, are better adjusted, and appear to benefit more from cochlear implants relative to children who have congenital or early-onset
deafness. Such differences clearly have complex origins and cannot be
attributed to any single cause. Lack of a meaningful and effective communication channel between parents and children, however, is clearly not
typical. Subsequent atypical development should not be surprising.

Early Social Interactions

We have seen that hearing loss may lead to differences in social interactions. Beyond socialization, an important part of any child's development
involves acquiring the roles, rules, attitudes, and values of one's society.
Both parental and peer relationships, therefore, are essential parts of education in its broadest sense. When parents and their deaf children have
better communication, regardless of whether they are deaf or hearing and
independent of the mode of communication, they have stronger and more
secure relationships compared to parents and children with poorer communication (Greenberg & Marvin, 1979). Several studies, for example, have
reported that hearing mothers tend to be controlling and directive in interactions with their deaf children, behavior that works against the establishment of a healthy mother–child relationship and can deprive children of
important trial-and-error learning experiences (see, e.g., Meadow et al.,
1981; Musselman & Churchill, 1993). Consistent with our expectations
about the importance of early interaction, mothers who have had the benefit of early intervention programs promoting effective communication with
their deaf children tend to be less intrusive than mothers who have not
had such experience (Greenberg et al., 1994; Lederberg, 1993). Maternal
dominance appears to be greater in situations where deaf children are raised
in oral-only environments, as compared to when sign and speech are used
together (Meadow et al., 1981).

Mothers' tendencies to control activities of their young deaf children
involving toys and other children may have several sources. Most obviously, mothers simply may be trying to establish lines of communication
(Lederberg, 1989). In the absence of effective communication, they might
be seeking to protect their children from harm or feel that their children
are unable to fend for themselves (Pollard & Rendon, 1999). Alternatively,
they might be trying to compensate for feelings of inadequacy or power-
lessnessss in dealing with their young deaf children. In any case, over-
protection and intrusion can happen in any parent–child relationship and
can result in a self-fulfilling prophecy. That is, children who do not have
the opportunity to explore and discover for themselves are likely to become
more dependent on their parents. Parents who have an effective means of

communication with their deaf children have less need for such control and can better gauge the ability of their children in various activities.

The experiences of children with other people thus cannot be separated from their experience with language. As they get older, linguistic interactions become even more important for their formal (in school) and informal (social) educations. It is through language that social norms and behavioral rules are communicated and social-emotional events are explained. Language provides for more effective and efficient transmission of social information than trial-and-error learning, facilitating the extension of social interactions outside the family and into peer relationships. Eventually, the establishment of effective social communication strategies will also contribute to academic success during the school years by virtue of its support for language and cognitive development. Deaf teenagers who report better communication with their parents, for example, also tend to have more positive self-esteem and greater academic success (Desselle, 1994; Gregory, 1995).

For hearing parents, effective communication tends to result in more satisfying interactions with their deaf children and less need for punishment. Families that use sign language with their deaf children also generally have greater emotional bonding (Kluwin & Gaustad, 1994). Such findings do not mean that sign language is essential for the social development of deaf children, but they do emphasize that language is an important part of social functioning both inside and outside the home.

Advocates of mainstreaming and inclusion often claim that deaf children benefit, both linguistically and socially, from being surrounded by hearing peers. A variety of studies, however, have shown that this is not necessarily the case (Anita, 1982; Lederberg, 1986; Stinson & Lang, 1994). Young deaf children clearly prefer to play and communicate with children who share the same hearing status, even though their social behaviors are much the same regardless of whether they are playing with deaf or hearing peers. Similarly, hearing children prefer to play with hearing peers rather than deaf peers (Lederberg et al., 1986; Vandell & George, 1981). The issue here is not hearing status per se. A variety of studies have shown that the quality and quantity of play interactions between deaf children and their deaf or hearing peers are related to communication fluency (Spencer & Hafer, 1998). Within the preschool setting, deaf children who have better language abilities are more likely than children with poorer language abilities to play with multiple peers at one time, to interact with teachers, and to use and receive more language from their play partners (Spencer & Deyo, 1993). Children who are enrolled in total communication programs also tend to get along better with deaf peers than children in oral preschools, showing less aggression and disruption in the classroom, presumably reflecting better social communication skills (Cornelius & Hornett, 1990).

Through social relationships, children develop secure bases for exploration, identify with others who are like them, and obtain instrumental and
emotional support.[11] Social relationships make children part of peer and
cultural groups. Students with positive social interactions in school tend
to have higher academic achievement, better mental health, and are more
likely to succeed in their careers. (Gregory, 1998). The availability of more
diverse social experiences also appears to enhance the flexibility of young
deaf children in dealing with later social interactions and the necessity of
growing up in a largely hearing world.

Experiential Diversity

A third essential ingredient of normal development is exposure to a variety
of experiences. It is through active exploration of the environment and experience with people, things, and language that children acquire knowledge.

Deaf children who struggle to communicate with others or who are
over protected by well-meaning adults might have less variability in the
kinds of experiences they are exposed to compared to hearing children.
Even in the same environment, deaf and hearing children may have qualitatively different experiences. Some such differences will be positive. For
example, deaf children are more likely than hearing children to use visuospatial coding in memory, a strategy derived from their reliance on visual
and spatial information. This is also a strategy that enhances recall of things
and locations (O'Connor & Hermelin, 1976). Other differences, in contrast,
may have a negative influence on a child development. We know, for example, that deaf children too often focus on only one dimension in tasks
that require simultaneous attention to two dimensions (e.g., balancing
different-sized weights on a scale; Ottem, 1980). This "cognitive narrow-
ing" may result from the willingness of teachers to accept superficial,
unidimensional answers from deaf students rather than encouraging deeper,
more extended discussions about things. All too often, deaf students are
allowed to get by with less than would be required of hearing students,
thus depriving them a valuable educational experiences.

Most of the time, subtle differences in the experiences of deaf and
hearing children have functionally the same outcomes, simply contributing to the complex mosaic that makes us all different from each other. To
the extent that there are individual differences as well as group differences
between deaf and hearing individuals in everything from brain organization to their experience with television, observed differences should not
be surprising. Nor should there be anything wrong with examining such
differences. Recognizing that differences between deaf and hearing children exist is an important step for parents, educators, and for researchers.
As much as hearing parents might want their deaf children to be like hear-

ing children, or at least treated like hearing children, raising and educating them exactly the same way as hearing children may not be the best way to facilitate their growth (Luterman, 1987). If deaf children are to receive support in those areas in which they need it, they must be appreciated in their own right, and they might need different educational experiences to derive the same benefits. Moreover, if deaf children are more heterogeneous than hearing children, there will be fewer applicable generalizations and greater need for individualized educational programming.

Language acquisition and cognitive development are both facilitated by experiences that show children the links between concepts and their labels. They are able to construct this primitive conceptual system in part because the language and behaviors of adults and older children already divides up the world in ways that make some cognitive, social, and cultural sense. The child thus can set about language acquisition and concept learning as problem-solving tasks, noting correspondences and underlying rules while filtering out irrelevant information. This active learning requires a diversity of experience.

> If deaf children are to receive support in those areas in which they need it, they must be appreciated in their own right, and they might need different educational experiences to derive the same benefits.

Restrictions on deaf children's experiences, therefore, may have broad implications. Research involving hearing children has shown that vocabulary development is positively related to the time spent with different adults in diverse settings. Vocabulary development also is greater in children who have mothers who are less controlling and provide more opportunities for exploration (Nelson, 1973). Similar studies have not been conducted involving deaf children, but comparable results would be expected as long as the relevant adults are able to communicate effectively with them.

Summary

Beyond similarities in their emotional reactions, parents vary considerably in their behaviors when they learn that they have a deaf child. Unless they are deaf themselves, understanding and accepting a child's hearing loss is not easy. Infants with hearing losses may respond differently to parents from children without hearing losses, and such differences in interactions often continue at least through adolescence. Parents and teachers may feel inadequate in dealing with a deaf child, and such feelings may lead them to inadvertently deny children opportunities for valuable exploration and experience. There are two things parents should do as soon as possible:

First, they should obtain information concerning hearing loss, assistive listening devices, communication, language development, and special education practices. Second, they should establish an effective means of communicating with their deaf child, keeping in mind that children will benefit from different modes of communication and education. There is no single right answer for all deaf children.

The different experiences children have will affect how they view and interact with the world. In the case of deaf children of deaf parents, a fuller range of natural experiences often leads to them passing through the various developmental stages at the same rate as hearing children. For deaf children of hearing parents, early experiences may not blend so readily into the background of family and community life. For them, the nature of their experiences may lead to differences in social, language, and perhaps intellectual functioning relative to hearing children.

Parents and educators of deaf children often overlook the overwhelming amount of language learning that derives from informal interactions and activities both in and out of school. A large proportion of children's vocabularies, for example, comes from classes on science, history, literature, and the like. To give these topics less attention than language-focused instruction all but assures that deaf children not only will have smaller vocabularies (Griswold & Commings, 1974), but that the vocabularies they do develop will be relatively concrete and specific (Blackwell et al., 1978).

The intertwining of language, social, and cognitive development is fundamental to deaf children's construction of knowledge about the world and the way it works. Nurturing these developmental domains in home, school, and community activities must be one of the highest priorities. We also must make every effort to better understand how deaf children's development is influenced by different learning situations, rather than focusing on the traditional debates over the effects of hearing loss or the use of sign language on development and academic success. We cannot continue to assume that deaf and hearing children will benefit in the same ways from similar interactions or instructional methods.

PART II

Educational Processes and Programs

What are the critical factors
contributing to language
development of deaf children?

How can we avoid losing valuable
time during a deaf child's optimal
years of language development?

5

FIVE

Language Development and Deaf Children

To understand the complex relations between language and learning, we have to look at both how children learn language and what it is that they learn that allows them to communicate with others. To accomplish this, we need to distinguish between apparent differences in language that are related to the modality of communication and actual differences in language fluencies observed among deaf children. It also will help to examine some relevant differences between deaf children and hearing children.

We have already pointed out that the distinction between spoken language and sign language, while a theoretically important one for researchers, is an oversimplification for most practical purposes. It is rare that deaf children are exposed only to spoken language or sign language, even if that is the intention of their parents or teachers. According to 1999 data, approximately 55 percent of deaf children in the United States are formally educated in programs that report either using sign language exclusively (just over 5 percent) or signed and spoken language together (just over 49 percent) (Gallaudet University, Center for Applied Demographic Statistics). Because almost half of all deaf children in the United States are missed in such surveys, however, these numbers only should be taken as approximate.

Comparisons of the language abilities of deaf children who primarily use sign language with those who primarily use spoken language represent one of the most popular and potentially informative areas in research relating to language development and academic success. Unfortunately, this area is also one of the most complex. Educational programs emphasizing spoken or sign language often have different educational philosophies and curricula as well as different communication philosophies. Programs may only admit children with particular histories of early intervention, and parents will be drawn to different programs for a variety of reasons. Differences observed between children from any two programs thus might be the result of a number of variables rather than, or in addition to, language modality per se.

Even when deaf children are educated in spoken language environments, they often develop systems of gestural communication with their parents (Greenberg et al., 1984). These systems can play a greater or lesser role in communication in different contexts, facilitating the later learning of a language, regardless of its mode (Volterra & Iverson, 1995). Far from there being a one-way transition from gesture to language, gesture plays an important role in communication throughout life for both deaf and hearing individuals. Deaf adults and children use gesture intermixed with their sign language as a highly flexible, descriptive tool, and gesture clearly is related to language growth and social communication in hearing as well as in deaf children.

A full understanding of language development in deaf children also may be clouded by the fact that many hearing parents who choose to raise their deaf children with sign language do not sign consistently, a situation also encountered if they use a form of an English-based sign system or cued speech. Parents often have only limited formal training in these methods and may be uncomfortable using them in public. Further, many parents use sign only when communicating directly with their child, not realizing how much language is learned indirectly from "overhearing" conversations of others. Young deaf children of hearing parents thus frequently do not have broad access to competent language models, either for sign language or for spoken language. This places them at a distinct disadvantage with regard to language development (Whitehurst & Valdez-Menchaca, 1988).

When dealing with deaf children, it will be useful for parents and practitioners to have a basic understanding of language acquisition as well as the larger context of the developmental and educational needs of deaf children. In this chapter, we focus on the needs and products of language development in deaf children. More complete discussions of language development can be found in textbooks dedicated to that topic (Crystal, 1987; Golinkoff & Hirsh-Pasek, 1999; Lightbown & Spada, 1993).

Foundations of Language Development

Perhaps the two most important variables in the development of deaf children are parental attitudes toward hearing loss and the quality of parent–child communication. These dimensions are related, of course. Parents who are more accepting of their children's hearing losses and more proactive in their child-rearing practices are more likely to be flexible and persistent in seeking ways to communicate effectively.

By the 1980s it was widely recognized that hearing children's language acquisition was strongly influenced by their interactions with their mothers or other caregivers. The search for solutions to the observed delays in deaf children's language acquisition therefore focused on comparisons of interactions of hearing mothers with deaf children to interactions of hearing mothers with hearing children. Typically, such studies found that hearing mothers interacted with their deaf children much differently from the way they did with their hearing children, and these differences were assumed to be responsible for the observed delays. Among other recommendations, parents were urged to expose their children to as much spoken and/or sign language interaction as possible. Underlying this recommendation was the implicit assumption that conditions that support language acquisition through audition are equally effective in supporting language acquisition through vision. There was little evidence to support this assumption, and we now know that the mechanisms of visual communication are different from those of auditory communication (see chapter 4). Thus, deaf mothers use significantly less language with their deaf children than hearing mothers do with their hearing children, but language development in the first two years proceeds at much the same rate (See Meier & Newport, 1990; Siple, 1997, for reviews).

Whatever its mode, shared communication greatly enhances language development and permits relaxed and effective parent–child interactions (Harris & Mohay, 1997). It also leads to early foundations in language which, in turn, support the acquisition of literacy and cognitive and social skills during the school years. Quality parent–child communication may be the single best predictor of language development, and it is clearly a central factor in later academic success (Drasgow, 1998; Hart, & Risley 1995). For the 90 percent of deaf children born to hearing parents, however, language acquisition through effective shared communication remains a significant challenge. Even when hearing losses are in the mild to moderate range, language development in those children frequently is delayed (Carney & Moeller, 1988; Gregory & Hindley, 1996; Johnson et al., 1989; Spencer, 1993a,b).

Studies have demonstrated that hearing mothers produce comparable amounts of speech to deaf and hearing children, regardless of whether they are also using sign language in a total communication format (that is, using signed and spoken language in addition to hearing aids). Hearing mothers also modify their spoken language to deaf children in much the same way as they do with hearing children (see Gallaway & Woll, 1994, for a review).

Quality parent–child communication may be the single best predictor of language development, and it is clearly a central factor in later academic success. The problem is that young deaf children are unable to benefit from spoken language in any way comparable to hearing children. For deaf children to acquire language, it needs to be unambiguous and visible to them on the lips, faces, and/or hands of their communication partners.

When acquiring sign language naturally, as a first language, deaf children of deaf parents pass through all of the stages typical of spoken language acquisition (Meier & Newport, 1990). But can hearing parents and others learn sign language well enough to promote its natural development? A variety of investigations has provided important insights into both language development of deaf children and the ways in which different language-learning environments can influence development in other domains. The available evidence indicates that, on average, deaf children who learn sign language as preschoolers show better academic achievement and social adjustment during the school years and have superior gains in English literacy (Calderon & Greenberg, 1997; Daniels, 1993; Gregory et al., 1997; Notoya et al., 1994; Strong & Prinz, 1997). Thus, the important factor for learning is not the ability to speak, but the ability to communicate through language, whatever its form, from an early age.

Precursors of Language

Most babies come into the world with the potential for hearing and producing a universal set of sounds essential to spoken language. Not all languages, however, consist of the same basic elements. In Italian, for example, the pronunciation of a shorter or longer /s/ sound can make for two different words (*sposare*, to marry, and *spossare*, to bore). This difference is one that native English speakers do not hear without practice. Similarly, when learning ASL as a second language, the difference between I WAS SICK REPEATEDLY LAST WEEK and I WAS SICK ALL LAST WEEK may not be immediately apparent (repetition of the sign versus repetition with a circular movement).

Through exposure to many examples, children learn the range of elements in their native language, whether they be sounds or sign components (handshapes, movement, sign location; see chapter 4). Meanwhile, they gradually lose the ability to discriminate and produce some language elements with which they have no experience. This process may explain in part why it is in some ways easier to learn a second language in early childhood than in adulthood, regardless of whether that language is spoken or signed. Learning a second language is influenced by age, environment, and motivation, as well as other factors relating to the two languages (e.g., their similarity).[1] Children seem to have an advantage when it comes to pronunciation (i.e., learning to speak or sign a second language "without an accent"), but in other respects adults seem to do just as well at learning a second language. Adults have longer attention spans and better-trained memories than children, and having learned a language, they are more accustomed to the ways languages organize words and expressions. In other words, the older learner is equipped to learn grammar faster than a child and already knows how to use language to get things done. At the outset, however, young children still have available the capability of speaking any language, and the sounds to which they are exposed help them to narrow the possibilities to the language(s) most important in their environment.

The ability of younger children to recognize the basic handshapes and movements of sign language seems to be comparable to that of recognizing the basic sounds of spoken language (Schley, 1991). The elements of the languages may be received through different senses, but the language learning processes of deaf and hearing children are much the same. That is, the elements fit together according to the same kinds of (but not specific) rules that govern all natural languages.

Babbling: A First Step?

Hearing infants start to home in on the sounds relevant to their native language during the first months of life, as evidenced in their *babbling*. At first, their productions are single units, consisting of combined loosely formed consonants and vowels (e.g., "goo" and "ah"). Not until six to seven months of age do hearing infants begin to produce the repetitions of well-formed syllables that are the hallmark of babbling (e.g., "bababa," "gagaga"). This *repetitive babbling* consists of the syllables that will be the building blocks of words. Perhaps just as important, babbling also elicits responses from parents who often see it as an attempt at communication. This, then, is the start of language-based, parent–child interactions.

Do deaf babies babble? It was long assumed that deaf babies babbled just like hearing babies up to the point when hearing babies start to produce words (see Marschark, 1993, chapter 5, for a review). The assumption was that deaf babies would not be socially reinforced by their parents for babbling, however, and thus any language opportunities were lost. While this scenario makes some intuitive sense, it is not what usually happens.

Deaf and hearing infants do produce similar early vocalizations, like crying and cooing. By the beginning of the babbling stage, however, they already differ. At seven months of age, when hearing babies are producing syllabic repetitions, deaf babies show a reduced frequency and complexity in vocal production. At 10 months, when the babbling of hearing babies becomes variegated (/magamaga/, /pakapaka/), the gap has grown further, even when babies have hearing aids and parents emphasize spoken language (Oller & Eilers, 1988; Oller et al., 1985). Repetitive babbling may still occur in deaf babies, but it starts later and is less frequent than in hearing babies. These findings indicate that babbling depends at least in part on audition. To the extent that babbling contributes to language development, they also point to a disadvantage for deaf children in learning spoken language, even before it normally emerges in hearing children.

There are, of course, other modes of communication available for hearing families with deaf children. By 7–10 months, hearing mothers and their deaf infants usually have developed regular patterns of interaction through physical contact (see chapter 4). They already may be using gestures and body language to communicate, just as deaf mothers do with their deaf and hearing infants. Usually overlooked by hearing parents is *manual babbling* by their deaf infants, which begins as early as 6 months (Lillo-Martin, 1993; Maestas y Moore, 1980; Petitto & Marentette, 1991). Whereas vocal babbling consists of the combined vowel and consonant sounds of spoken language, manual babbling involves the production or repetition of sign components, such as isolated handshapes or movements.

Early studies indicated that the first handshapes acquired consist of a relatively small set of configurations that appear to be uniform across deaf infants learning sign language as a first language (fig. 5.1; Boyes Braem, 1990). These handshapes make up the primary components of later signs and are found across all documented sign languages.

In one of the more extensive studies of manual babbling, three hearing children of hearing parents and two deaf children acquiring ASL from their deaf parents were observed (Petitto & Marantette, 1991). All of the children produced similar hand movements consisting of a subset of the potential elements of sign language. The deaf children's hand movements, but not those of the hearing children, appeared to progress through the stages characteristic of vocal babbling and were more complex and varied than those of the hearing children. Further, 98 percent of the deaf children's manual babbling occurred within a restricted space in front of the body, apparently a precursor to the use of normal signing space. The investiga-

Figure 5.1. Set of handshapes that appear consistently among deaf infants learning American Sign Language as a first language (© 1988, Sugar Sign Press; reprinted with permission).

tors argued that there must be an innate predisposition to discover the patterned input of language. Regardless of whether it is innate or learned, the similarity of vocal babbling in hearing children and manual babbling by deaf children, both including the building blocks of language, support the idea that babbling is intimately tied to the acquisition of language.[2]

In another study the babbling of three deaf children of deaf parents and two hearing children of hearing parents was analyzed, beginning as early as 7 months and continuing as late as 15 months (Meier & Willerman, 1995). No clear distinctions between the deaf and hearing children were observed in manual babbling. Deaf children did exhibit more handshape repetitions than the hearing children, but it was unclear what caused that difference. The authors concluded that babble–like gestures might be relatively common in all children, whether or not they have sign language input, and may offer no special advantage to deaf children (Schley, 1991; cf. Volterra & Iverson, 1995).

Because so few studies have been conducted concerning manual babbling, it is difficult to know how to reconcile such contradictory findings. Both studies involved very small numbers of children, suggesting that they may simply reflect natural variability. Regardless of how one interprets the relation between deaf children's early handshapes and manual babbling, those behaviors provide motivation for deaf parents or hearing parents who sign to engage in conversations with their deaf infants in the same way that babbling prompts hearing parents to talk to their hearing infants. Eventually, the language-relevant parts of such babbling will become incorporated into communication and, along with meaningful gestures, deaf children will be well on the way to acquiring language. Note, however, that the two are quite different: gestures are meaningful, while manual babbling, by definition, is not (see Meier & Willerman, 1995).

The Role of Gesture in Early Language Development

Gestures appear to be an essential prelude to language, establishing the rules and contexts of interpersonal communication for both deaf and hearing children (Bates et al., 1989). When used by hearing children, we can easily distinguish gestures from words. The distinction is somewhat harder to make when deaf children mix gestures with their signs, because the two forms of communication share the same channel. Nevertheless, gestures accompany the speech of hearing children in much the same way as they accompany the signs of deaf children (Marschark, 1994).

Three kinds of gestures are particularly common among deaf and hearing children. *Pointing* or *deixis* is frequently used to indicate a location in space, an individual, or an object of interest. Deictic pointing emerges about the same time as the first words, at 9–12 months. It also is used as a supplementary gesture, accompanied by linguistic description. *Iconic* or *object-viewpoint* gestures typically provide information about the way that something appears or acts, thus providing insight into the larger mental representation underlying the gesture (McNeill, 1992). Thus, a child might describe a cyclops, "drawing" the location of the eye on the forehead. *Character-viewpoint* gestures include pantomimic actions as well as the common gestures of offering, showing, or requesting.

> **For both deaf and hearing individuals, gestures are an essential component of communication during the first year of life and through adulthood. Denying the use of gestures to deaf children seems more likely to hurt rather than to help them.**

Young children's use of early gestures, and character-viewpoint gestures in particular, is generally assumed to pave the way for the eventual use of spoken words and signs, respectively (see Bates et al., 1989). When deaf children are at the point of using single words or signs (10–16 months), and when they move to using combinations of two words or signs (16–24 months), gestures continue to play an important role in language development. This is not to suggest that they will come to depend on gestures to the exclusion of signed or spoken communication; there is no evidence that this occurs when a more regular form of communication is available. Rather, for both deaf and hearing individuals, gestures are an essential component of communication during the first year of life and through adulthood (Marschark, 1994; McNeill, 1992; Stokoe & Marschark, 1999). The interesting issues are thus how young deaf and hearing children use gestures and how they function as part of later verbal behavior.[3]

Like more formalized language, gestures initially develop in children because of the need to communicate wants, needs, and desires, and one would not expect to see marked differences as a function of hearing status (Marschark, 1994; Yoshinaga-Itano & Stredler-Brown, 1992). In fact, most gestures used by deaf and hearing children are similar in their form and frequency until about the age of 2 years. This similarity could reflect either a biological predisposition for rule-governed verbal communication or the demands of social communication behavior. Comparisons of the gestural systems of deaf children and hearing children are likely to be informative in this regard, insofar as they would reveal commonalities of early communication behavior that are eventually replaced by more conventional signed or spoken systems (see Volterra & Iverson, 1995).

Investigations also have revealed changes in the frequency and purpose of gestures at various points of development. These changes appear to be related to early language exposure. Among young deaf children of deaf parents, for example, there is a noticeable change in use of pointing from its "immature" use as a gesture showing or requesting something to a "mature" form in the personal pronouns of ASL such as ME, HER, and YOU. At around nine months of age, both deaf and hearing children use pointing as a showing or requesting gesture. Then, at around 12 months, deaf children stop using pointing to refer to people, although pointing still can refer to things and places. Six to twelve months later, person-pointing comes back into use. At that juncture, however, pointing is used in the role of personal pronouns, such as setting up "she/her" in a particular location to refer to someone who is not present (Petitto, 1987). Such changes indicate that gestures and signs are distinct, even if they look the same. They also indicate the need for a better understanding of relations among early gestures, early signs, and early words.

The link between early gestures and a baby's first words have been of interest for a long time. If gestures are a kind of rudimentary attempt at language, growth in speech or sign vocabularies should be accompanied by reductions in gesture frequency. Alternatively, if gestures and words serve similar or complementary functions, there should be a positive relationship between the frequency of gestural and verbal productions as they come to be used in different contexts. These issues are particularly interesting given the claims of several researchers that deaf and hearing children learning sign language as a first language typically produce first signs earlier than peers learning spoken language first produce their first words. The question of whether there is truly an advantage for sign language in early childhood will be considered below.

As the first words come to be used by children, during the last quarter of the first year, they do not replace gestures. Rather, they tend to fill other roles in the language repertoire, regardless of whether a child is hearing or deaf (Caselli & Volterra, 1990). Older children and adults continue to use gestures, together with words and signs, as a means of highlighting important information or specifying spatial relations (Marschark, 1994). Gestures thus are a normal part of interpersonal communication throughout life. They should not be seen as only a characteristic of childhood.

First Signs, First Words

In an effort to clarify the fundamentals of sign language development, several studies have examined the emergence of early signs. One study, for example, focused on the early sign approximations made by children of deaf parents (8 hearing, 1 deaf; aged 6–14 months; Siedlecki & Bonvillian, 1993). Observations revealed that the first components of signs to appear with any regular accuracy were sign locations, followed by sign movements, and then correct use of handshapes. This sequence also has been found in other studies and appears to represent the order of phonological development within ASL.

In another investigation, deaf children who were acquiring ASL as a first language from their deaf parents were found to recognize that signs and their inflections are two different components of a single unit (Newport, 1988; see also Levy, 1997). This is similar to the verb-inflection distinction made by hearing children acquiring English (e.g., study+ing). Later learners of ASL, in contrast, tend to view sign+inflection combinations (e.g., STUDY CONTINUOUSLY) as a single unit. Seeing inflected signs holistically, rather than as made up of component parts, is rather like reading via the "whole word" method rather than by phonics (see chapter 9). Whole sign learning may be sufficient for the acquisition of vocabulary, but it is an inefficient means of acquiring a complete language.

One of the fundamental characteristics of natural languages is that they allow for *duality of patterning* (Hockett, 1958). This means that all languages have inventories of units (letters, sounds, or handshapes) that can be combined to produce potentially an infinite number of acceptable, meaningful combinations (i.e., into words or signs). These meaningful units, in turn, can be used to produce potentially an infinite number of higher-level combinations (sentences). It is through duality of patterning and the *openness* of language that human languages are creative, productive communication systems. We can say or sign things that have never been uttered before and, in principle, there is nothing about which we cannot construct a sentence. Implicit understanding of the *combinatorial rules* of language are thus necessary for true language fluency. Not understanding such rules in language learning would result in only limited abilities for language comprehension and production.

The transitions from referential gestures, to word and sign approximations, to intelligible language are not simple developments, and the language repertoires of individual children typically include a mix of the three during their second year. There appears to be considerable overlap among children between concepts previously communicated through gesture and those communicated through signs or words during this period (Acredolo & Goodwyn, 1988; Bates, 1979). Individual deaf or hearing children, however, tend to have either gestures or words for concepts at this age, but not both. Such findings lend support to the suggestion that gestures are an important accompaniment of sign language but distinct from it (see Stokoe & Marschark, 1999, for discussion).

Does Sign Language Have an Advantage over Spoken Language?

Hearing children of hearing parents normally produce their first words at around 9–12 months of age. Several investigators have reported, in contrast, that the first signs of native-signing, deaf and hearing infants can be seen one to three months earlier. Referred to as the *sign advantage*, this phenomenon has derived largely from parents' observations, and the data are far from consistent.

It is difficult to know when early productions should be considered signs. Like the first words, the first signs tend to blur with earlier approximations, a situation that resolves within a few months. One frequently reported early sign, for example, is the sign MILK, made by the opening and closing of the whole hand. Flexing of the unformed hand undoubtedly occurs frequently in infants, and it seems only a matter of time before it is produced in an appropriate context and interpreted as a sign (Boyes Braem, 1990). Nevertheless, the implications of such productions for social responding are comparable to those created by hearing children's first approximations to spoken words.

Although the notion of a sign advantage has been popular for some time, studies have yielded inconsistent findings about whether it actually exists. Considering both theoretical and methodological aspects of previous studies, it appears that the available evidence favors a small sign language advantage at the one-word stage of vocabulary development (Meier & Newport, 1990). The sign advantage apparently disappears by the two-word stage, however, when other factors come into play. For example, increased rates of touching and visual contact made between mothers and their deaf infants may have the effect of calling attention to their earliest sign productions in a more direct manner than is normally true for deaf mothers with deaf infants (Koester et al., 2000a). Later, however, touch and visual contact may be less important. Further, the component parts of signs—the distinctive features of the language—are completely visible to sign language learners. The components of speech, in contrast, are less readily observable without training for both producers and receivers.[4]

If one accepts that the visibility of signs is important, the sign advantage might be viewed as an artifact of prelinguistic communication in deaf children. That is, because gestures share the same modality as sign language, they could provide a smooth transition to language in the visual mode. Observers thus might be more likely to bestow linguistic status on

the prelinguistic gestures of children in sign language environments relative to the gestures of hearing children in spoken-language environments.
Consistent with that argument, the early gestures used by hearing children
have been found to be less likely than those used by deaf children to be
interpreted as real examples of communication by untrained observers
(Gregory & Hindley, 1996).

Relations Between Parent Language and Child Language

The existence of the sign advantage in children of deaf parents, assuming
that it exists, has not been shown to have any long-term impact on language development of deaf children. Even without it, deaf children of deaf
parents still have a significant advantage in language development relative to deaf children of hearing parents, because parental language usually is more accessible to the child (Nelson et al., 1993). Consequently,
parent–child interactions are more frequent and more positive, as well as
being generally more supportive of language development. Any language
advantages seen in deaf children of deaf parents therefore are more likely
due to the fact that a rich language-learning environment has been established rather than anything inherent in sign language itself.

Recent research findings generally are consistent with this suggestion.
One study, for example, examined the interactions of deaf toddlers with
their hearing mothers. The children ranged in age from 21 to 30 months at
the first evaluation, and there was a follow-up evaluation approximately
1 year later (Pressman et al., 1999). The children varied in their degree of
hearing loss and the mode of communication to which they were exposed,
but neither of these factors was reliably related to their expressive language.
Rather, the strongest predictor of expressive language was "maternal sensitivity" during interactions. It appears that those hearing mothers who
demonstrated extra flexibility and motivation to compensate for their deaf
children's communication needs were most effective in supporting language learning. As one group of investigators suggested, "Mothers who do
not get discouraged and withdraw from interaction when the children's
language development is slow may contribute to a child's long-term success" (Lederberg & Mobley, 1990, p. 301).

In a related study, the language abilities of profoundly deaf children
enrolled in total communication programs and auditory-oral programs were
examined (Musselman & Churchill, 1993). The children first were seen
when they were four-and-a-half years of age and again when they were
almost seven years old. Results indicated that the two groups did not differ in their expressive or receptive abilities at either evaluation. Those
children with mothers who were less dominant in conversational turn-

taking, however, showed greater gains in expressive language growth. This effect was observed regardless of the original starting point of children's language skills. Other research has shown that the use of signs by young deaf children is strongly related to the sign language production rates of their mothers (Spencer, 1993a,b). Although there is considerable variability across children, young deaf children whose mothers sign well thus often show expressive language at rates comparable to their hearing peers of the same age.

Findings of this sort emphasize that young deaf children are in no way doomed to the backwaters of language development, as long as specific efforts are made to ensure their access to effective communication with language models. When deaf children are enrolled in early intervention programs and are exposed to accessible language, they demonstrate more competent language development than children who do not receive those interventions (Calderon & Greenberg, 1997). Other factors are clearly involved as well, including characteristics of the children, their families, and the larger social environment. As children move beyond the earliest relationships with family members, these variables will have greater significance. Outside the home, children will encounter a greater diversity of language and other experiences that shape the course of development (Marschark, 2000). Those deaf children with effective communication skills will continue to develop and learn from formal and informal educational opportunities. Those children with poor communication skills will fall farther and farther behind throughout the school years.

Building an Effective Language

Thus far, we have focused on describing the broad essentials of language development, where social, pragmatic function was more important than form. During the toddler stage (ages one to two) of language development, the establishment of meaningful relations between words (signed or spoken) and their referents is more important than grammatically correct constructions (see Greenberg et al., 1984; Snitzer Reilly & Bellugi, 1996). We now turn to relations between learning signed or spoken language and the ways in which children come to understand and use language to refer to objects and events. In this context, links between language development and cognitive development also will emerge and, subsequently, connections will be made to literacy and academic success.

As deaf children move into preschool and other settings outside of the home, they usually have more varied sign language experiences. There are more people with whom they may sign, and the language learning context becomes more complex. For example, when young deaf children of hearing parents enter preschool programs, they are exposed to far more (and more natural) sign language than are their parents. Accordingly, the children tend to learn sign language at a faster rate than their parents. Of course, deaf children are also far more dependent on signing. For many deaf children, sign communication is the only efficient way to express their needs, desires, curiosity, and creativity, while their parents have a full range of spoken language at their disposal. This imbalance sometimes creates difficulty, as parents and teachers of deaf children often do not realize that they are communicating more information in their speech than they are in their signing. The two modes certainly can express the same information, but greater fluency in speaking tends to overpower lesser signing abilities in beginning signers. As a result, communication may suffer.

Similar challenges occur in the classroom. Although teachers vary in their simultaneous communication skills, studies have shown that 25–50 percent of a spoken message may be omitted from the signing of hearing teachers (MacKay-Soroka et al., 1987; Marmor & Petitto, 1979; Newton, 1985; but see Leigh, 1995). Even more troubling are those cases in which adults say one thing and incorrectly sign something else. Not only does the child fail to understand what is intended, but erroneous information is presented. As a result, the child might miss subsequent information while trying to figure out how the incorrect sign fits into the context. Much the same phenomenon occurs with children who rely on spoken language and are unable to discriminate individual words. Many deaf children thus not only start learning language later than peers who share a language with their parents, but they are confronted with less consistent and less useful language experiences when they do start. Language development thus may become a frustrating guessing game, and motivation to learn may suffer accordingly.

Learning to Use Language Efficiently

Before explicitly considering relations between deaf children's early language—whether signed or spoken—and their learning to read and write, it is important to examine the syntax and semantics of early language acquisition. The focus of this section is on the acquisition of sign language as the primary mode of communication for deaf children. The following section considers current research on the acquisition of spoken language as the first language. In both cases, it is important to keep in mind that (1) the way in which early knowledge/meanings are organized and interconnected will play a central role in later language and literacy skills, and (2) there are many similarities in the acquisition of languages, whether signed or spoken.

During the preschool years, from two to five years of age, deaf children who are naturally exposed to signing in the home rapidly increase the frequency with which they use conventional signs to communicate about objects and actions. Deaf two year olds exposed to ASL also appear to understand conventional sign modifications, such as verb inflections (e.g., GIVING to one person or to multiple people). By age three, they are modifying signs themselves, although their early modifications generally do not conform fully to the rules of ASL until they are about five years old. Nevertheless, deaf three and four year olds clearly know that signs can be altered to modify their meanings. Most of their modifications make sense, and, like the spoken modifications of words produced by hearing children, there is remarkable consistency across children.

The order in which new aspects of language are learned by deaf children of hearing parents is consistent with that of hearing children of hearing parents and deaf children of deaf parents, although it tends to lag some months behind. There are differences in what children know about individual word concepts, and even deaf college students may show differences in the organization of their lexical knowledge relative to hearing peers (McEvoy et al., 1999). Deaf three and four year olds, like their hearing age-mates, overgeneralize some irregular verbs and nouns that they previously used correctly. For hearing children, "went" may become "goed" and "children" may become "childrens." Although they have never heard such constructions, they presumably have learned the general rule and attempt to make similar words conform to it. Deaf children similarly are seen to overgeneralize grammatical rules. For example, some signs, like GIVE and SHOW are "directional," indicating both the agent and the recipient(s). A deaf three year old may overgeneralize directionality, adding it to nondirectional verbs such as DRINK or TICKLE.

Overgeneralizations of this sort are well understood by others when they occur in deaf children's signing and in hearing children's speech and may be responded to or corrected by others around them. Whatever the reaction, such errors are important because they indicate that the child is making sophisticated guesses about the grammar of the language and acquiring its component rules.[5]

By three-and-a-half years, deaf children begin to modify verb signs. They first use inflections to communicate directions and locations, then include qualitative and quantitative inflections to indicate, for example, how big, how good, how bad, or how fast something is. By age four, they are modifying signs and their meanings through conventional ASL facial expressions as well as inflections to indicate subjective meaning. In short, four-year-old children exposed to sign language early are fully able to express how and why things occur, their goals and intentions, and their likes and dislikes.

In addition to research about the content of deaf children's early language, interest in conversational and broader *pragmatic* uses of language is growing. In one study, for example, profoundly deaf children (of hearing parents) between four and seven years of age were found to be just as competent as their hearing peers in responding to requests for clarification in conversation (Ciocci & Baran, 1998). Deaf children in this study usually clarified their utterances by revising their statements, while hearing peers of the same age simply restated their utterances. Clarification strategies are a natural component of social conversation, and it is interesting that young deaf children appear to demonstrate this skill earlier than hearing children (but see Jeanes et al., 2000).

Another aspect of pragmatic language is revealed in children's signing or speaking to themselves during ongoing activities. The language of profoundly deaf four- and five-year-old children has been observed while they performed a construction task with their deaf mothers (Jamieson, 1995). Consistent with the frequent observation that deaf children of deaf parents have an overall language advantage relative to deaf children of hearing parents, this investigation found that deaf children with deaf mothers used more mature "private language" than deaf children of hearing mothers. Another examination of the private language of deaf preschoolers in a total communication setting found that those children were more likely to sign than to speak to themselves while looking at books, writing, and playing alone, and children who were more advanced in their literacy skills used more private sign language in such contexts both at home and at school (Cook & Harrison, 1995).

Learning to Speak versus Learning to Sign

As we described in chapter 2, perhaps the longest-running debate in the history of the education of deaf people has been the question of spoken language versus sign language. The "oral" and "manual" sides of the issue have never been short of supporters, even as the method of choice has varied. Historically, the debate became especially problematic when, instead of different schools adhering to different educational methods, delegates at the Congress of Milan in 1880 established the "oral method" as the official method of deaf education around the world.

By declaring the superiority of a single mode of communication in education, the congress ignored the possibility that different children would benefit from different modes of instruction. But the controversy has not subsided, and today the oralist position is often framed in similar terms: a preference for spoken language as a means to social integration in hearing society. By contrast, those favoring exclusive use of sign language, while fewer and less vociferous than those favoring spoken language, emphasize the importance of sign language to the individual and to the Deaf community and emphasize that sign language is fully appropriate for all purposes of day-to-day life.

As teachers and researchers, we have come to the conclusion that sign language can play a positive role in the educational, social, and personal development of most deaf children. This conclusion is based primarily on research findings described throughout this book, but it also is a function of what is not available. Despite the long history of emphasizing spoken language in the United States, empirical research concerning the development and teaching of speech skills to young deaf children has lacked theoretical coherence and generality with regard to normal conversation (Paatsch et al., 2001; Tye-Murray & Kirk, 1993; see also Commission on Education of the Deaf, 1988). In 1984, more than half of all school-aged children in the United States and Canada with hearing losses were described as having unintelligible speech (Cole & Patterson, 1984). More recent studies, especially those involving children with cochlear implants, have demonstrated significant improvements in the speech skills with extensive training, but impaired spoken language remains the norm for deaf children (Serry & Blamey, 1999; Tobey et al., 1994; Tye-Murray & Kirk, 1993). The acquisition of individual speech sounds, for example, generally proceeds in the same order for hearing children and children with implants; but the process is slower for deaf children, and those with congenital hearing losses rarely attain speech that is fully intelligible.

In part, this situation may result from the fact that most research studies in this area have been aimed at evaluating only a single means of speech therapy, and we do not have a body of literature concerning the relative utility of different approaches or the possibility of combining them (Moores, 1996). Further, because of the emphasis on speech reception and production rather than on language development per se, we have more information concerning the development of sign language than the development of spoken language in deaf children. This situation makes it difficult, if not impossible, to fairly evaluate the relative merits of spoken language versus sign language for young deaf children, especially with regard to semantics, grammar, and more complex aspects of language development. There is one safe conclusion, however: neither spoken nor sign language is inherently better than the other. We have to consider all of the needs of deaf children in various developmental and educational contexts to make appropriate decisions on an individual basis. In a later section, we discuss cochlear implants and language development of deaf children. It is in that arena that advocates of spoken language currently appear to be focusing their efforts.

Does Learning to Sign Affect Learning to Speak?

Closely related to the controversy over the use of sign language versus spoken language is the long-running debate about whether teaching young deaf children sign language will reduce their motivation or impair their ability to acquire or maintain intelligible speech. There really should not be much of a debate on this matter, as there is no empirical evidence to support such a claim. Several observers have indicated that ASL grammar sometimes intrudes into deaf children's speech and writing (Charrow, 1976;

Schiff & Ventry, 1976; Todd, 1976). Such intrusions are common among children and adults learning a second language, and there are no reliable data indicating any difficulty uniquely associated with sign language.

In fact, given the evidence indicating early linguistic and cognitive advantages in deaf children who have either deaf parents or competently signing hearing parents, early experience with sign language might be expected to have positive effects on spoken language development, regardless of hearing status. One recent study, for example, demonstrated that hearing children learning sign language as a second language showed greater visuospatial abilities, including visual and perceptual discrimination and recognition of spatial relations relative to a comparison group learning a second spoken language (Capirci et al., 1998). In the next section, we also provide evidence of an advantage in language development for children with cochlear implants who also are exposed to sign language. Some investigators have gone even further, predicting specific facilitative effects of early signing on subsequent acquisition of speech skills and the grammatical and morphological rules underlying spoken language (Caccamise et al., 1978; Daniels, 1993). At present, there appears to be no evidence to suggest the reverse—that early experience with spoken language facilitates development of sign language skills (but see Dodd et al., 1998).

> **Given the evidence indicating early linguistic and cognitive advantages in deaf children who have either deaf parents or competently signing hearing parents, early experience with sign language might be expected to have positive effects on spoken language development, regardless of hearing status.**

Does this mean that sign language is always the best early language alternative for deaf children? Not at all. It has been argued that approximately 90 percent of severely and profoundly deaf children could achieve proficiency in expressive and receptive spoken language under optimal conditions (Geers & Moog, 1978). Those conditions include strong family support, an educational program strong in support for oral and aural information, and at least average intellectual ability. However, only a minority of deaf children appear to develop spoken language skills that are adequate for the practical purposes of day-to-day life. Most children will not reach those levels of proficiency, and, at this time, we are unable to determine in advance which children will fall into which group.[6]

One relevant study examined the English-based sign and spoken English grammar skills of 168 deaf children enrolled in programs emphasizing spoken language and 159 enrolled in total communication programs (Geers et al., 1984). All of the children were between 5 and 9 years of age, had profound congenital or early-onset hearing losses, and had been involved in early intervention programs. No real differences in language skills were found between the oral and total communication groups when the latter children used sign only or when they used speech and sign together, although the total communication group showed significantly poorer spoken language performance than sign language performance (see also Geers & Moog, 1992). A later reexamination of a subset of the children compared children who had deaf parents with those who had hearing parents. Among five and six year olds, there were essentially no differences between the groups in either spoken or signed English ability. However, by seven to eight years, the children of deaf parents showed small but distinct advantages in both modalities (Geers & Schick, 1988).

It has been suggested that hearing as well as deaf children learning ASL as a first language might have significant advantages in vocabulary acquisition (Daniels, 1993). In one study, 14 hearing children of deaf parents, aged 2–13 years, were tested on the Peabody Picture Vocabulary Test (PPVT), a popular test of early vocabulary development. Those children obtained significantly higher scores than would be expected on the basis of the PPVT norms (i.e., for hearing children). Although generalizations across the wide age range examined are difficult, the results of this study suggest that the availability of both spoken and signed language at an early age might facilitate expressive vocabulary. That conclusion is supported by another study that examined vocabulary growth and sentence production in both sign language and spoken language of two four-year-old, profoundly deaf children enrolled in a total communication program (Notoya et al., 1994). Acquisition of signed vocabulary outpaced spoken vocabulary and was fully comparable to the rates of vocabulary growth in hearing peers through the stage of producing three-word sentences. Six months later, both children's reading scores on an early reading achievement test exceeded those expected of hearing children (see also Marschark, 1993, chapter 11). A larger investigation examined the speechreading abilities, speech skills, and language development in 16 preschoolers with severe to profound hearing losses. Assessments conducted over a three-year period indicated that children's early speechreading skills were strongly related to the development of both spoken and sign language skills (Dodd et al., 1998).

Results like these are encouraging in suggesting that when implemented in a balanced manner, the total communication philosophy can yield positive results, at least for some children. Keeping in mind that the quality of English language production by deaf students can vary depending on the kind of production elicited (Musselman & Szanto, 1998; Schick, 1997), such findings augur well for bilingual educational initiatives involving sign language and some form of English-based signing, together with spoken language, if desired (LaSasso & Metzger, 1999; Marschark, 1997;

Mayer & Akamatsu, 1999). Although bilingual programs may not be as effective for English literacy as some have expected (see chapter 8), it appears that they may ultimately contribute to spoken language abilities as well as general language fluency (Wilbur, 2000). Speech and sign skills often become increasingly intertwined in children who have experience with both modalities, improving speech production and comprehension as well as overall language ability. At the same time, it is well established that children raised in bilingual or multilingual spoken language environments have greater language competence compared to children from single-language environments (see Gregory et al., 1997). Sign language and spoken language thus should not be considered as mutually exclusive alternatives, but as potentially integrative strategies for fostering language development in deaf and hard-of-hearing children. Neither spoken language nor sign language has been shown to be a panacea for the observed lags in the language development of children with greater hearing losses.

During the first years of life, most children communicate about many of the same things, regardless of whether that communication is via gestures, signs, or spoken words. Such findings notwithstanding, there appears to be an inclination among younger children to use only one mode of communication at a time, that is, not to use simultaneous communication. Deaf preschoolers, for example, tend to prefer signed communication over spoken communication even when both languages are available, apparently because signing is more likely than speech to be successful. In later childhood and adulthood, some deaf individuals will become more comfortable with spoken language, while others may be more comfortably and competently bilingual. Deaf children's relative fluencies in the two modalities will depend in part on the age of onset and the degree of their hearing losses. Other factors, such as parental language abilities (signing by hearing parents, speech and signing by deaf parents) and the quality of early education and exposure to language also will make a difference. Most important, concerns of some parents and educators that sign language may impede the development of spoken language appear to be unfounded.

Cochlear Implants and Language Development

The combination of spoken language and sign language may be particularly important to deaf children who have received cochlear implants. Although parents often believe that implantation will improve deaf children's auditory perception and spoken production sufficiently to make them fully comparable to hearing children, those expectations are rarely met (Kampfe et al., 1993). Most often, deaf children with cochlear implants function more like hard-of-hearing children, showing improved auditory perception skills even if spoken language processing is still a challenge.

One relatively large-scale study, for example, followed the progress of more than 70 children who had received cochlear implants relative to 2 comparison groups using hearing aids: one group had 90–100 dB hearing losses and the other group had 101–110 dB hearing losses. The implanted children, all enrolled in a spoken language program, increased from 50 percent (chance) performance on an auditory perception test to 65 percent (just above chance) approximately 1 year later, surpassing performance predicted for the hearing aid group with greater hearing losses. Performance in the implanted group approached the performance of the group with lesser hearing losses (i.e., in the "severe" range). Although the implants clearly improved perceptual skills, these results emphasize the fact that children who receive cochlear implants do not become hearing children, but are still deaf by most definitions (see chapter 2). The authors acknowledged that differences in cognitive ability, socioeconomic status, and residual hearing also can influence speech perception scores, and they noted that it was unclear whether the groups were comparable initially (Meyer et al., 1988). Other studies have explicitly chosen participants who were good candidates for acquiring spoken language (Geers & Moog, 1994). So, although implants may be beneficial for many deaf children, they are not for everyone.

Until recently, research involving children who had received cochlear implants focused almost exclusively on speech perception and production rather than on language development. In part, this situation derived from the fact that funding for cochlear implants comes primarily from medical sources. Surgeons generally view the goal of implantation as improving the hearing of individuals with significant hearing losses, leaving the responsibility for language development to parents and teachers. At the same time, most candidates for implantation are drawn from programs emphasizing spoken language, and parents are often required to enroll their children in such programs if their children are to be implanted. Although this situation is changing, educational programs emphasizing spoken language largely have had goals similar to those of the doctors performing implantations—demonstrating significant improvements in speech perception and production—and more general concerns about language development often have been secondary.

Research findings in this area vary widely, and variability among children with implants frequently is so large that generalizations are difficult (but see Spencer in press). Although excellent language progress has been reported for some children, successes are far from universal. Still, the available research is informative. One group of researchers, for example, evaluated the expressive and receptive language development of 15 deaf children at 6 and 15 months after implantation and found that language development at both ages exceeded that based on preimplantation language abilities, with a larger increase occurring at the second testing (Robbins et al., 1995).[7] Because there was no comparison group of deaf children without cochlear implants, however, the researchers were able to conclude only that the implants promoted language development to a greater extent than would be expected from maturation alone.

In a well-documented study of 13 children with cochlear implants, advantages for those children in a variety of language domains were demonstrated, relative to both hearing norms and comparison groups using hearing aids or tactile aids (Geers & Moog, 1994). These advantages included greater linguistic complexity in spontaneous language and larger expressive and receptive vocabularies, although the children with implants still lagged well behind hearing children. Further, children in the implant and tactile aid groups were initially chosen for the study on the basis of having spoken language skills comparable to children attending a successful oral program.

Another investigation examined the English language achievement of 29 prelingually deaf children who received cochlear implants between 2 and 13 years of age and had them at least 3 years before testing. The achievement levels of the children were compared to those of another group of deaf children, aged 3–14 years, who wore hearing aids (Tomblin et al., 1999).[8] On measures of signed and spoken sentence comprehension, children with implants scored significantly above available norms, and language abilities of all but one child improved to the point where they were no longer linguistically comparable to children using hearing aids. On a test of expressive English grammar abilities, the children with implants again scored significantly better than the children with hearing aids when controlled for age (see also Spencer et al., 1998). Interestingly, 70 percent of the words produced in the storytelling task were spontaneously produced in simultaneous communication by the children.[9]

Similar results were obtained in a study involving 38 children with cochlear implants. All of the children were profoundly deaf, had been implanted before they were five years old, and had used their implant for a minimum of one year (Waltzman et al., 1997). All except one, who used total communication, had been exposed primarily to spoken language. Overall, significant increases in vocabulary development as well as in language production were observed relative to baseline performance (i.e., before implantation). Over a 36-month period, a subgroup of 33 children showed increases in expressive vocabulary equivalent to a 48-month improvement, and children implanted before age 2 were reported to show gains of 53 months. The number of children in this subgroup was not reported, however, and the basis for selecting the 33 children in the follow-up from the larger group of 38 also was not explained. So, again, the generality of the findings is unclear.

In any case, the available research evidence clearly indicates that cochlear implants improve speech perception at frequencies that might contribute to language processing. They also suggest that language development is enhanced by cochlear implants relative to preimplantation baselines, and that some children benefit more from implants than from hearing aids.

At present, however, it remains unclear how broadly we should interpret these findings. Participants in many studies have been chosen for their spoken language skills, and other studies have selectively analyzed data from particular subgroups. Contrary to the philosophy often expressed by supporters of cochlear implantation of young children, there does not appear to be any published evidence indicating that implanted children in spoken language environments acquire language faster than those in environments that include sign language. If anything, available data suggest that children enrolled in total communication settings have shown the greatest advances in language development. Even if children with implants eventually come to depend more on spoken language than on sign language, early access to language is essential for cognitive development and literacy skills. To the extent that sign language provides such access, it seems an alternative that should be available to deaf children and their families.

Finally, length of time with the implant is clearly an important predictor of speech and language success, and gains have been reported up to six years after implantation. Typically, this is a period of rapid language growth, and it will require considerable study to determine the optimal methods for fostering language development in deaf children with cochlear implants. Meanwhile, the selective nature of the available studies means that we do not yet have definitive data indicating who will benefit from implants and who will not. As the implantation of young children continues, new evidence concerning cochlear implants and language development in deaf children will be forthcoming.

Summary

Language is an essential component of normal human development and a means for discovering the world. However, because the majority of deaf children are born to nonsigning, hearing parents, many of them do not have full access to the language of their world until they have passed the most critical ages for language acquisition. Available research indicates that for children with greater hearing losses, exposure only to spoken language often falls short of giving children the linguistic tools they need for academic and social purposes. Although access to English may be essential for literacy, it is most important that deaf children, like hearing children, be able to communicate with their parents from the beginning. From babbling and gestures, to first words and signs, to more complex language, it has been shown that normal language development depends on frequent and regular communication between deaf children and those around them, regardless of whether it is through signed or spoken language.

In young deaf and hearing children, gestures serve practical communicative functions, and the gestures deaf and hearing children use are

markedly similar. As both deaf and hearing children develop, their vocabularies grow and their gestures are complemented by conventional language.
Although gestures may have a special role within ASL, they are natural
and normal for both deaf and hearing children. There is no evidence that
preventing their use by deaf children has any positive impact on their
spoken language skills, and it may even work to their disadvantage. There
also is no evidence that early sign language learning impedes or prevents
spoken language learning. Sign language may even provide a bridge to
spoken English, although different children will excel in and prefer different modes of communication.

Many deaf children acquire spoken language, but it is more common
among those with lesser or later-acquired hearing losses. At present there
does not appear to be sufficient research to be able to evaluate claims about
how deaf children acquire spoken language, the best ways to educate them
in the oral mode, or the utility of spoken language for their educational or
social success. This is not to say that spoken language lacks value in these
domains, many deaf children will thrive in oral environments, and spoken
language can increase opportunities for interactions with hearing individuals (including classmates, teachers, and, eventually, employers). Nevertheless, advocates of spoken language have not yet proven the case nor provided support for the position they have held for more than 100 years.

The best predictors of language development and academic success, at
least in the early school years, include effective mother–child communication, enrollment in early intervention programs, and early use of sign language (Calderon & Greenberg, 1997). This is not to say that sign language
will be the appropriate mode of communication for all deaf children. However, on average, deaf children who are exposed to sign language during
infancy and preschool years have more effective communication experiences
and surpass their deaf peers in language, social, and cognitive development.

Early indications also suggest that children with cochlear implants benefit
from exposure to sign language. Evidence is scarce, but initial findings indicate that those children function more like hard-of-hearing children than
hearing children. Impressive language gains have been reported in some studies relative to preimplantation baselines, but language skills continue to improve over time (in contrast to findings with adults who received cochlear
implants), and relevant research is just beginning in this important area.

For many people, the most frustrating finding concerning language
development of children with hearing loss is the fact that we have not yet
found *the* one approach that supports deaf children across the domains of
social functioning, educational achievement, and literacy. A single such
approach is unlikely, given the heterogeneity of deaf children as a group.
Educators and researchers alike thus continue to seek a balance between
effective early communication skills, usually best achieved through sign
language, and the English skills needed for academic success.

Does hearing loss influence the
development of thinking skills?

Does hearing loss affect memory?

6

Cognitive Development and Deaf Children

There is a long history of investigations reporting that deaf
children lag behind hearing peers in learning, problem solving, and creativity. In this chapter we describe the kinds of
evidence that led to such conclusions and the extent to which
they appear to be valid today.

Early research concerning cognitive development in deaf
children often was aimed at understanding intellectual growth
"in the absence of language." Other investigations involved
tasks that required comprehension of English or histories of
reading. More recently, we have come to understand that both
kinds of evaluation might be biased against deaf children.
Still, ways in which deaf children's atypical histories of language functioning and educational experience might influence their cognitive development are largely unexplored.

There have been a variety of studies dealing with deaf
children's cognitive skills, and especially memory, sometimes
including consideration of language fluencies and degree of
hearing loss. More recently, various tests of cognitive ability
have been developed that are nonverbal in nature or can be
administered through sign language. The extent to which
those tests accurately reflect the thinking skills of deaf children still remains poorly understood, as does the question of
whether such tests tap the same skills that they do in hearing
children. Further, some people still make the appealing but
dubious assumption that cognitive development is essentially

the same for deaf and hearing children (see Braden, 2001; Marschark & Lukomski, 2001, for discussion).

Studies of intelligence and academic abilities of minority and underprivileged children during the 1960s and 1970s led to a concern about the lack of cultural *fairness* in testing. It was recognized at the time that the nature of children's early environments could influence later performance on intelligence measures and academic achievement. This issue was never adequately

addressed with regard to deaf children, most of whom clearly have early childhood experiences that could cause differences in test performance. As a result, deaf children were often described as "deficient" or as "concrete, literal thinkers" who were unlikely to be able to grasp the kinds of abstract concepts necessary for academic success.

Research focusing on specific aspects of cognitive development, such as classification and concept learning, have yielded contradictory results. Using nonverbal assessment techniques, researchers sometimes have eliminated differences between deaf and hearing children on these tasks. Nevertheless, delays in these domains have been demonstrated both in deaf children who have been educated in spoken-language environments and those exposed primarily to sign language. One might expect that deaf children of deaf parents would perform comparably to hearing peers on most cognitive tasks, but these expectations are not met with any consistency. More research is needed with larger numbers of children before conclusive findings can be obtained.

The lack of any simple causal link between language delays and cognitive abilities in deaf children indicate that there are undiscovered factors that influence evaluations of cognitive development in deaf children. It may be that the ranges of language skill examined have been too narrow to evaluate the issue fairly or that the connection simply is not as direct as it might seem. That is, aside from language delays, the quality and quantity of language-based interactions should foster various components of cognitive growth (Hart & Risley, 1995).

For example, we know that early access to effective language is essential for normal cognitive development and academic success in both deaf and hearing children. We also have seen that early use of sign language is a good predictor of cognitive development and academic success among deaf children (see chapter 4).[1] In one study, for example, language development was found to be the best predictor of success in various memory tasks (Bebko & McKinnon, 1998). The number of years of effective language exposure in the primary communication modality fully accounted for the age differences in performance, but the total number of years of language experience was not as good a predictor. The contribution of developing language skills, and especially automatized (unconscious) language skills such as the activation of word meaning has also been shown to be an essential contributor to other complex cognitive abilities (Bebko & Metcalfe-Haggert, 1997). Taken together, such findings emphasize the need for care in evaluating language development, cognitive growth, and academic performance, while recognizing that they are rarely independent.

In this regard, LaSasso (1999), an experienced educator of deaf students, pointed out the need to be especially careful of differences between deaf and hearing students in test-taking strategies and skills (e.g., reading strategies, test format, type of information assessed). LaSasso noted, for example, that on tests where students have to read a passage and select the correct answer from several alternatives, deaf students are more likely than hearing students to select answers simply by matching words in answers with words in the text. This kind of strategy is not always available, and, even when it is, it does not always yield the right answer. The way in which test questions are written thus may affect performance, whether or not the students understand the test material. In addition, relative to hearing peers, deaf students may be more likely to guess at answers rather than to work through alternatives as a problem-solving situation, resulting in lower performance that may not reflect either content knowledge or the ability to use problem-solving strategies (Marschark & Everhart, 1995; see also Marschark & Mayer, 1998). Finally, differences in the abilities of deaf and hearing children to maintain or integrate verbal information over short periods of time are likely to have implications for overall cognitive functioning and for reading and writing in particular.

We now know that although cognitive differences are observed between deaf and hearing children, these often are related more to how they go about various tasks than to absolute differences in ability. Deaf children are still found to lag behind hearing peers in some areas, but these lags usually can be linked to barriers to information access in the home or early educational experiences and are not a function of hearing loss per se. The notion of deaf children as concrete, literal thinkers has now been replaced by a better understanding of the interactions of language and intellectual development in deaf children. As this chapter will reveal, the relationship is anything but a simple one.

Foundations of Learning

Children come into the world equipped with the "hardware" (nervous system) and "software" (basic perceptual and cognitive processes) necessary for learning and for constructing meaning during interactions with the world. In chapter 5, for example, we saw how infants can distinguish their mothers from other women and can distinguish familiar language from unfamiliar language at birth. Basic learning mechanisms thus lead to developing relationships with caregivers, the rapid tuning of perceptual and neuromotor mechanisms, and the blooming of development. This intimate interaction between heredity and the early environment is often described in terms of *nature* and *nurture* (Akamatsu et al., 2000; Wahlsten & Gottlieb, 1997).

Some data indicate that children with hereditary deafness (reflected either in having deaf parents or family histories of hearing loss) demonstrate consistent advantages in early assessments of intelligence relative to other deaf children (Akamatsu et al., 2000; Zweibel, 1987). While this finding might suggest a hereditary contribution, cultural and linguistic factors in families with genetic deafness also influence early cognitive development. A deaf child born into a family with deaf members, for example, often is exposed to sign language early in life, and deafness is not viewed as negatively as it might be in a family with no such history. We return to this issue later in the chapter, when we discuss intelligence.

Visual Processing and Sensory Compensation in Deaf Individuals

We do not have sufficient space to go into extensive detail concerning the neurological (primarily brain) and neuropsychological (brain and behavior) development of deaf children (see Emmorey, 2001). Beyond interactions with heredity, however, early experience clearly has an impact on the development of the nervous system and organization within the brain which, in turn, may affect learning. A common assumption in this regard is that because they lack hearing, deaf people are particularly adept in the visual domain, an example of *sensory compensation*. The situation is rather complex and easily misinterpreted, so we provide a brief overview of the issues here, insofar as they relate to learning and cognitive development in deaf children.

Earlier, we described several medical causes of congenital or childhood hearing loss that might also result in neurological damage (e.g., meningitis, high fevers). Children who have suffered such damage may vary both with regard to the location of injury and its possible effects. Although it is not our intention to discuss the effects of brain damage per se, it is noteworthy that children's brains are remarkably resilient and plastic. This means that they are able to accommodate and adjust to various brain traumas to some degree (Kolb & Wishaw, 1996; Lenneberg, 1967). Such flexibility continues at least until adolescence, and there is increasing evidence for considerable neural plasticity (*accommodation*) into adulthood. This should not be taken to imply that hearing loss related to neurological damage may somehow recover over time. Sensorineural hearing losses typically involve specific nerves that do not repair themselves. Still, for the minority of deaf children who have some brain damage related to the etiology of their hearing losses, physiological mechanisms and teaching strategies can reduce the long-term impact of the damage on learning.

Our focus relates to something more subtle than the presence or absence of brain damage: the extent to which deaf and hearing children's brains may develop different patterns of organization or functioning as a result of differences in early experience. We would expect such differences because lack of hearing will influence the development of other systems as well. In particular, the use of a visual-spatial language demands greater use of brain areas normally associated with vision, spatial processing, and perhaps kinesthetic (motor feedback) input. This situation points to the possibility of sensory compensation, either physiologically or pedagogically over time, and may provide information on structuring teaching-learning situations for deaf children and on choosing the most effective kinds of instructional materials.[2]

The visual modality is certainly important for deaf children. Overall, however, there is no evidence indicating that deaf people make better use of vision than hearing people. That is, deaf people do not seem to demonstrate any generalized sensory compensation. Depending on the specific kind of task used, deaf people have been found to perform better, worse, or the same as hearing individuals. For example, in a series of studies involving severely to profoundly deaf children, aged 6–16 years, they surpassed hearing peers of the same ages on the compound stimulus visual information task. This test requires short-term memory for complex visual materials and subsequent performance of actions based on different dimensions of the figures. The only case in which the performance of hearing children exceeded that of deaf children was when the task involves serial presentation of parts of a stimulus and serial (ordered) recall (Todman & Cowdy, 1993; Todman & Seedhouse, 1994).

Deaf college students also appear to be more flexible than hearing students in their ability to redirect attention from one spatial location to another, better at detecting motion in peripheral vision, and they show enhanced ability to perceive and remember complex visual signs (Corina et al., 1992; Parasnis & Samar, 1985). Younger deaf children, however, generally show poorer visual attention than hearing children, particularly in situations in which they are liable to be distracted (Quittner et al., 1994; cf. Spencer, 2000).

This latter finding is particularly important because it suggests that, at least with younger students, reliance on visual materials in the classroom should not be taken as a panacea. Clearly, visual materials are important for communication and learning, but care must be taken to ensure that the learning environment is constructed in such a way that visual materials are both available and accessible. For example, when materials like slides or transparencies are presented to hearing children (or adults), presenters often talk about them, explaining or elaborating the content. Deaf individuals need time to be able to read the material and then to shift attention back to the presenter (or the interpreter) to follow what is being communicated. Yet, we frequently see teachers not pausing long enough for deaf students to finish reading material before continuing a presentation. Regardless of whether they are signing or speaking, this creates a conflicting, distracting situation for the learner.

At a more general level, if interactions between hearing and vision are normal components in human development, deaf children might be expected to show somewhat different paths in the development of visual attention. This suggestion was supported by a study involving deaf children aged 6–13 years. They were found to have more difficulty than hearing children in a visual task that required selective responding to a specific number embedded among other numbers (e.g., a 7 in a long string of other digits), even though the task did not involve use of sound. Interestingly, those children who had cochlear implants were better at attending selectively than were children without implants, at least after a year of implant use (Quittner et al., 1994). The authors suggested that to the extent that cochlear implants influence children's perception and interactions with the world, they may create new opportunities for making connections between concepts missed by other deaf children.

Better visual attention skills also have been observed in deaf children with deaf parents. Although more research is needed, such findings suggest that visual attention may be linked to better language skills among deaf children or when more direct connections between language and vision occur in the environment (Harris, 1978; Quittner et al., 1994; Spencer, 2000). In any event, the development of visual attention skills—and cognitive abilities more generally—are likely to be enhanced by environments rich in stimulation and connections between different sense modalities. Cochlear implants would contribute to such connections, whether or not they provide for language comprehension.

Although sound appears to contribute to some aspects of perceptual and cognitive development, sign language does, too. Overall, users of American Sign Language (ASL) tend to be superior to deaf and hearing people who do not sign in their abilities to discriminate faces (Bettger et al., 1997), to identify emotional facial expressions (McCullough & Emmorey, 1997), and in their performance on mental imagery tasks involving mental rotation, image generation, and image transformation (Emmorey, 1998). Deaf children unfamiliar with sign language do not demonstrate such enhanced visual-spatial abilities, lending support to the conclusion that this is not a simple case of sensory compensation (Parasnis et al., 1996). Rather, exposure to sign language appears to result in a neuropsychological organization that has advantages in some domains. In other visual-spatial domains, such as face recognition and overall face-processing abilities, sign language users and individuals who do not use sign language are comparable (Emmorey, 1998).

At a more general level, there is now considerable evidence that the richness of the environment has a direct impact on brain development and, by extension, flexibility in learning and cognition. In animal studies, rats that are raised in environments that contain wheels, climbing apparatuses, and other interesting things have more densely interconnected brain cells and tend to be better learners than animals raised in less enriched environments. It is unlikely that there is any simple comparison to humans in this regard, and specifically to children who may be lacking one sensory modality, but there is sufficient circumstantial evidence from both deaf and hearing children raised in stark institutions or in isolation to indicate that a diverse linguistic and nonlinguistic environment provides an important foundation for learning.

Circumstantial evidence also suggests the possibility that differences in language exposure between deaf children with deaf parents and deaf children with hearing parents might be at least in part related to parallel differences observed in several academic domains. If deaf children of hearing parents do not have effective communication with their parents during their early years, their social and educational interactions are likely to be less rich than children who share a common language with their parents, regardless of whether that language is signed or spoken (see e.g., Volterra & Erting, 1990).

By understanding how deaf children learn, remember, and solve problems, we should be better able to structure everyday situations in ways that promote the cognitive development of deaf children and make learning interesting. In addition, such knowledge should allow us to train teachers and design educational methods that help deaf children fulfill their academic potential. We therefore now turn to several essential aspects of learning, both in academic contexts and elsewhere. We then consider the topic of intelligence, what it means, and what it does not.

Memory

Studies of memory have been one of the most dominant research emphases involving deaf persons over the past 100 years. The popularity of memory studies originally derived from an assumption that deaf children grow up with only nonverbal memory codes. Two errors underlying that assumption have been pointed out, both relating to mistakenly equating *language* with *spoken language*. First, deaf individuals clearly are not without language, even if they lack skills in the spoken and written vernacular. Second, memory does not require spoken forms of language, although there are some differences observed in memory performance as a function of whether people use signed or spoken languages. To most clearly indicate the potential impact of memory functioning on educational performance, it will be worth considering the two primary components of memory separately.

Working Memory

A variety of studies concerning *short-term memory* or *working memory* have shown that deaf and hearing individuals may encode information in qualitatively different ways. With lists of simple stimuli such as words, pictures, or numbers, for example, hearing people tend to rely on speech-based verbal coding, usually linked to the order of the information to be remembered (Baddeley, 1986). Deaf people, in contrast, have been shown to rely more heavily on visuospatial short-term memory codes, such as remembering locations rather than the temporal sequence of objects presented. This is not to suggest that any particular memory code or way of organizing information is any better or worse than another; different memory codes and memory strategies presumably have differing strengths for processing various kinds of information.

Early studies indicated that memory for letters and words by deaf children exposed only to spoken language was closely linked to their spoken language skills and inversely linked to their degree of hearing loss (Conrad, 1972, 1979). That is, children with more speech and hearing showed better memory performance. More recently, a strong relation has been shown between language development and the use of memory rehearsal by deaf children. Rehearsal emerges as a memory strategy at about 7–8 years for hearing children, 10–11 years for deaf children exposed primarily to spoken language, and 12–13 years for students in total communication programs (Bebko & McKinnon, 1990). Overall, however, it is the use of memory strategies, rather than the modality of any particular memory code, that most influences deaf children's memory performance.

There is no particular reason that one language modality or another should have any advantage with regard to memory strategies. At face value, the advantage should go to whatever communication system optimizes the child's access to teaching, learning, and interpersonal experience. Nevertheless, a variety of studies have demonstrated that deaf children and deaf adults tend to remember less in various short-term memory tasks than do hearing peers (see Marschark & Mayer, 1998). The basis for this finding appears to lie in the fact that although deaf students can recode printed words into sign-based codes, thus removing the apparent bias of using print materials, working memory seems to function best with speech-based memory codes. Further, this advantage holds for both deaf and hearing students.

Several studies, for example, have reported that deaf students with better speech skills tend to rely primarily on speech recoding as a strategy in memory tasks, whereas deaf students with low to moderate speech-coding abilities tend to use both speech and sign strategies (Hanson & Lichtenstein, 1990; Lichtenstein, 1998; see also Campbell & Wright, 1990). Those students with better speech skills also tend to remember more, although it is important to remember that correlation does not imply causation. Sign language fluency has also been found to be inversely related to memory span in deaf students, while spoken language fluency is directly related to memory span (Marschark & Mayer, 1998). What are the causes and implications of such findings?

Educators and researchers have suggested that deaf individuals may use visual imagery in place of verbal codes for memory, but several studies have shown this not to be the case (Bonvillian, 1983; Conlin & Paivio, 1975). Deaf individuals with better sign language skills do make use of signs in memory coding, but this appears to the more of a linguistic code than a visual imagery code. Thus, for example, signs made with similar hand-shapes tend to disrupt memory performance among deaf individuals just as words that sound the same disrupt memory performance among hearing individuals (Bellugi et al., 1975; Hanson, 1982; Poizner et al., 1981). Such findings lead to the interesting prediction that just as variation in English fluency may affect the frequency of phonologically based coding in deaf individuals, variation in sign language fluency should affect the frequency of sign-based coding.

In one of the earliest published studies on memory and deaf individuals, a classic 1917 investigation demonstrated that deaf people generally have shorter memory spans than hearing people, and that deaf people who use spoken language have longer memory spans than deaf people who use sign language (Pintner & Patterson, 1917). Originally, those results were interpreted as indicating limited memory capacities and language-related cognitive deficits in deaf people. Our current understanding of working memory has provided a more specific and reliable interpretation. Working memory is now known to include an *articulatory loop* that limits memory span to the amount of information that can be articulated in roughly two seconds. This means that fewer long words than short words can be remembered, a prediction that has been supported many times in a variety of studies.

The time-limited nature of working memory also means that languages in which digits take longer to produce will yield shorter digit spans than languages in which the digits take less time to produce. As it happens, ASL is one language in which it takes longer to produce digits than in English, even if the rate of information transfer in terms of propositions is the same for the two languages (Marschark & Mayer, 1998). Therefore, it should not be surprising that deaf people using sign language-based coding in working memory demonstrate shorter memory spans than deaf or hearing people using speech-based coding in working memory. Deaf and hearing individuals have the same working memory capacity, roughly the amount of information that can be articulated in two seconds, but fewer ASL signs than English words can be fit into the articulatory loop in that amount of time.

These findings have two potential implications for educating deaf students. First, deaf students who tend to rely on spoken language may have better memory for material that is presented in a rote (list) manner, as compared to students who rely primarily on sign language. Rote memorization may be useful in some situations, such as learning multiplication tables or poetry, but it generally is not an ideal learning strategy. Nonetheless, it is frequently adopted by students (both deaf and hearing), even if it puts them at a disadvantage relative to using more integrative, conceptually based strategies (Richardson et al., 1999).

A second implication of the above findings is that just as longer and more complex grammatical structures pose a greater problem for deaf than for hearing readers, the same may be true for students who are more oriented toward sign language than spoken language. More complex grammatical structures put greater demands on working memory, and a reduced working memory span will have negative implications. One could argue about cause and effect in that case, and other factors are likely involved in the difficulty deaf students have with more complex grammatical structures. For example, consistent with rote rehearsal strategies, deaf students have been found to sometimes focus more on words and ideas within texts rather than on relations among them. Such *item-specific processing* reduces both comprehension and memory for text and may be a major factor in deaf students' showing poorer memory when reading than their hearing peers (Banks et al., 1990; Marschark et al., 1993; Richardson et al., 1999). A complete theoretical explanation and practical implications of these findings are still being sought, but the language used in short-term memory coding does appear to have an impact on reading.

Semantic Memory

Thus far, we have been dealing only with working memory. *Long-term memory* or *semantic memory* also has an impact on learning in a variety of ways. Information that we have learned through a variety of external sources, or figured out for ourselves, not only has to be retained in long-term memory, but also has to be retrievable if it is to be utilized. Access to information in long-term memory normally happens spontaneously, as it is needed, in the context of ongoing behavior. Although there are times when memory access fails, such as when we are unable to associate a name

with a familiar face, other things such as remembering how to ride a bi-
cycle, our home telephone number, the sum of 2+2, or the meaning of
"duck" do not typically require us to pay much attention. Of course, "duck"
may mean different things depending on the context, but there will be other
cues to tell us which is relevant, and it is only rarely that such decisions
reach consciousness (for example, when we realize that "submarine" means
"under water" and "antiseptic" means "against germs").

Because of the need for automatic, rapid access to long-term memory
information, the organization of our semantic memories is important both
when we are trying to remember something and in a variety of processes
including reading, problem solving, and working memory. Research with
hearing individuals has provided insight into the ways in which organization and retrieval processes occur, particularly in response to individual
words presented either in lists or in text. For the present purposes, it is
important to recognize that people vary in how much they know about
different things, how that information is organized, and that organization
can affect the accessibility and availability of information.

We expect that organization of general knowledge is roughly the same
for most individuals: We know that a canary is a bird, France is in Europe,
and Lyndon Baines Johnson was a president of United States sometime after
Abraham Lincoln. Not surprisingly, people who are experts in an area may
have different ways of organizing relevant information in that area, thus
improving its accessibility and availability. Children also may have different, and sometimes comical, ways of organizing information that reveal its
incompleteness and the fact that it is not yet well interconnected (e.g., a worm
may not be considered an animal, because it does not have eyes). Ultimately,
however, the structure of our memories usually takes care of itself and thus
you, as a reader, are retrieving meanings to the words of sentence as you are
reading it, with little difficulty or awareness. Your semantic memory and
your related ability to do *top-down processing* (see chapter 9) allows you to
fill in gaps, like in the preceding sentence, where a word is missing.

If we could be sure that deaf and hearing students know roughly the
same amount of information and that the information is organized in
roughly the same ways, we would not need this section of the chapter.
Given what we know about differences in the early experiences and education of deaf and hearing children, however, such assumptions may not
be correct. At the very least, it might be expected that deaf students, as a
group, are likely to be more variable in the content and organization of their
long-term memory stores as compared to hearing students. As with other
topics we have considered, differences may be small and unrelated to learning or academic achievement. In areas such as reading and problem solving, however, even relatively small differences may be important.

Few studies have investigated the link between the memory performance of deaf individuals and the breadth and organization of their con-

ceptual knowledge, and none has yet examined the way in which those differences might affect performance in school. The few studies conducted through the 1970s found only small differences in the knowledge bases of deaf and hearing students, at least when highly familiar stimuli were used. Both deaf and hearing students were found to organize familiar objects in similar ways, as reflected in the way they sorted objects or words into groups and the way similar items were clustered together in memory tasks (Hoemann et al., 1974; Tweney et al., 1975). Deaf students tended not to use meaning-based strategies in recall, however, and typically recalled less than hearing peers, even when they did (Koh et al., 1971; Liben, 1979).

Research has shown that although deaf students recognize and attempt to use semantic relations to improve memory, they might lack flexibility in fully unpacking the meaning of an item (a duck can be an animal, a thing that swims, a thing that walks, a potential meal, a noise maker, or a bug catcher) or automatically recognizing a concept's place in a hierarchical taxonomic structure (a duck is an animal, a bird, a farm animal). Deaf students know these things, but as a function of their prior experience, they may not automatically activate less familiar information in memory. How can we determine the extent of such differences?

A recent study examined the organization of knowledge by deaf and hearing college students (McEvoy et al., 1999). A single-word association task was used in which students wrote down the first word that came to mind in response to each of 80 printed words. Responses of the two groups were remarkably similar overall. Nevertheless, there also were significant differences on several dimensions reflecting coherence or consistency in memory organization. All of the differences were in the same direction indicating that deaf students' verbal concepts were less homogeneous than those of hearing students. There was significantly less consistency in associations across the deaf students, who had broader and less well-defined sets of associations with other concepts. The results suggested that during memory retrieval, problem solving, or reading, deaf students' activation of meaning in semantic memory may not be as directed as that of hearing students. Such findings should not be taken to imply that deaf students always will be faced with reading difficulties. Instead, they should be seen as emphasizing the need for a more complete understanding of deaf students' cognitive skills and knowledge if we are to foster educational success.

The above findings indicate that there may be differences in both knowledge organization and the strategies involved in accessing that information between deaf and hearing students. Although there is considerable overlap in their knowledge of concepts, there also appears to be a tendency of deaf students not to apply some aspects of their knowledge in situations that would benefit from such application (e.g., to improve memory or help solve a problem; Marschark & Everhart, 1999). This situation could reflect insufficient depth and breadth of knowledge or a failure to strategically apply such knowledge spontaneously. Alternatively, deaf learners may use some nonobvious strategies that have not yet been described. In any case, the learning and academic performance of deaf (or hearing) students clearly will suffer when conceptual information from memory is needed but is not used successfully in a particular task. Research into these questions is just beginning, and it will be some time before we have a complete understanding of the content and structure of deaf students' knowledge, the influences of individual differences (such as educational histories, degree of hearing loss, and age of onset), and the reasons deaf students sometimes may not transfer their knowledge across contexts.

Creativity and Problem Solving

Dealing with the environment—from visual identification, to social interaction, to reading—requires marshalling a variety of cognitive resources, sometimes in ways never used before. Introducing a variety of novel situations during childhood seems likely to provide children with greater flexibility in dealing with novelty later (fig. 6.1).[3] It also may give them a richer experiential repertoire from which to draw in problem solving and reading and writing. We may not know how, precisely, such flexibility is gained, but we know that diversity of experience and effective access to interpersonal and written information are important contributors.

The previous sections have indicated that there are differences as well as similarities in the skills and knowledge bases of deaf and hearing students as a function of both linguistic and nonlinguistic experience. In this section, we focus on the way in which knowledge and experience are applied in new situations through the use of memory. We will see that differences in the social and object-centered experiences of deaf children relative to their hearing peers may influence their problem-solving skills in several ways. In this broad sense, *problem solving* refers to the use of previous experience, knowledge, and skills to satisfy the demands of an unfamiliar situation. We therefore are suggesting that any observed differences in deaf and hearing children's knowledge about people and things have the potential to influence the way they go about dealing with novel situations.

Problem solving is best seen as a collection of related abilities, from the simple generalization involved in labeling similar things with the same name to complex situations such as transferring turn-taking rules from one game to another or using knowledge of mathematics in an engineering course. Studies of problem solving rarely involve complex, real-world situations primarily because these situations are extremely complex. Instead, research more often focuses on tasks that have clearly defined answers in

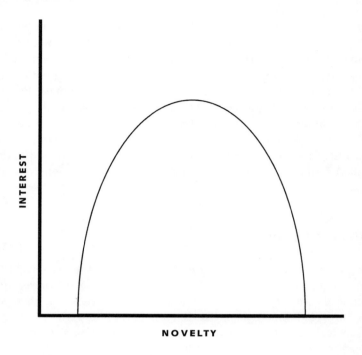

Figure 6.1. Inverted U function of interest relative to novelty.

clearly defined "problem spaces." Investigations of this sort typically involve the research methodologies in vogue at the moment. In the case of deaf students, the majority of problem-solving research was done in the 1960s and 1970s, when most popular tasks involved the acquisition of simple single- or multidimensional concepts and Piagetian conservation (relating to children's abilities to consider problems or situations from alternative perspectives). Many of those studies involved nonverbal materials and responses in order to avoid any confounds due to deaf children's language abilities.

The early body of research demonstrated that across concept learning tasks, classification tasks, and conservation tasks, deaf children lagged behind hearing peers. Given the presumed generality of these basic learning tasks and their popularity as measures of cognitive development, these studies suggested that deaf children were lacking some important earlier experiences. One classic study, for example, involved deaf eight year olds and hearing six year olds and eight year olds in a weight conservation task (Furth, 1964). In the usual weight conservation task, children are shown two identical balls of clay. After children agree that they are equal in weight,

Functional Fixedness

You are standing in a room that is empty except for a small table holding a pair of scissors and an empty glass. Two strings are hanging from the ceiling. You can't reach both simultaneously, no matter how you stretch, but your task is to tie the two ends of the strings together. How do you do it? (Hint: Think of alternative uses for objects in the room.)

one of the balls is changed by breaking it into pieces or flattening it into a disk. The child is then asked if the changed piece of clay is heavier, lighter, or the same weight as the unchanged clay. They also have to justify their answers.

In the nonverbal version of the task used in this study, children moved their hands horizontally for "same weight" or lowered one hand or the other to indicate that one of two pieces of clay held by the experimenter was heavier, thus eliminating the need for understanding the terms "lighter" and "heavier." After training with pieces of clay of various sizes, children saw nine different transformations performed on one of two same-sized balls of clay, including the critical test trials in which a ball was transformed into a snake shape, a ring, and a disc. Overall, the eight year old deaf children correctly said "same" on approximately 45 percent of the trials. In comparison, hearing six year olds did so on about 41 percent of the trials and hearing eight year olds responded correctly on 90 percent of the trials.

The findings of this study and many others have indicated that deaf children's conservation performance lags behind hearing peers by two to four years. Because nonverbal versions of the tasks appeared to rule out any linguistic confounds, many investigators have claimed that these studies reflect deaf children's concrete thinking, usually attributed to lack of experiential diversity in the real world. As we have seen, however, another possible explanation for deaf children's difficulties in such tasks—as well as many classroom tasks—may be that they are easily distracted (Luetke-Stahlman & Luckner, 1991; Quittner et al., 1994).

Considering the dozens of studies along this line that have involved deaf children, it appears that their performance is essentially equivalent when successful performance requires attention to a single dimension (for example, the size of a piece of clay). When a task requires simultaneous attention to two or more dimensions (for example, the size and shape of the clay), deaf children routinely perform more poorly than the hearing peers of the same age (Ottem, 1980). The difficulty is not that deaf children are unable to form coherent concepts or categories, because they clearly do so in tasks involving only one dimension. There appear to be at least three alternative explanations for such findings, none of which has yet been ruled out by available research.

One possibility is that the dimensions on which concepts are to be formed in such tasks are not as obvious or salient as they might be for hearing children. This situation could result either from a failure to notice and label items as having a particular value on some dimension (e.g., elephants are smart as well as large). The previously mentioned findings indicating that concepts are less interconnected for deaf students than hearing students is consistent with this suggestion. A second possibility is that deaf children have less experience with contexts in which such concepts are relevant and have to be balanced against each other (Gershkoff-Stowe et al., 1997; Marschark & Everhart, 1995). This could result in their not being able to find the effective strategy for a problem, even if they have all of the requisite knowledge.

A third possibility is that the difficulty of multidimensional tasks for deaf children may derive from them having a different threshold for frustration or motivation to persist in such tasks, leading them to respond incorrectly when they are unsure of an answer, even if they have partially solved the problem. One teacher recently gave us an example of this that she encounters frequently in testing deaf students. She described a multiple-choice testing situation in which a child had already correctly ruled out answers A and B and was trying to decide between C and D. When he was unable to do so, he picked A. The teacher asked why he had chosen an answer that he already knew was wrong. The student responded that he did not know the right answer, so it did not matter (Elaine Moore, personal communication, August 18, 2000).

These alternatives, of course, are not mutually exclusive, and they may all be involved in the performance of a particular child or group of children in a problem-solving study. The situation can be clarified somewhat, however, by tasks that provide a "trail" indicating how children go about solving a problem. One study of problem solving by deaf and hearing students, for example, used a version of the 20 questions game in which children had to discover which of 42 pictures of common objects the experimenter has selected (Marschark & Everhart, 1999). Examining the questions that children ask in a situation like this should provide some insight into how they go about solving the task. The primary indicator of sophisticated problem solving, in this case, was the frequency with which children used alternative-limiting questions such as "Is it an animal?"

Deaf children, aged 7–14 years, rarely used alternative-limiting questions in the twenty questions game, and, in fact, did not show any consistent strategy short of making specific guesses ("Is it the sailboat?"). Deaf and hearing children who had played twenty questions or similar games before were equally likely to use the alternative-limiting strategy. Inexperienced hearing children typically discovered the "correct" strategy, whereas their inexperienced deaf peers did not, resulting in the overall differences between the two groups. The results of the study were interpreted as indicating lags either in the organization of knowledge or access to that knowledge, both fundamental parts of successful problem solving in a variety of different contexts. Alternatively, it may be that treating each question in the task as a separate event, rather than stepping back and viewing the whole game as a set of related parts, may leave deaf children "not seeing the forest for the trees." In either case, children who are less likely to make use of relations among the aspects of a task often will be less likely to succeed. This holds for social situations as well as academic situations such as reading.

The transfer of knowledge and strategy from one domain to another, as in the tasks described above, is one hallmark of flexible thinking. Together with creativity, these abilities largely define intelligence. Meanwhile, perhaps the most general and frequently invoked characterization of deaf children is that they lack flexible thinking, even when those concepts involve nonverbal domains (Furth, 1966; Liben, 1978; Myklebust, 1964; Oléron, 1953; Quigley & Paul, 1984). Direct tests of deaf children's nonverbal creativity are rare and generally do not support this conclusion (Marschark & Clark, 1987). Considerably more literature is available concerning deaf children's creativity in language, although most of the relevant research has involved their creativity within English.

In general, studies of deaf children's flexibility within English have demonstrated that many of them can understand figurative language only when the relevant tasks are simplified and carefully structured. This is a critical point that needs to be recognized by teachers in all subject areas because a large portion of written English is nonliteral. In contrast, studies that have evaluated deaf children's creativity within sign language have indicated that they are at least as creative as hearing peers (see Marschark & Everhart, 1995, for a review). Unfortunately, communication barriers and lack of understanding about deaf children's knowledge and skills can result in teachers' and parents' unwittingly suppressing their natural creativity because they fail to recognize creativity expressed in sign language or less-than-fluent English. Such findings again suggest the need for culturally fair tests in order to fully understand to children's cognitive abilities and optimize the teaching-learning process. With that important caveat, we now look at the issue of intelligence testing with deaf children and the extent to which it reliably and validly reflects their cognitive abilities.

Intelligence

Thus far, we have considered several pieces of the mosaic of the deaf learner. Many parents concerned about their deaf children's academic achievement are most likely to think about the relevance of intelligence. For psychologists, *intelligence* is the repertoire of abilities that allow an individual to deal flexibly with novel information and situations at a particular age—that is, it is cognitive flexibility. In the present context, the relevant question thus is not what kind of scores deaf children make on intelligence tests, but what they can achieve. IQ (*intelligence quotient*) scores are sometimes reliably related to achievement in deaf children, but those relationships typically are not very strong (Hirshoren et al., 1979). Further, it is not at all clear that intelligence tests are tapping the same things in deaf and hearing children.

With the advent of intelligence testing in the early 1900s, especially in North America, it was not long before psychologists became interested in the performance of deaf children. Early studies indicated that deaf children were about two years behind hearing peers on the new tests. Those findings were taken to account for about half of the four to five-year educational lags seen in deaf children, and language deficits were presumed to account for the other half (Pintner & Patterson, 1917). During the 1920s and 1930s, performance tests of intellectual abilities were developed specifically for the purpose of better evaluating the mental abilities of deaf children. Despite the apparent nonverbal nature of these tests, deaf children still generally scored lower than hearing peers, even though the differences were small.

It is now clear that many of those early nonverbal tests were not correctly constructed or used, and they may have been biased against anyone who lacked the sociocultural experiences of hearing, white, middle-class children. More recent tests are more language independent. This means that they can be conducted without the necessity of understanding spoken or signed instructions. They also are more culturally fair, at least within western cultures. Nevertheless, even now, when samples of deaf and hearing children are shown to perform similarly on some (usually nonverbal) intelligence test, the deaf children often lag behind hearing peers in school-related academic performance. Findings of this sort demonstrate that there are important factors other than intelligence that influence academic achievement in deaf children. Nonverbal tests may ensure that intelligence measures are not biased by a child's fluency in a particular language, but they do not address the fact there are also some nonlinguistic skills and knowledge typically learned through language.

Earlier in this chapter, we discussed the potential advantage in intelligence for deaf children with hereditary hearing losses relative to those with acquired losses. Recent findings related to that possibility support an earlier study of nonverbal intelligence and verbal achievement in deaf students (Kusché et al., 1983). That investigation involved high school students who had at least one deaf parent and evidence of hereditary deafness, a second group that had hearing parents and either deaf siblings or deaf cousins and other indications of hereditary deafness, and two groups with hearing parents and no evidence of hereditary deafness. Overall, the two groups with evidence of hereditary deafness had significantly higher IQ scores than the matched students with nonhereditary deafness. Because only one of the groups with hereditary hearing loss had hearing parents, the observed difference could not be attributed to the role of sign language in early language stimulation or the quality of parental communication. Instead, the investigators suggested that some kind of cultural, historical selection could have resulted in higher nonverbal intelligence for individuals with hereditary hearing loss.

These alternatives were clarified in another study of the relation of familial deafness and intelligence (Zweibel, 1987). Consistent with the previous findings, deaf children with hereditary hearing losses obtained significantly higher IQ scores than deaf children with acquired hearing losses. At the same time, deaf children with deaf parents obtained higher IQ scores than deaf children with hereditary hearing loss but with hearing parents and deaf siblings, whereas deaf students with hereditary hearing loss, hearing parents, and hearing siblings did not differ from deaf children with all-hearing families and no evidence of hereditary hearing loss. This pattern of results led to the conclusion that early experience and exposure to effective language may be a more important predictor of intelligence than heredity, but all of these variables are likely involved.

Other studies have examined deaf children's performance on various intelligence tests. For the present purposes, we note only that on nonverbal intelligence tests designed explicitly for deaf children, deaf and hearing children typically obtain comparable scores. Of course, the tests were designed to yield exactly that result, and it is more interesting to note those places where deaf and hearing children show different patterns of scores on subtests (see Braden, 1994). It appears that most of that variation occurs in tasks involving sequencing or temporal ordering (favoring hearing children), but such findings have never been linked to any kind of academic or social differences.

Before leaving the issue of intelligence, we should caution that there are significant difficulties of interpretation with regard to intelligence tests and deaf students. The use of nonverbal intelligence tests may seem fair and appropriate because most deaf children with severe to profound hearing losses are not fluent in English. But if nonverbal tests tell the whole story, it should not be necessary to use verbal intelligence tests, even for hearing individuals. Verbal intelligence tests may help to further our understanding of deaf children's ability to deal with the abstract, symbolic nature of language. Administering appropriately normed intelligence tests to deaf children using sign language should accomplish this goal just as well as spoken language administration, assuming that sign language fluency is shared by the student and test administrator. This common fluency is not easily or often achieved, creating continuing difficulties for both interpretation and educational administration. Nevertheless, eliminating language abilities from assessments of deaf children would result in our tapping only one part of intelligence as it is typically understood. Most of what is learned in both formal and informal educational settings is acquired through language, and thus deaf children may be able to achieve high scores on nonverbal tests but still be struggling in school. In this case, intelligence tests and the demands placed on children in school settings are different, and one may not be a predictor of the other.

Metacognition

The flexibility to be able to use knowledge in different situations often requires that we consider alternative hypotheses, set up a mental "problem-solving space," and reflect on how we can bring our knowledge to bear on a problem. This thinking about thinking is referred to as *metacognition*. Metacognition plays an important role in a variety of problem-solving contexts, including mathematics, science, and reading. In reading, for example, we monitor our own comprehension processes, (hopefully) recognizing when they break down. We notice when we come upon words that we do not know and attempt to figure them out on the basis of context. Alternative meanings of ambiguous passages are mulled over, and we attempt to understand them in the context of our background knowledge and the intention of our reading (see "Metacognitive Strategies").

Studying metacognition can entail diverse methodologies, from simply asking children "Why did you do that?" or "When you wrote that, what were you thinking?" to more complex tasks that reveal the use of alternative strategies and hypotheses (e.g., the twenty questions game described earlier). Although a number of studies have examined metacognition among hearing children, far fewer studies have explored the topic with regard to deaf children. Available research suggests that deaf students might be less likely than hearing students to consider alternative approaches to a task before undertaking it or while working through it. In domains such as reading and mathematics, deaf students frequently apply strategies that are inappropriate or fail to apply strategies that we know are in their repertoires (Kelly & Mousley, 2001; Marschark & Everhart, 1999; see also Marschark & Mayer, 1998; Strassman, 1997).

A likely explanation for many deaf students' relative lack of metacognitive skill is that their teachers may take a more concrete and focused approach to problem solving, hoping that their students will have a clear understanding of a particular strategy. Allowing students to discover their own strategies and the relative utility of different approaches while discussing them with others is a much more time-consuming teaching tech-

Metacognitive Strategies

Understand the goal or purpose of the task (problem solving, reading, etc.)

Relate new information to existing knowledge

Consider a passage or text to see if it makes sense in a particular context

Distinguish important from unimportant information in a problem-solving task

Evaluate understanding/comprehension

Determine the loci of comprehension problems and apply "repair strategies"

Learn to recognize common mistakes

Read for meaning, integrating parts of a text

Match the strategy to the learning or problem-solving task

Ask for help (instrumental dependence)

Visualize a problem

Eliminate unlikely alternatives in comprehension or multiple-choice questions

Learn to think outside the box (divergent thinking)

nique, but one that provides for more flexible thinking and the development of metacognition. Earlier studies in the area of creativity and problem solving tended to support the view that deaf children are concrete and literal in their thinking (i.e., unlikely to be able to master metacognitive skills), thus leading to several textbooks encouraging teachers to focus on more narrow approaches to teaching-learning (e.g., Blackwell et al., 1978; Luetke-Stahlman & Luckner, 1991). This set up a self-fulfilling prophecy, as the failure to encourage diverse problem-solving skills led to limited metacognitive skills, not the other way around.

Summary

In this chapter we considered several cognitive components that make up learning. In the domains of visual attention, memory, problem solving, and creativity, research has provided evidence of differences between deaf and hearing learners. In some cases, these differences are likely to have impact on academic performance, although most of them reflect differences that could be reduced or eliminated through changes in instructional methods. Research in these areas not only improves our understanding of deaf children's learning abilities and learning challenges, they provide us with important information for enhancing the teaching-learning process. Although the claim that deaf learners are more literal or concrete than hearing peers may be warranted for some deaf children in some domains, the reasons for that characteristic may be due more to the way in which they have been educated than anything directly related to deafness.

Research concerning the neuropsychological development of deaf children, and ways in which it is affected by the use of sign language versus spoken language, also can provide insight into potential differences in learning by deaf and hearing students. Deaf individuals who use sign language have been shown to have some enhanced visual-spatial skills relative to deaf and hearing individuals using spoken language, but they are similar in other skills. While the extent to which such findings can be utilized in educating deaf students is not yet clear, we now know that the two populations are not strictly comparable in many respects. This means that expectations, interactions, and educational methods appropriate for hearing children may not generalize to deaf children.

Deaf students have language skills that are sometimes not reflected in assessment of English skills. It also should not be surprising if their concept and category knowledge—or the use of that knowledge—differs from hearing students. This means that teaching deaf children as though they simply are "hearing children who cannot hear" is doing a disservice to them. We have already seen that deaf, hard-of-hearing, and hearing children may have different knowledge bases, cognitive strategies, and experiences. Rather than ignoring such differences, we must carefully take them into consideration when teaching, particularly in mainstream classrooms, where the learning styles of diverse students may be quite different.

The research described in this chapter may lead to a variety of suggestions for practice. Teachers of deaf students, for example, should find it useful to expand discussion of vocabulary to include semantic fields or networks, perhaps through the use of concept maps. Teachers and parents also should be able to foster cognitive development and language development by discussing and encouraging the use of multiple meanings of words, perhaps through word games, noting how context influences the way that a word or concept is interpreted. Problem-solving games, encouraging language creativity, and the use of fantasy and imagination also will contribute to flexible cognitive functioning. Exercises of this sort not only foster improved performance on academic problem-solving tasks such as analogies and word games, they should lead to improved performance and reading and other domains, as long as they are introduced early and revisited regularly.

Deaf children should not be taught as though they were hearing children who cannot hear.

What kind of school is best for deaf children?

What factors should we consider in deciding on a school program for a deaf child?

7

Educational Programs and Philosophies

In this chapter we explore the continuum of educational alternatives available for deaf children and emphasize the need to consider a variety of factors in determining the best placement for a particular child. Although we focus on schooling, it is important to keep in mind that learning has strong social roots in interactions with adults and peers. The ability to profit from both formal and informal instruction at school requires that children have skills in areas such as attention, problem solving, turn taking, and memorizing and have a positive attitude toward learning. Children must also have a firm foundation in language to access information in the classroom and learn from it. Although a variety of nonverbal, social interaction strategies are available and useful for young deaf (and hearing) children when they enter school, it is through language that the give and take of education really occurs.

Parents often find the information available to them in making the school decision both confusing and contradictory. As we described in chapter 2, federal legislation has sought to make access to education easier for deaf children and their families, but the laws often are misinterpreted or overinterpreted by state, regional, and local authorities, making the results less than helpful for parents. Further, there is much disagreement about whether there is one educational setting or format that is best for deaf children, with the issue of residential (i.e., separate) schools versus mainstreaming being the most heated.

The school debate is now decades old, and yet the matter is not yet resolved; there is no evidence to indicate that one educational setting is uniformly better than another. Meanwhile, on one issue there appears to be almost unanimous agreement: the importance of early intervention programs for deaf children. Such programs provide communication instruction,

parental counseling, and enriching social and cognitive experiences for deaf children. Yet, even with regard to preschool programs, there are some complex decisions to be made because different programs may influence language, cognitive, and social growth in a variety of ways.

The characteristics of parents, teachers, and school programs, as well as the children themselves, are all important in considering appropriate educational placements for deaf children. Sometimes, there also are interactions among these characteristics that may escape notice. For example, one recent study examined motor development in deaf children between four and ten years of age (Dummer et al., 1996). Overall, a small delay in motor development was observed in these children relative to hearing peers. Among the four year olds, however, who were not yet in school, the deaf children performed better than hearing children. Among the school-aged deaf children, those attending schools that were more sports oriented showed better performance than those who were in a less sports-oriented school environment.[1] Clearly, the ways that deaf children's environments are structured play a central role in their development, and such factors may account for some of the observed differences between them and hearing peers of the same age. At the same time, some of those differences may be more apparent than real.

Abandoning Myths

Before considering available educational alternatives for deaf students, we should dispense with several myths that have dogged the field for the last 200 years. For example, there appears to be a lingering belief held by many parents of deaf as well as hearing children that placing their children in daycare somehow harms them or is not as beneficial as having them at home with their mothers. At a time when the majority of middle-class mothers work and welfare reform in the United States is pushing more mothers into the workplace, this issue is both politically and emotionally charged. A variety of recent investigations, however, including a recent longitudinal study of 1200 children, has shown that hearing children attending daycare programs develop just as quickly and normally as children who stay at home (Scarr, 1998). Even the relative quality of daycare seems not to be as important as once thought, apparently having little or no impact on development during the preschool years and no long-term effects at all.

Rather than being a potential liability in their preschool years, early intervention programs for deaf children provide opportunities for them to interact with other (deaf and hearing) children, offer important information and support for parents, and foster the development of effective communication skills in both children and parents. The value of such programs for social, cognitive, and language development has been uniformly supported by research over the past 20 years with both deaf and hearing children (Calderon & Greenberg, 1997).

A second myth is that early use of sign language somehow impedes the development of speech and speechreading (Schiff & Ventry, 1976; Todd, 1976; cf. Jones & Quigley, 1979). This issue was examined in chapter 5 and is considered only briefly below as it relates to educational programming for deaf children. Many children grow up with two or more languages (outside of language-chauvinistic countries like the United States, anyway), and there is more evidence for bilingualism providing educational and personal benefits than there is for it creating any long-term negative impact on learning or development. Some educators have even claimed that sign languages like American Sign Language (ASL) help provide deaf students with smooth access to spoken-written languages like English, a complex issue we consider in chapter 8. In any case, the once common practice of not allowing deaf children to gesture or sign is at best unproductive and at worst an unnatural impediment to language acquisition, regardless of whether children are learning to sign, speak, or both. Although, historically there has been some contradictory evidence with regard to the benefits of spoken versus sign language in childhood (Battachi & Montanini-Manfreddi, 1986; Brasel

> **Early intervention programs for deaf children provide opportunities for them to interact with other (deaf and hearing) children, offer important information and support for parents, and foster the development of effective communication skills in both children and parents. On this, at least, there is no disagreement.**

& Quigley, 1977; Geers et al., 1984), the preponderance of recent evidence with regard to language development favors exposing deaf children to sign language as early as possible (Calderon & Greenberg, 1997).

A third common myth in deaf education is that placing deaf children in regular, mainstream classes will foster their integration into the larger hearing society. This assumption makes intuitive sense, but we have found no research evidence to support it. To the contrary, a number of studies indicate that children in mainstream settings report problems of self-identity, emotional security, and establishing friendships (Kluwin & Stinson, 1993; Stinson & Lang, 1994; cf. Furstenburg & Doyal, 1994). Because of communication barriers, many deaf students are frustrated in their attempts to interact with their hearing classmates and thus may focus more on relations with teachers and deaf peers (Lederberg, 1991). This is not an unusual finding for minority students who are prevented from having full access to classroom participation. In the case of deaf children, this situation has important implications for the development of autonomy and self-esteem (Marschark, 1993).

Previous attempts to compare the language development or academic achievement of deaf children in one kind of educational program with those of children in another kind of program have been problematic. Comparisons of deaf children in mainstream programs with children in segregated (residential or separate school) programs often have assumed that all other things are equal. But all other things are seldom equal when it comes to deaf children. Most investigations of this issue have not taken into account the intellectual abilities, language fluencies, or social skills of children before entering particular programs. It is difficult to control all of these factors given the relatively small groups of children normally involved, but they clearly influence the findings, and ignoring them can lead to erroneous conclusions.

A fourth myth is that children who are enrolled in programs with one kind of language orientation or another remain pure in their language use. In reality, this rarely happens. Children in settings emphasizing spoken language, for example, may use speech in the classroom and with their families. But they also often communicate in sign language with their peers, whether or not their parents and teachers are aware of it. Similarly, deaf children in settings emphasizing sign language are almost always exposed to both signed and spoken modes of communication by virtue of living in a largely hearing society. Such interchange will play an important role in the language models available to and utilized by deaf children as well as their access to what is happening in learning situations.

Having set some myths aside, we now examine in more depth the kinds of educational programs available for deaf children and the range of philosophies parents may counter when searching for an appropriate educational environment.

Early Intervention Programs

The growth of early intervention programs over the past 25 years has provided important social, cognitive, and language experiences for deaf children and critical information and support systems for their parents. Such
programs vary in their language and educational orientations as well as
their offerings relative to daycare. There are now several models of bilingual–bicultural early intervention intended to emphasize spoken and sign
languages and the cultures of both hearing and deaf people. Most early
intervention programs, however, emphasize one communication mode or
the other.

Early intervention programs may be administered by public school
systems, state health and human services departments, residential schools,
or private organizations. Many school systems also offer home-based, "itin-
erant" preschool education, in which local teachers work with parents,
children, siblings, and other family members at home (Rupp, 1998; see
Ballman, 1995, for hearing children). In providing services for parents as
well as for children, preschool programs focus on language development,
parent-child communication, social skills, and appropriate support for
children to learn to use any residual hearing through testing and possible
fitting for hearing aids. Teachers generally provide parents with strategies
for enhancing their children's development, including instruction in sign
language, spoken language, or both. Classes tend to be small and offer a
variety of specialized curricula. For example, the home-based SKI*HI program focuses on enhancing cognitive and communication skills and the
use of residual hearing (Strong et al., 1992, 1994). The PATHS program
focuses on social-emotional development in academic as well as in social
situations (Greenberg & Kusché, 1987), and the Diagnostic Early Intervention Program (DEIP) promotes family-oriented partnerships with experienced and knowledgeable professionals (Moeller & Condon, 1994; see
Calderon & Greenberg, 1997, for a review).

Research on the impact of these programs has shown that they promote healthy emotional development and effective social functioning
among deaf children in both school and family settings. The more opportunities deaf children have to interact with peers, the more they develop realistic and flexible social strategies. Deaf children who attend
early intervention programs thus have been found to have social skills
comparable to their hearing peers and superior to deaf peers who do not
attend such programs (Lederberg et al., 1987). Meaningful communication with diverse adults also fosters language growth and curiosity. Indeed, research has indicated that exposure to sign language and early
involvement in an intervention program are two of the most potent predictors of deaf children's academic success (Calderon & Greenberg, 1997).

Among hearing children, those with more preschool experience have higher achievement scores, fewer behavior problems, and are less likely to be required to repeat a grade. More preschool experience is also positively associated with children's literacy and mathematics skills (National Center for Education Statistics, 1995). Presumably, similar results will emerge from current research involving deaf children.

The social and communication skills acquired in early intervention programs are clearly related. Deaf children who have not yet developed fluency in language use a variety of communication devices in interacting with hearing and deaf peers (e.g., gesturing, modeling). Deaf children who have developed better communication skills, however, appear more adaptive and more likely to benefit from their rich environments. Compared to children with poorer language skills, these deaf children are more likely to play with multiple peers at one time and use and receive more language from their peers. They also interact more frequently with teachers in ways that support educational achievement (Cornelius & Hornett, 1990; Lederberg, 1991; Spencer & Deyo, 1993). In one study involving deaf kindergarten children, half were enrolled in a program that included both spoken language and sign language, and the other half were enrolled in a program emphasizing only spoken language (Cornelius & Hornett, 1990). The children exposed to both modes of communication showed significantly higher levels of social play and more frequent dramatic play than their peers in the spoken language environment. The children enrolled in the spoken language-only program were reliably more aggressive and disruptive in the classroom.

In general, the earlier children are enrolled in intervention programs, the better they develop social and language skills, regardless of the language orientation of the program. Earlier enrollment also tends to lead to children being better prepared to enter school (Calderon & Greenberg, 1997; Calderon et al., 1998; Strong et al., 1994). The long-term impact of such programs on academic achievement remains to be determined, but findings clearly indicate their value during the early school years.

School Choices for K-12 Deaf Children

There is no single answer to the question of what kind of school is best for deaf children. Programs differ, and what may be good for one child may not be good for another. Parents thus are faced with some difficult decisions. The choice of one particular school program over another may have long-term implications for academic achievement and career success. With this in mind, we now examine the educational options available for deaf children and what we know about their benefits in terms of educational and social-emotional growth.

Residential Schools

Residential schools for deaf children have a long history in the United States. They have played a central role in Deaf culture and the Deaf community (see chapter 2; Padden & Humphries, 1988). For years, most states had only one or two schools for deaf children, often located in outlying areas. Children whose homes were far away lived in these schools with houseparents during the week, returning to their families on weekends and vacations. Although still referred to as "residential schools," most of them have commuting students. Deaf parents, who fondly remember their own residential school days and remain part of a community with their former teachers and classmates, often place their own deaf children in these schools.

Some deaf adults proudly identify themselves with the residential school they attended. Many of those who were children of hearing parents, however, tell stories about being taken to residential school and left without any explanation and not knowing when (or if) they would see their parents again (see "Tales from Residential School"). Despite the difficulties experienced in such separations, most of those children eventually discovered a thriving culture where they felt at home. Residential schools provide deaf children with role models, fluently signing and socially competent peers, and environments in which they are on a level playing field with their classmates.

Although early intervention programs may provide deaf children with some exposure to ASL and to deaf adults, residential schools can play an important role in maintaining a social, cultural, and academic context that provides older deaf children with supportive learning environments. A similar case likely can be made with regard to children attending "oral" schools, such as the Clarke School and the Central Institute for the Deaf, but studies concerning the sociocultural workings of those programs are unavailable. Interestingly, there also does not appear to be much research concerning life in the oral deaf community, although there have been several autobiographies by oral deaf adults. This situation may reflect oral deaf

---

Deaf in America: Voices from a Culture
(Padden & Humphries, 1988)

"In the dormitories [of residential schools], away from the structured control of the classroom, deaf children are introduced to the social life of Deaf people. In the informal dormitory environment, children learn not only sign language but the content of the culture."

Tales from Residential School:
Marie (40), Looking Back

"My parents managed to communicate that we were going on a trip and that I should pack my suitcase. I could not understand why my suitcase was the only one in the car, and was very confused . . . but that was nothing new. It was only after I saw them drive away [from the residential school], that I realized they were leaving me there—alone."

individuals striving to be assimilated into the hearing world, but given the existence of social-political organizations like Self Help for the Hard of Hearing (SHHH) and the AG Bell Association for the Deaf and Hard of Hearing, the lack of documentation is surprising.

Within the residential school classroom, the teaching-learning environment is structured with the needs of deaf children in mind. Activities are conducted in small groups, and seating is arranged to allow clear line-of-sight of the teacher at all times. Language activities, particularly those that emphasize children's expressive language, are built into class schedules. This kind of experience is very different from removing children from the (mainstream) classroom for language training, which impacts self-esteem and deprives deaf children of the opportunity to experience everything in the classroom that their hearing peers experience. A residential school may embrace ASL, total communication, a bilingual-bicultural approach, or other language orientations for students with diverse backgrounds. Most important, the language of the classroom also will be the language of the playground, the cafeteria, and adults serving as models in the environment. In contrast to regular public schools, access to school language for deaf children is not overlaid on teaching designed for hearing children; it is part of the ongoing, everyday way of doing business.

In chapter 2, we described how residential school enrollment peaked at around 60,000 in the early 1970s, partly as a result of a rubella epidemic. At that time, more than a third of all deaf children attended residential schools, and another third attended special school programs for deaf children. According to the Gallaudet Research Institute Annual Survey of Hearing Impaired Children and Youth, of the more than 40,000 deaf and hard-of-hearing children included in their 1999 survey, only about 25 percent attended residential schools full-time. Another 26 percent were in self-contained classrooms for deaf students in public schools, and 44 percent were in mainstream classrooms.[2]

The Gallaudet survey includes only about 60–65 percent of deaf and hard-of-hearing children in the country. Legislation since 1975 has sought to ensure that all children with disabilities are educated in "the least re-strictive environment." The inclusion movement was begun primarily by parents and supporters of mentally retarded children, who wanted them to be educated in public schools, but it has led to increasing numbers of deaf children attending local public schools. As a result, many residential schools have closed. The identification of 44 percent of deaf children being educated in mainstream classrooms is thus clearly an underestimate.

As we have seen, a variety of factors related to school placement (de-gree of hearing loss, early intervention experience, and parental factors) make it difficult to draw general conclusions about the relative utility of residen-tial school programs as compared to other programs. There are several areas in which their impact appears fairly clear, however, and these are discussed below. In any case, the primary goal should be to identify the individual needs of a child in choosing the most appropriate kind of academic place-ment. For that to occur, there must be a range of alternatives available.

Public School Mainstreaming and Inclusion

Mainstreaming and inclusion both involve placing deaf students (or others with special needs) in regular public school classrooms. Mainstreaming often involves children also attending some special classes, whereas inclusion entails students being "fully included" in all aspects of public school set-ting. Mainstream programs also frequently involve the availability of a spe-cial resource room, ideally with specially-trained teachers or aides, whereas inclusive programs attempt to offer support services within the regular school classroom itself. In some cases, a child's individualized education plan (IEP) calls for partial mainstreaming, where the child spends part of the day in a residential school setting and part of the day in a public school.

Are mainstream programs working? The stated goal of mainstreaming is to provide students with disabilities educational opportunities equiva-lent to those of their hearing peers. In order for mainstreaming to be suc-cessful, therefore, children need to be integrated into both the social and academic processes of the classroom (Kauffman, 1993). Many mainstream programs, however, appear not to provide the equality in education that their supporters claim. Deaf students are often placed in regular classrooms only for nonacademic courses, while taking their core curricula either in separate classrooms or at other schools to which they have to commute during school hours, taking away from valuable class time. Students ex-periencing such partial segregation may be stigmatized in ways American immigrants once were by being required to attend remedial education classes. As in that case, deaf children who receive such dual-track educa-tions may have more difficulty with social and academic integration than those who are consistently taught in one setting or the other (Kluwin & Stinson, 1993; Musselman & Mootilal, 1996).

Children in mainstream settings need not suffer from the problems of programs that provide only superficial integration. For some students, a mainstream classroom with appropriate academic support services can provide excellent educational opportunities. Mainstreaming is not for all deaf students, but then no one type of program is. Parents must not only identify the best program for their child, but they must closely monitor the child's academic and social progress for indications of the program's appropriateness. Through involvement in IEPs, parents now have a greater role in determining the course of their children's education, and they need to make sure that they take advantage of the opportunity.

Contrary to what is sometimes believed, neither mainstreaming nor inclusion was part of the Individuals with Disabilities Education Act (IDEA). The 1975 law (PL 94-142) and related legislation that followed mandated early identification of hearing losses in school-age children, unbiased evaluation of deaf children using a variety of alternative communication methods, including sign language, full access to public education, and educating students with disabilities in classrooms with nondisabled students to the maximum extent possible. Recognizing the importance of accessible language to the educational success of deaf children, the IDEA Amendments of 1997 (PL 105-17) further specified that in the development of IEPs, the IEP team should

> consider the communication needs of the child, and in the case
> of a child who is deaf or hard of hearing, consider the child's
> language and communication needs, opportunities for direct
> communications with peers and professional personnel in the
> child's language and communication mode, academic level,
> and full range of needs, including opportunities for direct
> instruction in the child's language and communication mode
> (Sec. 300.346, iv).

Bilingual–Bicultural Programs

One educational alternative of interest to both deaf and hearing parents of deaf children is the *bilingual–bicultural* ("Bi-Bi") program. The bilingual–bicultural approach seeks to educate children in both the language of the local Deaf community (e.g., ASL) and the language of the local hearing community (e.g., English), while ensuring that children experience and learn about sociocultural aspects of both communities. Underlying bilingual–bicultural programs are several basic principles (Pickersgill & Gregory, 1998):

- Recognition of the language and culture of Deaf people
- Recognition of the value of linguistic and cultural pluralism within society

- Recognition of the need to remove oppression and to empower deaf people
- Equality of opportunity regardless of language, disability, ethnicity, or gender
- Use of language which reflects the fact that Deaf individuals form a linguistic and cultural group.

One primary goal of bilingual–bicultural programs is to provide children with appropriate levels of both sign language and written language that will fully support their development, further education, and eventual employment. Some observers are concerned that this orientation may favor one language/cultural orientation over another and, indeed, most bilingual programs emphasize ASL as children's first language (Singleton et al., 1998). The aim, however, is to provide deaf children with a natural first language that is fully accessible and use that base to support the transition to reading and writing (and perhaps speaking) English (see Marschark, 2001b; Wilbur, 2000).

Bilingual–bicultural programs need to recognize the continuum of language skills that allow children to reach their potential, and special care should be given to the needs of each child within the program. Staff should be fully competent in both signed and spoken languages and well-versed in both Deaf and hearing cultures, since both deaf and hearing individuals will have the same responsibilities and professional demands. When a bilingual–bicultural program adheres to its principles and provides balanced education, the result should be graduating students who are not only capable, but tolerant and enlightened with regard to diversity. Evaluations of bilingual–bicultural programs with regard to language development and literacy are just beginning, and broader investigations concerning social and personality development have not yet been conducted (Padden & Ramsey, 1998; Singleton et al., 1998).

Bilingual–bicultural programs, whether in residential schools or other settings, often attract teachers who are either deaf or familiar with the Deaf community. Ideally, hearing adults would make up approximately half of the staff, with all staff fluent in both languages. Both deaf and hearing staff thus provide children with role models, and they are able to see deaf and hearing people working together as partners.

Comparing Alternative School Placements

Given what we know about different school placements, it might be expected that we would have a clear understanding of which kinds of programs are best for subgroups of deaf children. Several factors obscure the true relation between school program placement and achievement, however, making comparisons of programs difficult. One such factor is that

children placed in a particular school may already have certain characteristics that favorably match that school's program. They may be better students or have more background knowledge before they enter the program.
Those in mainstream programs may have less severe hearing losses, later
age of onset, or more parental involvement in their education. A combination of these characteristics also might be responsible for differences observed in academic success.

With regard to mainstream programs, exposure to signed and spoken
communication could be more beneficial than exposure only to spoken
language or sign language in separate schools (Akamatsu et al., 2000; Brasel
& Quigley, 1977; Strong, & Prinz, 1997). Alternatively, the possibility that
such settings might deny deaf students access to fluent language in either
spoken or sign modes may create a barrier to learning (Johnson et al., 1989).
Finally, teachers or parents may have higher (or lower) expectations for
children in particular educational settings. It is therefore difficult to determine the extent to which observed differences in academic achievement
are due to characteristics of the programs themselves or to the kinds of
students they attract.

Whatever the reason, we know that deaf children in special educational
placements generally have different characteristics from those in mainstream settings. Deaf students in special school settings have been described
as more likely to be male and from minority groups. They more often come
from families with lower incomes, and they tend to have greater hearing
losses and to be less emotionally mature. When such factors are taken into
account, there still appears to be a slight academic advantage for students
in mainstream settings, however (see Kluwin, 1993, for a review).

One large-scale, longitudinal study of deaf students in various school
placements found that high school students in mainstream programs were
more likely to be functioning at grade level in English, mathematics, science, and social studies (Kluwin, 1993). This difference largely appeared
to be due to the fact the mainstream students took more academic classes
than students in special school settings, versus courses like art and vocational training, although the other factors noted above likely were relevant
as well (degree of hearing loss, background knowledge, etc.). A more recent investigation found no differences between deaf children attending
residential schools and local public schools in reading achievement, typically the most difficult educational challenge for deaf children (Padden &
Ramsey, 1998).

At least one study has reported that mainstreamed students scored
higher on a series of academic outcome measures relative to students in
special education programs, while there was no difference in their levels
of social-emotional functioning (Furstenburg & Doyal, 1994). The latter
finding conflicts with a larger body of evidence suggesting that deaf students in mainstream settings are not as socially and emotionally secure as

their peers in separate school settings (see Kluwin & Stinson, 1993, for a review). Some early observers suggested that the relatively limited social context of residential schools should interfere with social development, particularly in the area of self-responsibility and social maturity (Liben, 1978; Meadow, 1976). While that might be true, relative to hearing peers, investigations also have indicated that younger deaf children enrolled in public schools show less social adjustment and emotional maturity than peers enrolled in residential schools (Kluwin & Stinson, 1993; Marschark, 1993). Mainstream deaf students often report feeling socially isolated, rejected, and lonely (Lowenbrau & Thompson, 1987; Stinson & Lang, 1994).

It thus remains unclear whether there are consistent academic or psychological differences between deaf children attending separate school programs and those attending local public schools. There is at least one area in which differences observed among deaf students in higher grades have their origins, at least in part: in the educational system itself. Whether due to their characteristics at program entrance or their academic progress, deaf children in full mainstreaming or inclusion settings tend to take more advanced courses than students in residential or special school settings. Among hearing students, the academic rigor of a student's high school courses is a much better predictor of college graduation than entrance examination scores, high school grade point averages, or class rankings, (Adelman, 1999), and the same pattern seems to apply to deaf students.

Classroom Challenges and Solutions

Residential schools and bilingual–bicultural programs are specifically designed around the educational needs of children who are deaf or hard-of-hearing. This is not the case in mainstream settings, where deaf students have more difficulty following classroom lectures and discussions. Students with mild to moderate hearing losses can often follow classroom instruction fairly well by sitting in the front row, but communication can be disrupted in several ways. For example, a teacher may talk while facing the blackboard or while wandering around the room, thus reducing both the volume of visibility and facial cues needed for speechreading. There may be more than one person speaking at a time with questions and answers flying back and forth. This kind of interaction in the classroom requires rapid switching of attention by deaf students, placing them at a disadvantage relative to hearing classmates. Teachers and hearing peers also may not speak clearly enough for a deaf student to follow.

For students with greater hearing losses, following a speaking teacher directly is almost impossible. Even if a student's speechreading skills are moderately proficient in one-on-one conversations, that strategy can quickly become ineffective in a classroom full of multiple visual stimuli and distractions.

Some students with more severe hearing losses are able to use spoken language as their primary means of communication and can succeed in such settings without communication support. These students, however, often succeed despite going to class, through the assistance of their parents, friends, and supportive teachers. Other deaf students have speech skills good enough to lead teachers to assume (erroneously) that they have comparable hearing or speechreading abilities. This phenomenon is similar to what happens when foreign language speakers' expressive skills are better than their receptive skills. A carefully rehearsed question about directions to a particular landmark can result in a fluent and overwhelming answer!

Many deaf students in mainstream classrooms depend on sign language interpreters. Qualified educational interpreters have received extensive training in sign language and its variants. They are prepared with regard to special aspects of educational interpreting (as opposed to legal or medical interpreting) and are bound by a clear and detailed code of ethics. Unfortunately, there are not enough interpreters available to serve all of the deaf students who would benefit from them. At the same time, the diverse skills and qualifications of interpreters working in the field sometimes results in mismatches with the needs or preferences of deaf students. More problematic is the fact that schools frequently use less skilled individuals whose fees are lower than those of professional interpreters. Knowing sign language does not translate to competence in interpreting in the classroom or interpreting for other school activities (see Seal, 1998).

Another important service for deaf students is note taking. Deaf students obviously have to rely on visual communication. When hearing students look down to make notes, they still are able to follow the lecture or classroom conversation because they can hear it. Deaf students who rely on signed communication do not have that luxury. Each time they look down to write something, part of the spoken or signed message is missed. The alternative of not taking notes at all puts the deaf student at a clear disadvantage, especially as students progress through school and material becomes more complex and technical. Hearing students are often asked to volunteer to share their notes with deaf classmates, or teachers may copy their class notes or overhead transparencies for deaf students. Hearing as well as deaf students benefit from such opportunities, and once teachers have prepared hearing students to take notes for a deaf student, many will continue doing so in future classes.

Real-time captioning in the classroom provides an alternative means of access to spoken language. Where most captioning is added to movies and television programs after they are produced, real-time captioning is done live. Usually, real-time captioned television shows, such as news broadcasts, involve a captioner using stenographic-style equipment of the sort used by court reporters. The captioner either can be present or at a remote site connected via a telephone line. This kind of captioning generally is too expensive for use in individual classrooms where the number of deaf students is relatively small, but technology is providing alternatives. Steno-based or Computer Assisted Real Time (CART) was first introduced in the early 1980s. One such system, C-Print, for example, allows an assistant with competent typing skills, but without the extensive training required for stenographic systems, to provide real-time captioning on laptop computers. Afterward, the C-Print files can be printed as class transcripts, thus eliminating the need for a separate notetaker (Stinson et al., 1999). The limited amount of training necessary for C-Print operators and its relatively low cost is making it an increasingly popular means of providing deaf students with access to information in the classroom. Still to be determined is the extent to which real-time captioning improves learning by students who may have reading difficulties.

There is a variety of other support services and effective classroom management strategies that can be useful for deaf students, both inside and outside the classroom (see chapter 9). Deaf students' reliance of visual information makes the use of overhead transparencies, video projection, and similar teaching tools indispensable. In addition to the assistive listening devices described in chapter 3, classrooms can be designed to be user friendly to deaf students, allowing unhindered views of the instructor and blackboards and offering good acoustics for students who use residual hearing.

Taken together, support services and appropriate teaching-learning environments help to give deaf students equal access to learning situations they have been promised under Section 504 of the Rehabilitation Act of 1973, IDEA, and the Americans with Disabilities Act. But education is not simply a matter of sitting in a classroom. Effective teaching and learning require clear communication between students and instructors and the opportunity to ask questions and interact with other students. In addition to providing educational and career information, academic support services allow deaf students to be integrated into their schools and communities to an extent that would otherwise be nearly impossible.

Parental Involvement in the Education of Deaf Children

In chapter 4, we discussed some of the ways in which education begins at home. No chapter on educational programming for deaf children, however, would be complete without some explicit discussion of the importance of parental involvement in their children's educations at school. From an interpersonal, social-emotional perspective, parents serve as role models for children, and young children will identify with and emulate physical and behavioral characteristics of their parents that appear to be valued. From a legal perspective, the fact that parents now have the right and the moral responsibility to be involved in designing the educational programming of their deaf children (through the IEP process) helps ensure that those children are receiving the quality of education guaranteed by federal legislation. From an educational perspective, there can be no doubt that parents' involvement in their children's education is one of the single best predictors of academic achievement.

A variety of studies involving hearing children has identified specific parental behaviors that help foster educational success (Hart & Risley, 1995; Janos & Robinson, 1985). These behaviors include

- Provision of quality language interactions
- Spending time with children talking about school activities and helping with school work
- Involvement in academic and extracurricular interests
- Answering questions about formal and informal academic issues in a supportive manner
- Fostering curiosity and creativity.

Parents' involvement in their children's educations, both at home and at school, can also instill in children a sense of the importance and value that their parents place on learning. Academic achievement and locus of control (that is, whether individuals see their lives as under their own control or as under the control of others) are critically related for children during the school years. Children notice their own achievements and are motivated to master new skills and achieve even more. Academic success thus breeds academic success (Greenberg & Kusché, 1987).

To this point, investigations concerning academic achievement and personality variables such as *locus of control* and *achievement motivation* have not been conducted with students who are deaf or hard of hearing. We have already seen that early intervention programs for deaf children sensitize parents to their need to be involved in their children's educations. Still, because of the impediments to effective communication between most deaf children and their hearing parents, active, hands-on involvement of parents in deaf children's educations is relatively infrequent. In one recent study, hearing parents of deaf children and hearing children reported being equally involved in their children's education (Powers & Saskiewicz, 1998). But although the parents of deaf children reported observing their children in the classroom more frequently than parents of hearing children, they were less likely to volunteer to participate in classroom activities. The results showed that parents recognize the importance of their involvement in school activities if their deaf children are to succeed, even if they do not always follow through. Parents may hesitate because of feelings of helplessness, their lack of confidence or comfort with their communication skills, or their concerns about intruding on teachers, "the experts."

Schools also vary in their encouragement of parental involvement. Resistance to parental involvement on the part of teachers often derives from the fact that most of them are accustomed to hearing from parents only when they have complaints, but teachers also may be less sure of their abilities when working with deaf children than with hearing children. More positive interactions with parents are likely to make educators less defensive and more open to collaborating in all aspects of the educational process. We consider this issue further in chapter 9.

Deaf Students in College and University

Older deaf adults still talk about the days of working in the print shops, steel mills, and heavy industry, but they want something more for deaf children today. Partly as a consequence of the legislative initiatives with regard to deaf education, described in chapter 2, and partly due to the advocacy of the Deaf community and deaf and hearing parents of deaf children, there is a now full array of educational opportunities available for deaf students in community colleges and in four-year colleges and universities. The Americans with Disabilities Act, in particular, attempted to guarantee deaf students, as well as other individuals with disabilities, full access to public and private services, including the college classroom.

According to the National Center for Educational Statistics (NCES), there are more than 20,000 deaf and hard-of-hearing students enrolled in post-secondary educational institutions in the United States, approximately 93 percent of them at the undergraduate level (NCES, 1995). That number is most likely an underestimate, as many college-age students choose not to identify themselves as deaf or hard of hearing. The NCES report indicates that approximately half of the 5,000 2-year and 4-year post-secondary educational institutions in the United States enroll 1 or more students who identified themselves as deaf or hard of hearing, with the numbers increasing annually. Almost 50 percent of all two- and four-year institutions have identified themselves as serving at least one deaf or hard-of-hearing student, and among larger colleges and universities this number is around 95 percent.

Approximately one-third of the 5,000 post-secondary educational institutions covered by the NCES report provided special support designed for students with significant hearing losses, and 80 percent of students who identified themselves to their college or university as being deaf or hard of hearing received those services. Even so, deaf students attending college are much less likely to graduate than hearing students. Around 35 percent of deaf students graduate from two-year programs, compared to about 40 percent of their hearing peers; and around 30 percent of deaf students graduate from four-year programs, compared to about 70 percent of their hearing peers. In part, these differences reflect the fact that even if deaf students are provided with academic support services within the classroom, they may have had unmet educational needs before the college years.

To be successful at the college level, deaf and hearing students have to bring with them an array of academic and personal skills that frequently are not characteristic of younger deaf children (see Stinson & Walter, 1997). Those undeserving deaf students who are regularly passed into the next grade by teachers are unlikely to be accepted to or succeed in college. Entrance to and graduation from college requires that students have succeeded in particular courses during their high school years. Unfortunately, because lags in language development and gaps in academic skills tend to increase as deaf children reach higher grades, deaf students are less likely to take more difficult, intensive courses than are their hearing peers, and thus are less well prepared for college. Clearly, the answers to such challenges cannot be found on the college or university campus, but must be part of students' entire educational careers.

Summary

The most important message from this chapter is that there must be a continuum of placements for deaf children and that parents and teachers need to collaborate to determine which placement is best for a particular child. Federal legislation protects deaf children from discrimination in education and mandates that they are fairly and appropriately evaluated, placed, and academically supported. Parents now have an opportunity to play a central role in planning their deaf children's educational placement, and they need to be informed about their options and the implications of those options.

Early intervention programs are available across most of the United States and in many other countries. Children who attend such programs tend to be advantaged both academically and socially when they enter school, and there are no disagreements about the importance of these programs. The kind of school program a deaf child later attends presents a more complex challenge.

Regular public school teachers often are not prepared, mentally or methodologically, for teaching deaf children in their classrooms and may have difficulty in handling this situation. Most frequently, this difficulty is not an active or conscious opposition to including deaf children in the teaching-learning process. No matter how willing and supportive teachers are of having deaf children in their class, most have little or no special educational preparation and may be unsure or even resistant to making modifications to their established routines. Interpreters may be seen as teachers aides, or worse, as interlopers. It may be initially uncomfortable or burdensome to always face the class when talking, to slow the pace of discussions with each child taking a turn and leaving time for interpretation, and to develop visual materials for most topics. Teachers may feel that these classroom management strategies are disruptive for both themselves and for other children in class (although there is no evidence that this is the case). It thus is not surprising that teachers have supported the idea of mainstreaming and inclusion even if they are less supportive of having students with disabilities in their own classes (Scruggs & Mastropiere, 1996).

Even the best-intentioned teacher in a regular school classroom is likely to assume that deaf and hearing children are essentially the same, except for issues relating to communication and the need for visual materials. We showed in chapter 6 that this is not the case. Deaf children have different experiences, backgrounds, and knowledge which clearly will influence educational needs. Teachers who have received training in the education of deaf children and educational settings that have been designed with deaf children in mind are more likely to best match the strengths (and weaknesses) of deaf learners. Specially trained teachers also are more likely to communicate better with deaf students, to provide appropriate role models for deaf children, and have an understanding of cultural and historical issues relating to people who are deaf.

These issues notwithstanding, many deaf children clearly do thrive in mainstream settings with appropriate academic support services such as sign language interpreters and note takers. Beyond the fact that children with less severe hearing losses and those with better language skills are more likely to succeed in mainstream classrooms, there do not appear to be reliable predictors of mainstream success. Deaf students who are mainstreamed for half of each school day or more tend to show better academic performance relative to those mainstreamed for less than half a day or those in residential schools, both because of the better utilization of time and better cross-fertilization among courses. The problem is that it is still unclear whether fully mainstreamed students perform better because of something inherent in the programs, because better students tend to enter those programs in the first place, or because teachers and parents have higher expectations for children in those programs. The finding that mainstreaming is related to better academic performance does not mean that sending a deaf student who is unprepared for the public school classroom into such a program will make them better students.

For many deaf students, mainstream settings fail to foster social development in the ways that are important for normal, healthy development. Deaf children often are excluded from social interactions with hearing students by virtue of communication barriers and because of the fact that, whether we like it or not, they are different from their hearing peers. New technologies may provide access to information that is more blind with respect to student disabilities. Support for deaf students, through interpreting, visual technologies, the Internet, and distance learning may help to level the educational playing field.

One might expect that deaf children who attend residential schools, and especially those who have deaf parents, would display a variety of educationally relevant advantages over peers who do not have a fully accessible and supportive learning environment. In contrast, some investigators have suggested a possible negative impact of residential schools on social-emotional development of deaf children, and any time children are educated in a separate environment, there will be questions about quality and comparability of their curricula (see Johnson et al., 1989; Vernon & Andrews, 1990). We therefore consider these issues in detail later. There is little research on this issue, however, and at least one recent study found no differences between residential school children and public school children in reading achievement, typically the most difficult educational challenge for deaf children (Padden & Ramsey, 1998). Unfortunately, given the political sensitivity of this issue at both the (state and local) governmental and (Deaf and educational) community levels, definitive statistics in this regard are unlikely to be provided any time soon.

The question of whether there is something about residential schools, per se, that might account for deaf students' academic difficulties or whether such findings are the result of confounds such as teacher skills or the availability of technology is interesting, but not easily answered. Some investigators have argued that the social milieu of residential schools could interfere with social development, particularly in the areas of self-responsibility and social maturity, and provide only limited opportunities for social and cognitive experience that would contribute to both the content and process of learning (Liben, 1978; Meadow, 1976). However, deaf children enrolled in public schools have been found to show less social adjustment and emotional maturity than peers enrolled in residential schools, and one could argue that the more accurate self-images and positive self-esteem gained by deaf children in residential schools should enhance educational outcomes (Kluwin & Stinson, 1993; Lowenbraun and Thompson, 1987). At the same time, parents may have different expectations for children in residential and mainstream settings, related to the children, the programs, or their own beliefs. This possibility has yet to be explored systematically (see Marschark, 1993; Sisco & Anderson, 1980).

The relative benefits of alternative school placements are also obscured by the fact that children attending residential schools tend to have more severe hearing losses, come from homes with lower income and socioeconomic status, and have poorer spoken language skills. Residential schools also have greater representations of children from minority families and deaf families (Marschark, 1993). Most important, it is clear that different school programs will be more or less beneficial for children with different needs. As we describe in chapter 9, the field of deaf education is sorely in need of teachers who are better qualified in their content area, as well as in sign language. More deaf teachers are needed to serve as role models and to be fluent communicators with children who are deaf or hard of hearing. Only when we can match accessible teaching strategies and materials to the needs of deaf learners can we really say that we are providing them with fair and appropriate educations.

How well do deaf students read and write?

How do we teach students who cannot hear to read and write English?

8

Reading, Writing, and Literacy

Language is an essential component of normal development and a means for discovering the world. As we have seen, however, deaf children frequently do not have full access to communication until they have passed the most important ages for language acquisition. Parents and educators of young deaf students thus often struggle to find a balance between fostering effective early communication skills, which research has shown is usually best achieved through sign language, and the provision of English skills needed for literacy and academic success.[1]

Despite decades of concerted effort, most deaf children progress at only a fraction of the rate of hearing peers in learning to read. Current data indicate that, on average, 18-year-old deaf students leaving high school have reached only a fourth to sixth grade level in reading skills. Only about 3 percent of those 18 year olds read at the same level as the average 18-year-old hearing reader, and more than 30 percent of deaf students leave school functionally illiterate (Traxler, 2000; Kelly, 1995; Waters & Doehring, 1990). At the same time, there are clearly many deaf adults and children who are excellent readers and excellent writers. How can we account for these differences? What are the implications for educators developing English curricula for deaf students?

To answer these questions, we first need to consider what is meant by *literacy*—that is, what is it we are asking students to acquire? Then, we have to understand how deaf students read, at both descriptive and procedural levels. In this chapter, we consider only literacy relating to print materials (reading and writing); other possibilities will be considered in chapter 9. But is the question whether deaf students read well enough to fulfill the needs and expectations of their teachers? Is it important to know how well various subgroups of deaf learners read compared to each other? Or, do we want to know how well deaf students read, as a group, compared to hearing students of the same age?

English Literacy

The National Literacy Act of 1991 defines literacy as "an individual's ability to read, write, and speak in English and compute and solve problems at levels of proficiency necessary to function on the job and in society, to achieve one's goals and to develop one's knowledge and potential" (Farstup & Myers, 1996, p. 4). Consistent with this definition, the *Standards for the English Language Arts* (1996) were established by the International Reading Association and the U.S. National Council of Teachers of English. The *Standards* are intended to ensure that students are sufficiently knowledgeable and proficient in language that they can succeed academically, find challenging and rewarding work, and appreciate and contribute to our culture. In essence, this is a definition of *functional literacy,* often considered a basic goal for elementary and secondary education.

In terms of reading skills, functional literacy corresponds to somewhere between the fourth- and eighth-grade reading (U.S.) levels according to standardized reading tests. This is the level of skill needed for reading newspapers and simple instruction manuals and to use information from those sources in work settings (McLaren, 1988). Realistically, however, gaining and keeping a job in today's "information age" requires more: at least the ability to function at an eleventh or twelfth grade level in reading and writing (Waters & Doehring, 1990). A 1992 study of more than 2,000 deaf individuals 10 years after high school graduation indicated that 49 percent were employed as blue collar workers, or approximately 30 percent more than is typically found among hearing individuals at the same point in their careers (MacLeod-Gallinger, 1992). Poor literacy skills were cited as a primary factor in the relative employment disadvantage of these deaf people.

Functional definitions of literacy have been challenged on the basis that literacy is a socially constructed phenomenon, dependent on the values of the culture that defines it (Bloom, 1987; Hirsch, 1987; McLaren, 1988). The notion of *cultural literacy* includes the belief that knowledge of literature and history obtained through reading are necessary for informed participation in society. Would readers in the U.S. be the same without *Moby Dick*, *The Diary of Anne Frank*, or *Tom Sawyer*? The question is worthy of debate, but most of us would agree that such classics should be available and accessible to everyone, whether or not they choose to read them.

Another position holds that writing skills should allow us to express and make sense of our experience within society. This position sees literacy as thoughtful, practical, and critical, and the written word as a tool that may be used for the purposes of social change. The term *critical literacy* is used to refer to this ability to use reading and writing to understand one's place in history and society and thus increase the likelihood of change.

Curriculum Standards

However literacy is defined, we need to ensure equitable educational requirements for literacy across various settings and provide guidelines for establishing relevant curricula. Toward this end, the *Standards for the English Language Arts* (1996) includes a 12-point outline of what students should know about and be able to do with language. Students who meet the standards will be able to read a wide variety of literature and written texts, write effectively for different audiences and for different purposes, and use various resources to gather information. They also will be able to use language for their own purposes, including enjoyment and critical analysis. Finally, the *Standards* indicate that students should develop an understanding and respect for language diversity and be able to use their first language (if it is not English) to develop competency in English language arts and the other academic content areas.

For deaf children, as well as for hearing children whose first language is not English, the *Standards* state that

> The first step in literacy education . . . is not to assume, as has been done too frequently in the past, either that all students bring a common core of literacy knowledge to school, or that those who do not bring what is customarily expected are deficient. Rather, the first step is to respect each student's home

language, prior language, and cultural experience and to determine what he or she already knows and can do upon entering school. Teachers must then provide appropriate and rich instructional support on that basis. (p. 20)

This position clearly coincides with our theme that "different" should replace "deficient" in the way that deaf learners are viewed. On a more practical level, however, it assumes that schools will provide bilingual education programs for students from non–English-speaking homes to allow effective use of their first language. Considering the voter rejection of bilingual education in California in June 1998 and controversy surrounding many bilingual programs for deaf students, support for such goals clearly is not universal.

Another assumption underlying the *Standards* is that in bilingual education a child's first language provides the most effective bridge to English. As we shall see, that assumption has not yet been met in the case of students who are deaf. Nevertheless, the *Standards* provide a convenient starting point for thinking about teaching reading and writing to children who are deaf or hard of hearing. We therefore turn to consideration of reading and writing, followed by discussions of instruction and assessment methods for deaf students.

Components of Reading

Most of us can remember our early (if not later) struggles with learning to read. Regardless of the quality of early instruction, reading is complex and challenging for young children. It requires a variety of skills at different levels, and the difficulty of learning to read for children who do not have English as a (fluent) first language should not be underestimated. To better understand the task faced by young deaf children, we briefly consider three levels of reading reported to give them difficulty: decoding of individual words, vocabulary, and grammar.

Word Decoding

At its most basic level, reading requires recognition of the words on a printed page. This can be achieved either by recognition of whole words or *decoding* of their component parts. The first strategy is the essence of the "whole word approach" to reading, while the second is more commonly known as "phonics." In either case, readers take words from the printed page and store them in a mental, linguistic form which is held in working memory (see chapter 6). Interactions between working memory and long-term memory provide the meaning of what is being read in the context of other words in the text, the reader's content knowledge, and the purpose of the reading. Once the reader arrives at meanings for groups of words or sentences, they may be stored more permanently as ideas or impressions in long-term memory and/or continue to be held in working memory while the exact wording of the text is forgotten.

Phonological decoding, the basic process underlying the phonics approach to reading, is usually based on the sounds of individual letters or letter combinations. How can children who are deaf make use of a phonics approach to reading? Children who are hard of hearing are better at phonological processing than children with greater hearing losses because they can make use of word sounds (Perfetti & Sendak, 2000). Among children with more severe losses, however, phonological skills do not appear to be related to degree of hearing loss; so there must be another route to the decoding of individual words (Miller, 1997). In fact, research has shown that deaf readers can access phonological information through information accumulated from lip-reading, fingerspelling, articulation, and exposure to writing, no one of which is sufficient in itself (Dodd, 1980; Hanson et al., 1983; see Leybaert, 1993). At the same time, phonological proficiency is clearly related to reading development. We can see the use of phonological processes, for example, in older deaf students' being more likely to make phonologically accurate misspellings (e.g., "pakige" for "package") than younger deaf students. Children with good articulation also make such errors more frequently than children with poor articulation. Such findings are not limited to children who use spoken language, but are found also in students who use sign language (Hanson, 1986; Leybaert, 1993; see also Padden, 1991).

With experience and practice, certain letter combinations become familiar, and recognizing them as syllables and words becomes routine. The faster and more routine the better, because, as we have seen, working memory is limited to approximately the amount of information that can be articulated in two seconds, regardless of whether that information is stored in the form of speech or sign language. If individual words or meaningful parts of words (e.g., the morphemes "sub" and "marine" in the word "submarine") are lost before a meaning has been assigned to them, phonological processing becomes less efficient, less accurate, and may break down all together.

Vocabulary

Vocabulary knowledge is another primary component of reading that might be expected to present particular challenges for deaf students. As we saw in chapters 4 and 5, many deaf children lack full access to language during the early years, and they have fewer social interactions that involve opportunities for word learning. Young deaf children of hearing parents

thus have been shown to have fewer labels for things than hearing children of hearing parents, and deaf children of both deaf and hearing parents
are less likely to gain such verbal knowledge from reading (see Marschark,
1993, chapter 11, for a review). Further, several studies have demonstrated
that vocabulary knowledge among deaf children and young adults is not
as consistent or effectively organized as it is in hearing peers of the same
age (McEvoy et al., 1999).

Deaf readers typically show their largest reading-related deficits in the
area of vocabulary knowledge, although they perform better on tests that
include context than they do on tests that involve words in isolation. Not
only do they have smaller vocabularies than hearing peers, but the classes
of words they know are often different. Deaf children, and especially those
with hearing parents, are more likely to understand and use concrete nouns
and familiar action verbs rather than more abstract or general words with
which they may have less experience. Deaf readers also have considerable
difficulty with multiple meanings of words and rely heavily on local context in a passage to determine which meaning is appropriate. It may be that
this dependence on local context interferes with comprehension of an
entire text (see Banks et al., 1990).

Regardless of the causes, poor vocabularies in either deaf or hearing
children are likely to impede higher level reading processes both by slow-
ing or disrupting the determination of word meaning and placing a heavy
load on available cognitive resources. One result of such limitations would
be the disruption of grammatical processing, as working memory becomes
overloaded and inefficient. It thus would not be surprising to find that deaf
children also exhibit difficulties in grammatical aspects of reading.

Grammar

During the 1960s, the focus of many teachers and researchers interested
in deaf children's reading turned to the explicit teaching of grammatical
structures and rules. Although the motivation for that focus may have been
misplaced, the many studies of deaf children's understanding of syntax
provided more thorough analyses of their grammatical knowledge than
previously had been available (Quigley et al., 1976; see also Marschark,
1993, chapter 11). That research indicated that there were categories of
grammatical structure that were particularly troublesome for young deaf
readers, with the largest differences occurring in grammatical structures
such as questions, pronouns, and embedded clauses or phrases.
It is unclear whether such difficulties are attributable to the lack of
grammatical knowledge, the memory demands involved in dealing with
particular structures, or some other factor (Mayer & Wells, 1996). In any
event, results from those investigations also demonstrated that a combination of sign language and exposure to English was generally the most

beneficial language environment for deaf children learning to read, at least with regard to the acquisition of grammatical abilities and text comprehension (Brasel and Quigley, 1977; Schlesinger & Meadow, 1972). This finding, which was obtained for children with both hearing parents and deaf parents, is inconsistent with both the frequent assertion that deaf children of deaf parents are generally better readers than those with hearing parents and arguments against combining sign language and English in instruction (e.g., Johnson et al., 1989; cf. Akamatsu et al., 2000; Mayer & Akamatsu, 1999). The issue is quite complex, and we will return to it later.

Characteristics of Deaf Readers

How do deaf students read? A variety of investigations have indicated that deaf readers, like hearing readers, use a combination of whole-word recognition, phonological or sound-based recoding, and orthographic (spelling-based) recoding to hold information temporarily in working memory (see chapter 6; Hanson & Fowler, 1987; Hanson & McGarr, 1989). Some deaf readers also recode English print into sign, at least some of the time (Marschark & Mayer, 1998; Treiman & Hirsh-Pasek, 1983).

Most hearing children begin reading by building up a limited sight vocabulary of words from television, road signs, and books (for example, *STOP* and *dog*) (Frith, 1985; Marschark & Harris, 1996). Then they gradually develop a sound-based (phonological) strategy for figuring out new words. The result is a growing inventory of sound–letter correspondences that supports decoding of text. A similar, if delayed, process appears to occur in many deaf readers, who come to use phonics as well as sight vocabulary (Miller, 1997). There is a positive correlation between speech intelligibility and reading during the first year of school, as young deaf children who are more consistently and accurately producing speech tend to read better than those who do not (Harris & Beech, 1998; see also Hanson, 1986). Improved articulation and speechreading are not enough to account for improvements in reading over the long term, however, and exposure to fingerspelling and writing experience also may be necessary to maintain reading progress (Campbell, 1992; Padden, 1991; Wilbur, 2000). Hence, there is a need for mixing alternative reading strategies.

One study involving deaf college students clearly demonstrated the combination of word decoding strategies used in reading (Lichtenstein, 1998). Analyses of experimental results and questionnaire responses from 86 first- and second-year students indicated that the meaning of text, as it was read, was retained in a speech-based code (in working memory). This "speech in the head" was supplemented by the use of signs and fingerspelling and, in fact, students were more likely to report using two or more codes rather than only one. Deaf students who made use of speech coding also were better able to remember and reproduce a sequence of English words. This latter result reflects the now-confirmed finding that speech coding appears to be the optimal means of briefly retaining linguistic information in working memory, a central component of reading comprehension as well as the mechanism underlying memory span (Perfetti & Sendak, 2000).

In young deaf readers, the development of phonological coding skills appears to lag behind that of hearing readers, occurring sometime around the fourth or fifth grade (age 9–11 years; see Marschark & Harris, 1996; Padden & Hanson, 2000). Meanwhile, many deaf children appear to use a decoding strategy based on the way words look on the printed page (an orthographic strategy). This approach to word decoding, although perhaps not as flexible as phonological decoding, offers the dividend of supporting spelling skills. Several studies have indicated that deaf children's spelling abilities are surprisingly good, exceeding other reading skills beginning around the second grade (see Marschark & Harris, 1996, for a review).

Some investigators have demonstrated an association between fluency in American Sign Language (ASL) as a native language and reading achievement, suggesting that fingerspelling is the element associating knowledge of ASL with the ability to read English. However, research shows little support for the possibility of fingerspelling codes during reading (Treiman & Hirsh-Pasek, 1983; Padden & Hanson, 2000). Rather, it appears that fingerspelling serves as a kind of platform for the development of rudimentary phonological coding. Through fingerspelling, deaf children become aware that words are made up of segments and groups of segments (syllables) that correspond to particular spelling patterns.

How does knowledge of the vocabulary and syntax influence deaf students' reading? We have already seen that knowledge of vocabulary is one key to figuring out the meaning of a text, and beginning readers get much of this knowledge at home. Several studies have demonstrated that exposure to both English and sign language provides strong support for the acquisition of reading skills, and stronger vocabulary knowledge appears to be an important product of that combination. In one study, for example, children who had experience with both English and sign language from their hearing parents scored higher on the word meaning and paragraph meaning subtests of the Stanford Achievement Test than those who were exposed only to ASL (as a first language by their deaf parents) (Brasel and Quigley, 1977; see also Schlesinger & Meadow, 1972). However, even familiar vocabulary may not be recognized as quickly by deaf readers as by hearing readers. For fluent reading comprehension, the rapid access to the meanings of words during reading has to be automatic rather than conscious and deliberate. Several studies have suggested that deaf children's lack of experience with reading reduces the spontaneous nature of decoding (Fischler, 1985; Kelly, 1995).

Deaf students who have had extensive exposure to English text appear to read in ways similar to hearing readers. Proficient deaf readers have been found to process complex sentence structures, such as relative clauses, and retrieve stored content knowledge, which supports subsequent processing of words in the text, like hearing readers (Cooley, 1981; Kelly, 1995; Lillo-Martin et al., 1992). Relatively less skilled deaf readers also use such strategies, but they are more likely to use local context in the passage to make guesses at the meanings of words rather than taking into account the full content of the text (Banks et al., 1990). As a result, their recall of material often contains the same amount of information as that of hearing peers, but in a less organized and disjointed way that clearly reflects a lack of global comprehension (Marschark et al., 1993).

How Should We Teach Reading to Deaf Children?

Children bring a considerable amount of relevant knowledge to school when they learn to read. Beyond the information they already have about the content of what they are reading, both deaf and hearing children should already understand what reading is about. In contrast to older views of reading (and about development at large) which assumed that children could not acquire various skills until they were ready, we now know that children know a great deal about reading and writing before they acquire those abilities.

Watching a young, prereading child "read" a book to someone else demonstrates that the child has both a general understanding of reading and some specific reading-related knowledge. At a general level the child knows that most books tell stories, contain language similar to spoken language, and that most people find pleasure in reading. At a more specific level, the child knows things like which way is right-side-up when reading a book, that sentences are continued across pages, and the direction that one reads, both on a page and across pages. Before they receive formal instruction, children can recognize some letters and words, and, in the case of hearing children, understand that there is a relation between spoken and printed words.

Although there do not appear to have been any studies comparing the prereading knowledge of hearing and deaf children, it is quite possible that deaf children have somewhat less knowledge in this regard than hearing children—unless, of course, they are enrolled in early intervention programs or their parents begin reading to them at an early age. Such a situation might suggest that deaf and hearing children need different kinds of instruction in the basics of reading and writing. Alternatively, children may just need more of whatever it is they have not already received at home: the availability of print materials, having someone read to them, and reading role models. In any case, it is not surprising that different views of what deaf children need to acquire effective literacy skills have spawned several different approaches to instruction. Let us consider some general examples.

Materials-Driven Approaches

Because many deaf students are learning English at the same time they are learning to read, some educators and investigators have argued that texts written with carefully controlled vocabulary and grammar would be most effective. Materials can become more advanced as reading skills improve (Quigley et al., 1976). Others argue that real or authentic texts are more appropriate, giving young deaf readers a full and accurate picture of what reading is all about (Dolman, 1992).

Use of simplified texts geared to the hypothesized sequence of deaf students' learning English is quite common. Various studies have indicated that at least 80 percent of teachers use such *basal readers*, and some investigators have suggested that the frequency is greater than 90 percent (Commission on Reading, 1989; LaSasso & Mobley, 1997). For the most part, these readers are linked to the research orientations of the individuals who developed them. One basal reading series, *Reading Milestones* (Quigley & King, 1982) (see fig. 8.1), is used in most programs that use such simplified readers. *Reading Milestones* is based on a body of research conducted by Stephen Quigley and his associates at the University of Illinois during the 1970s. In the series, syntactic structures used in each story appear in an order of difficulty derived from testing large numbers of deaf children and adolescents on the *Illinois Test of Syntactic Abilities*. Stories at the basic level contain single clause, subject-verb-object sentences; those later in the series include more complex constructions such as the passive voice and relative clauses.

Another way to construct simplified texts is through the use of *readability formulas.* Commercially available readability programs combine indices of word frequency (in print), sentence length, and sentence complexity to arrive at an average reading level for an input text. Although such formulas are informative for some purposes, they are problematic in constructing texts for deaf readers. Frequency in print generally is not a good indicator of vocabulary knowledge for those students. For example, grammatical function words like "the," "if," and "to" are particularly challenging for these students, even though they occur frequently in print (Walter, 1978).

The usefulness of basal readers and other grammatically simplified texts appears problematic for other reasons as well. Sentence length is not a reliable index of grammatical difficulty because sentences with subordinate clauses typically are harder to comprehend than sentences with coordinate clauses, even if they are the same length. Pronouns and their re-

Henry thought about his father's story. He decided not to daydream while they were sailing. He would do his job and become a good sailor. Henry walked back to the sails, and he helped his brother and sister with the sails. It was late afternoon, so they turned the boat back toward the shore.

When they were on land again, Mr. and Mrs. McBride told their children, "You did a very good job today. We are proud of you."

"All of you are becoming good sailors, and soon you will be ready for solo sailing. But, you must remember to be careful," Mrs. McBride said. "Henry, no more daydreaming, okay?"

Figure 8.1 Sample from *Reading Milestones.*

lated constructions present particular difficulties for deaf readers, but they are often removed from basal texts. Although this modification may simplify the structure of the material, research suggests that such texts may be more difficult for deaf students to understand than authentic text (Israelite & Helfrich, 1988; see also Strassman, 1997).

Another approach to improving reading comprehension is to use authentic texts with accompanying aids for comprehension. Meaning-preserving pictures accompanying text have been used to facilitate comprehension in children's readers for many years, but there have been few evaluations of their effectiveness with deaf readers. In one study, investigators explored the difficulty encountered by deaf readers in understanding nonliteral constructions (e.g., "He saved his money like a squirrel preparing for winter") (Iran-Nejad et al., 1981). The researchers suggested that deaf children might well be able to comprehend such expressions if they possessed the relevant knowledge of syntax, vocabulary, and the world. The reading materials thus were a set of short stories in which those variables were controlled at levels appropriate for their deaf 9- to 17-year-old participants, accompanied by a picture depicting the main point of the story. After reading the stories, the students had to select the sentence that best completed each story from a set of four alternatives including literal sentences, similes, and metaphors. Overall, even the youngest deaf students were able to select nonliteral choices as best completions for the stories, indicating that the picture and simplified structure facilitated comprehension even for nonliteral content.

A related study involved deaf college students who varied in their reading abilities. They each read a short text on the anatomy of the human eye and were asked questions about the content (Dowaliby & Lang, 1999). Some of the students viewed video clips capturing the content of the paragraph, while others viewed clips showing the text translated into sign language. In an adjunct question condition, students read part of the text, answered a multiple-choice question central to the meaning of the passage, and received feedback on their responses before proceeding. The results indicated that lower ability readers who were given adjunct questions performed as well as higher ability readers who read the text alone.

We are now seeing the beginning of a movement away from basal readers toward the use of real texts selected to be appropriate for young deaf readers. Basal readers remain popular, but their use has not appreciably improved the reading skills of deaf students over the past 25 years, as grammar has proven to be neither the insurmountable problem nor the solution that was previously believed. Further, the use of simplified texts moved the reading enterprise into the realm of artificially constructed language, lacking the cohesion and interest of natural text. Strategies for teaching reading to deaf children, meanwhile, have become more focused on the use of language in context. Perhaps the best example of this is the whole language approach to reading instruction.

The Whole-Language Approach

One popular approach to teaching reading to deaf students, known as the *whole language movement*, is based on a *transactional* (interaction) model of education rather than a *transmission* (from teacher to student) model (Ewoldt, 1985; Weaver, 1990; cf. Tiberius, 1986). That is, in the whole language approach, the teacher's role is not to transmit knowledge or meaning to the students, but rather to construct new meaning with the students. Students may read original texts produced by other students or written by professionals. They may attend a presentation or other event, discuss it with classmates, and then write about it. Proponents of the whole language approach maintain that students create meaning by interacting with a text and with other readers (Edelsky et al., 1991; Goodman et al., 1987; Weaver, 1990). The idea is that young readers want information and young writers want to express themselves—that content, not process, motivates them. The challenge for the teacher then is to make the reason for process or language instruction clear and keep the content in the foreground. This is most likely to occur in a content-rich classroom, where learning about one's classmates and the world is paramount and where reading and writing are presented as tools for that purpose.

The whole language movement accompanied a broader interest in language development based on the work of Vygotsky, Piaget, and Halliday, that developed in the mid to late 1970s. Beyond the structural emphasis of North American studies of language development, the whole language approach emphasized language in context, and the need to understand the whole child as a socially and cognitively active participant in the world. Consistent with this broader perspective, the whole language approach for deaf children grew from dissatisfaction with years of structured approaches to reading instruction that focused mostly on isolated sentences rather than on connected discourse (see, e.g., Livingston, 1997; Paul, 1998; Schirmer, 2000).

It appears that reading instruction focusing on isolated sentences (i.e., without either linguistic or real-world context) is at least partly responsible for the apparent difficulties with grammar demonstrated by deaf students. Further, the constant drill and practice inherent in such approaches removes the enjoyment of reading for even the most interested student (Wilbur, 1977). At the same time, an overemphasis on the whole language approach has its own difficulties. Teachers emphasizing whole language may give less attention to areas needing more focused instruction, such as complex syntactic structures (Dolman, 1992; Kelly, 1995, 1996). There is no methodological contradiction if a teacher focuses on word decoding skills, reading strategies, writing, and grammar in the context of a whole language approach, but strict adherents to the whole language approach do not always see it that way.

Balanced Literacy

In response to the extremes of both drill and practice and a whole language approach, a number of educators have adopted a *balanced literacy* approach to reading instruction. As Pressley (1998, p. 283) noted:

> Whole language is like Little League baseball if players only played games. Their playing of whole games would be substantially impaired by lack of skills. Just as bad, skills emphasis is like Little League baseball if it involved mostly infield, outfield, and batting practice. As good as players experiencing such an approach might be in picking up grounders, running down fly balls, and hitting consistently, they would not be baseball players. They would not know how the components articulate as part of an entire game.

Balanced literacy follows a set of heuristics compatible with one of the fundamental themes of this book: that language, learning, and instructional strategies need to be viewed and dealt with in an integrated manner. Schirmer (2000, pp. 101–102) succinctly summarized the principles of balanced literacy as follows:

- All forms of expressive and receptive language work together (reading and writing are interrelated processes)
- The emphasis is on the meaning of written language in authentic contexts (classroom reading and writing should involve real-life materials)
- Classrooms are communities of learners in which literacy is acquired through the use of reading and writing skills
- Children are motivated when given choices and ownership in reading processes
- Literacy processes are more important than products
- The development of literacy skills is part of an integrated curriculum
- Reading behaviors of skilled readers reflect what instruction should accomplish.

In short, the balanced literacy approach to teaching reading and writing takes the best of different instructional techniques and combines them in a way that recognizes children as active learners. Fully in accord with a social constructivist approach to education, balanced literacy represents a way of thinking about what we want children to learn in order for them to be able to appreciate and take advantage of the written word. There is no instructional manual for balanced literacy, no basal readers, or workbooks. It is, fundamentally, a commonsense approach to education.

Assessment of Reading Skills

Assessment of reading has long been accomplished primarily by means of standardized tests. Although useful as a relative indicator of overall reading ability, such instruments do not conform to the view that reading is a constructive process. Standardized reading tests also do not tell us whether any difficulties observed in reading comprehension are the result of a lack of background/content knowledge or of the inability to apply decoding strategies to a particular text. Standardized test scores thus may be useful in determining placement in a program or general achievement, but they are unlikely to be the best way to match a child with appropriate reading materials (Schirmer, 2000). For classroom instruction, assessments that are descriptive, functional, and content related are more appropriate (see, e.g., Stewart & Kluwin, 2001; Yore, 2000).

When we are teaching reading to young deaf students, we are teaching skills, but also habits and attitudes. Students need to discover and become comfortable with strategies for decoding text and ways to construct and to understand information. At the same time, we are teaching ways of approaching reading and text materials. These approaches should lead young deaf students to view reading as a source of enjoyment as well as a way to obtain knowledge. To accomplish this goal, classroom instruction will not be enough. Reading behavior must be modeled early, there must be print materials in the home, and deaf children need to understand that reading is a valued activity. Understanding the cognitive and metacognitive processes, such as word decoding, retrieval of knowledge from memory, and inferencing, which underlie the diverse reading skills of deaf students will contribute to these efforts (see chapter 6), and rigorous studies of teaching methods and outcomes are needed. Assessments of reading skills therefore need to be tailored to individual children just as carefully as teaching methods.

Characteristics of Deaf Students' Writing

Writing ability is even harder to quantify than reading ability, and there is far less systematic research on the writing of deaf students than on their reading. Nevertheless, there is a variety of useful information available concerning the writing skills of deaf learners, including both analyses of their writing and, more recently, some explorations of the processes that go into it. Looking ahead, the intimate relationship of reading and writing is such that deaf children's performance in the "input" (reading) domain generally is paralleled by their performance in the "output" (writing) domain. But the issue is much more complex and much more interesting.

When asked what kinds of writing they did outside of school when they were growing up, deaf college students report writing things like thank-you notes and the minutes for youth group or club meetings (Albertini & Shannon, 1996). Parents and children, both hearing and deaf, leave notes to inform others of their whereabouts, to make requests, and to express affection. Clandestine notes passed in school serve informational and social functions. Creating stories and poems and writing journal entries serve personal and artistic functions.

For the American Deaf community, writing has also served cultural functions (see, e.g, Panara et al., 1960; see also Maxwell, 1985). For many years, the only form of long distance communication available to most deaf people was personal letter writing (see chapter 2). In the late 1880s and first half of the twentieth century, newspapers published by schools for the deaf across the country (known as "The Little Paper Family") provided news, opinion, and social cohesion to local Deaf communities (Best, 1943; Buchanan, 1991). In the latter part of the twentieth century, the development of an acoustic coupler by three deaf entrepreneurs made telephone communication possible for deaf people (see Lang, 2000). More recently, fax machines, messaging systems, and electronic mail have expanded opportunities for immediate, written long-distance communication, and writing remains a part of the personal and cultural lives of American deaf people.

Contrast the above functions of personal writing with the kinds of writing done in school, determined by either the curriculum or the teacher. Most frequently, deaf students are asked to write reports on various topics or to engage in writing drills that focus on vocabulary and grammar. Consistent with this orientation, most investigations of writing by deaf school children over the past 50 years have focused on their structural, linguistic characteristics. Such analyses still indicate that deaf students generally produce shorter and less structurally variable sentences than hearing peers, when they produce complete sentences at all. Although they are generally as competent as hearing peers in the use of punctuation and in spelling, deaf children tend to use "stock" words and phrases repeatedly in a text, and they use more articles and nouns and fewer adverbs and conjunctions. Words are frequently omitted, and sentences generally are less syntactically complex and less well interconnected in compositions than those of hearing peers (Cohen, 1967; Heider & Heider, 1940; Simmons, 1962; Yoshinaga-Itano & Snyder, 1985).

Findings of this sort have been replicated in a variety of different contexts and across the school years, leading to the general conclusion (similar to that in the reading literature) that the average deaf 18 year old writes at a grammatical level comparable to that of a hearing 8 to 10 year old. However, when we look beyond English grammar and vocabulary, we see that the meaning and conceptual structure of deaf students' writing is often fully comparable to that of hearing students.[2] Writing with deaf students interactively (e.g., in dialogue journals) or allowing them to write on themes that interest them similarly has shown that deaf students are capable of producing coherent prose when they have control of the content and a motivating reason for writing (Albertini, 1993). In one relevant study, deaf and hearing students aged 8–15 years wrote stories on themes such as what they would do if they were picked up by a UFO. The two groups produced stories that were essentially equivalent in the structure of their underlying meanings, but the deaf students produced stories with shorter and simpler sentences, fewer adjectives and adverbs, and less frequent use of pre-positions and conjunctions reflecting less complex English structure (see "Being Picked up by a UFO") (Marschark et al., 1994).[3] Deaf students' stories also were almost exclusively composed of literal and concrete language, even while signed stories from the same children contained nonliteral constructions and were remarkably creative. Hearing students, in contrast, used similar levels of nonliteral, figurative construction in their writing and their spoken language (Everhart & Marschark, 1988).

One alternative to a structural perspective on deaf students' writing includes thematic and rhetorical analyses of their writing. This newer view of writing sees it as a process of discovery and shaping of the writer's thought. Analysis of deaf students' writing about their own experiences and feelings reveals much about their thinking and attitudes, even it often lacks the formal correctness and fluency of more experienced writers (Albertini, 1990; Albertini et al., 1994). Studies of this sort demonstrate that deaf students can write with remarkable clarity and force when they know their audience, are authorities on a topic, and have a clear purpose in mind.

Although such investigations have expanded our knowledge about deaf students' writing abilities, little information is available on how they actually compose what they write. In one interesting study, the com-

"Being Picked up by a UFO," Written by a Deaf 11 Year Old (from Everhart & Marschark, 1988)

"When I get in ufo They look funny. They have long pointed ears and have round face They speak different from our. They brought strange foods and Purple beverage. When I taste it I spill and begin to cought. I taste like dog food. But It was very pretty inside with many feather and clothes were very pretty. But one thing people in ufo stare at me because they never see large musclar and can pick up Heavy thing like weight, people or table. They feel it and said wow and start to teach me how to talk but they speak Russian language. I hate to learn Russian language. So I stay in ufo for 5 hours so they stop to place where they take me and drop their and they sent me a dog with long sharp teeth and was very tame I egan to cry and miss them."

posing processes of two 13–year-old deaf students was investigated over the course of two years (Mayer, 1999). Observable composing behaviors were documented by videotaping the students as they wrote; and an interview was conducted immediately after writing, using the videotape to prompt recall of the composing process. Both students were seen to mouth their words, one student doing so as he wrote and the other as she reread her writing. Both also used mouthing in conjunction with signing and fingerspelling, reflecting English-based composition strategies. Neither student was observed to sign while writing, even though they were both skilled users of ASL, and they expressed surprise that they were even asked about it.

One important assumption underlying bilingual (ASL and English) programs for deaf students is that ASL might serve as an important tool in reading and writing (see Mayer & Wells 1996). In a general sense, that assumption is clearly true, as fluency in one's first language appears an essential prerequisite to being able to articulate thoughts and feelings to others. However, the above study and all the reports we have about writing in a second language indicate that translation at the point of composing is not a very useful technique. Such an approach requires that the writer sit with either a dictionary or mental lexicon at the ready and translate from one language to the other unit by unit. As anyone who has tried this in any two languages knows, it is a slow, laborious process that leads to inaccurate and sometimes humorous results. Thus, one of our students wrote that over the weekend he stayed in his room and stared at his "four Caucasian walls." In short, choosing words and grammatical structures when one composes is analogous to a bottom-up approach to reading—the forest may be lost for the trees.

Even advanced learners are occasionally misled by dictionaries when working in their second language. One of our students once wrote that over the weekend he stayed in his room and "stared at the four Caucasian walls."

Composition wholly within the second language seems more efficient and likely to produce a smoother and more coherent passage. Given that composing is a combination of cognitive and linguistic activities, it is helpful to view writing, like reading, as involving the interaction of top-down and bottom-up processes. As in reading, a certain level of language proficiency (knowledge of the vocabulary, word formation rules and sentence formation rules) is necessary to allow fluent processing and encoding of thought. The question of how we can foster these in deaf students' writing is an issue that we consider in the next section.

How Should We Teach Writing?

Children typically learn to read before they learn to write. By the time most children want to encode thoughts into written words, they know print is related to speaking and can recognize a limited set of printed words. For many children, this transition happens before the child has reached school age. Not only can they recognize words, but they can also write a few, and they know that notes, newspapers, and TTYs are ways of communicating with others.

Writing is a process, but it need not be a lock-step sequence. How individuals write varies according to their goals and personalities, among other things. One way of looking at this process presents writing as a set of cognitive, linguistic, physical, and social activities. In the act of writing, these levels of activity interact. The double-headed arrow in figure 8.2 indicates the interaction between levels and between the writer and the text in progress. The single-headed arrow indicates the goal of the process: a published text. With an eye toward teaching, the levels in the model are

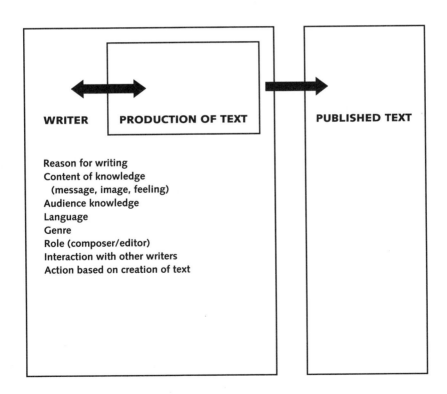

WRITER   PRODUCTION OF TEXT   PUBLISHED TEXT

Reason for writing
Content of knowledge
  (message, image, feeling)
Audience knowledge
Language
Genre
Role (composer/editor)
Interaction with other writers
Action based on creation of text

Figure 8.2. Interactive Model of Writing.

arranged to indicate that interaction between the writer and the text occurs before the writer "publishes" or shows the text to a wider audience.

Genre also affects the outcome of writing projects. In one study, deaf adolescents were asked to write in two different genres: a letter and an essay. The two types of writing then were compared for number of idea units and number of words they contained, among other characteristics (Musselman & Szanto, 1998). As in other investigations, this study found that deaf students had considerable difficulty with the vocabulary and syntax of English. However, they also found that the genre affected written performance, as the letter elicited higher levels of performance than the essay (see also Schick, 1997). The investigators therefore suggested that instruction should focus on writing tasks that are meaningful and purposeful for the students and urged a curriculum where content, form, and use are integrated—in other words, a *process approach* to writing.

Although it has been around for more than 100 years (see chapter 9), the process approach to writing represents something of a paradigm shift in the way that writing is taught today (Hairston, 1982). Teachers of freshman composition courses in open enrollment universities, such as the City University of New York during the late 1960s, were faced with classes of students from non-middle class, non–English-speaking backgrounds. Many of these students were simultaneously learning English, and most had no experience with genres like the expository essay (Shaughnessy, 1977). Classical Eurocentric models of such genres were meaningless and irrelevant to these students. Their instructors thus were forced to reconsider the way they taught writing. Rather than appealing to formal models of writing based on the classics, they had students write from personal experience. Students were asked to use writing as a way of mining memory to produce images, understanding, and meaning. Instructional time was focused on process first and product second. Publication and evaluation of the product were seen as the final stages of the process. Attention to content became primary and form became secondary, and the teaching of writing became the process of using the writing to stimulate thought. Consistent with strategies for teaching deaf students used decades ago, this approach fit well with the notion of the teacher as someone who encourages learning as a social and cultural activity (see chapters 1 and 9).

Changes in the teaching of writing have led to a reexamination of traditional notions of writing. Though writing is a solitary act, the activity need not be a lonely one, and the student does not need to be isolated from other writers. The romantic idea of the poor poet writing alone in a leaky garret has been tempered by scholarship showing that accomplished writers have often sought the help of other writers or worked in groups (e.g., the Brontë siblings). Thus, in contemporary classrooms, hearing and deaf students are encouraged to write freely, assuming the role first of composer and then editor; they are taught how to work with other (supportive) writers on early drafts.

A student who writes only to have a paper read and graded by the English teacher (a tradition with which most of us are all too familiar) comes away with a narrow conception of the function of literacy. Instead, we need to encourage students to take action based on their writing. This occurs often enough outside of the classroom: we make a list and go to the store or we write a letter of protest and have it published. The acquisition of such *dynamic literacy* is seen as just as important as being able to decode words on a page and encode words to put down in writing (*basic literacy*) or to interpret data or analyze a film (i.e., critical literacy) (Morris & Tchudi, 1996).

Linking writing to action is a way of linking English with content courses in the curriculum, such as social studies and science, and educators recently have shown considerable interest in the use of writing to foster learning in other areas (Yore et al., 1994). These *across the curriculum* approaches have encouraged the collaboration of English teachers and other professionals at secondary and post-secondary levels. Proponents of the approach claim that the advantages of collaboration justify the effort it takes to overcome logistical and discipline barriers in the schools.

In the interactive model of writing shown in figure 8.1, collaboration in writing can take a variety of forms. For example, a science teacher provides the purpose and motivation to write, and also the content of the writing. The English teacher negotiates the genre or type of writing and language appropriate to the purpose and audience with the science teacher and students. Together, the teachers also determine the type(s) of interactions and actions involving the students. For example, if the science teacher wanted the students to predict the outcome of a chemistry demonstration, students would record observations and predictions as a journal entry in the their personal science journals. The goal would be to accurately record all the relevant details and to use them to form hypotheses. Later, the student and English teacher could use the journal entry as the basis for a lab report that would be turned in and graded. Thus, writing tasks in the science class may vary from freely written journal entries to formal reports.

In this collaboration, the science teacher provides motivation, context, and content for the writing, and the English teacher provides instruction in the process of writing and language use. Such a collaboration demonstrates to the student that writing can be a tool to enhance observation, reasoning, and decision making (Lang & Albertini, 2001; Yore, 2000). In such a setting, a teacher's assessment or evaluation of writing is more authentic and valid. That is, the assessment reflects a student's knowledge of content and context as well as form.

Assessment of Writing Skills

Writing ability usually is not included in national reports of literacy levels. This may be the result of the diversity of expectations regarding what constitutes good writing or the fact that educators have disagreed on the best ways to assess writing. At the same time, many states are now instituting competency or graduation exit examinations that include writing components. Data that we have seen from programs involving deaf students in the United States, as well as recent studies of the writing of deaf students in the United States, Italy, and Canada, suggest that deaf students' general lack of knowledge of the vocabulary and grammar of their national languages limits their ability to communicate in writing (Fabretti et al., 1998; Kluwin & Kelly, 1991; Musselman & Szanto, 1998). There is far more to the issue, however.

At the outset, it will be helpful to make a distinction between *assessment* and *evaluation*, two related but distinguishable processes. Assessment is best viewed as the documentation of change. When a teacher periodically collects samples and records observed changes in a student's skills, use of different strategies, attitudes toward writing, and related self-perceptions, a student's growth as a writer can be assessed and documented. Evaluation, in contrast, involves judgment about the product of writing per se: A teacher scrutinizes observation notes collected over time and evaluates writing samples to decide on a grade, need for future instruction, or placement. Teacher's logs, checklists, and portfolios are forms of documentation that support evaluations such as grading and ranking.

At the school level, it is important to know whether a student is ready to enter a writing program, where to put the student in that program, and whether the student has the requisite skill to move out of the program. Most frequently, writing assessments involve either multiple-choice tests, essay tests, or portfolio assessments. Multiple-choice tests provide lexical, grammatical, and stylistic options within a given sentence or short passage and ask the student to select the best alternative. Such tests are referred to as *indirect* measures of writing ability insofar as they tap writing knowledge without actually obtaining a writing sample. In *direct* measures of writing ability, a student usually is asked to write a short essay on a particular topic. The essay is then read and evaluated by the teacher or other professionals. In some cases, the writing samples are blinded so that the reader does not know which student produced them.

Multiple-choice tests and evaluation of writing samples are the two methods most widely used to evaluate and place deaf students. Recent research, however, indicates that indirect measures are less valid as indicators of the writing ability for college-age deaf students than are direct measures (Berent et al., 1996).

A third method of writing assessment is portfolio assessment. A writing portfolio contains samples of a student's work from the beginning of a course or an academic year to the end that program. The portfolio includes a variety of written works chosen by the student and the instructor, including different genres, and commentary by the writer on the samples selected.

Sometimes this commentary will take the form of an introductory letter to the reader, although the student may provide comments on each individual sample. Proponents of portfolios claim that it allows a more valid assessment of attitude and understanding of the process as well as writing skill development (Belanoff & Dickson, 1991; Hart, 1994). Studies of the reliability and validity of portfolios as assessment tools apparently have not yet been conducted.

The Continuing Challenge of Developing Literacy

Clearly, teaching the national or majority language has been a preoccupation for educators of deaf students for more than 100 years. Have we learned anything from the various methods and approaches we have tried? Have we succeeded or failed in teaching reading and writing to deaf students? Some contend that the reading and writing skills of deaf students have shown little improvement. For example, the Commission on Education of the Deaf, better known as COED, was established by the Education of the Deaf Act of 1986 to study the quality of education being received by deaf persons. In its 1988 report to the Congress and the President of the United States, the Commission reported being "deeply distressed by the striking lack of discernible progress in reading and other language achievement levels by deaf children over the past 20 years" (Bowe, 1991, p. 12).

According to the framers of the COED report, teachers and researchers have failed to find the right way to teach literacy skills to deaf students. An alternative perspective is that, given the increased demand for literacy to function in today's society, the problem has been failing to keep up with the demand. A greater variety and sophistication of reading and writing is required of today's students than was required in the past; and greater sophistication and creativity is required on the part of today's teachers and parents. Literacy education is not the province of just the parents or just one teacher. It belongs in the content classrooms as much as it does in the English or language arts classroom, and it needs to pervade all aspects of a child's educational career. Only by taking a holistic approach to language and literacy will deaf students overcome the long-standing challenges and be able to meet the new demands.

To understand fully the challenges faced by deaf students in the literacy arena, it is important to take into account several factors presented earlier in this book, including the variation among deaf children as language learners, the influences of early language environments, and interactions of hearing loss and access to reading-relevant information. Unfortunately, previous curriculum efforts devoted to improving literacy of deaf children frequently have focused on trying to teach them the particular skills and strategies that work for hearing children, even though deaf and hearing children often have very different background knowledge and learning strategies. Frank Bowe, who chaired the COED group, expressed his concern about this situation and the attempts to teach language to deaf children rather than support their learning (Bowe, 1998). He suggested that schools make use of all possible strategies to encourage reading during childhood to promote the natural acquisition of both language and English literacy among younger deaf children. Older children, he argued, can be taught particular language skills later, in one modality or another.

In this regard, we should distinguish between child language acquisition and adult language acquisition. Remedial speech and language programs generally are based on psycholinguistic research in first language acquisition. That is, investigators have documented the order of acquisition of the sounds, meanings, structures, and functions of language and proposed typical milestones so that therapists and teachers can speak of stages of acquisition. To a great extent, second language learning programs at the elementary level are based on the order of milestones observed in first language acquisition. Underlying this order is a premise that as the child matures cognitively, he or she is able to construct ever more sophisticated categories of meaning and complex language structures. For adolescents and adults, cognitive maturity and previous language learning experience have altered the reality of what is "simple," "complex," and "relevant," and thus the premise of a developmental order based on first language acquisition research may be pointless and even counterproductive for older children. For them and for young adults, organization of language learning by content and function may be more appropriate (Albertini & Samar, 1983).

To be in a position to learn the structure and function of English, a deaf (or hearing) learner has to have access to that target language. First, therefore, students must be provided with natural and accurate models of the English language. Second, deaf students must have available written materials that are authentic and well-written. Third, the language used in instruction must be clear and accurate. That is, both the first and the second languages must be accessible to the learner, something that is not always true for deaf children.

Although an increasing number of classrooms make use of ASL as the language of instruction, some form of English-based signing may be more effective for literacy instruction (see chapter 4). We have already noted that there is much debate about the use of natural versus artificial sign systems in the classroom. With regard to communication in the home, the issue of whether to use English-based signing systems is largely academic because most parents and teachers are far more proficient in one of those systems than they are in ASL. There is clearly a role for English-based systems, in any case, as means of reading aloud, rehearsing for writing, and in proofreading. It is important, however, for native and near-native users of ASL, that discussion of the content of writing still may be richest and most efficient if conducted in ASL. Teachers therefore need to be proficient in both ASL and an English-based sign system, as well as spoken and/or written English. Effective communication with deaf students is the basis for the acquisition of literacy skills as well as other academic, personal, and social skills.

⌈ Teachers' proficiencies in ASL and English-based signing do not guarantee the deaf student access to literacy, however. Just as important as access to the language and content of instruction is the fact that deaf students learn both language and its content through interaction with peers, native speakers, and experts in various domains. Consistent with a social constructivist perspective, therefore, we believe that the acquisition of literacy skills must be seen as a process of dialogue in a community of learners rather than as transmission of information from teacher to student. In this view, the teacher takes into account the experience, skills, and knowledge each learner brings to the classroom. The learner looks to the teacher for prompts, resources, and guidelines for learning. Together, they bring the language alive as a shared experience. ⌋

For this to occur, the purpose of acquiring literacy skills must be apparent to the student. A natural language is never learned in a vacuum, and any instruction that focuses too long on form or pattern practice (drills) risks becoming meaningless and rote for the student. Whenever possible, language instruction therefore should be connected to specific objectives: for example, reading to understand an exciting new discovery in a field interesting to the student (e.g., dinosaurs or oceanography) or writing to report on an interview with a famous deaf person. Unfortunately, some educators still hold the view that content instruction should be delayed until the deaf student has achieved a certain level of English language proficiency, a belief that has led to unacceptable delays in content instruction. Different people read for diverse reasons on various occasions. Rather than dictating what material is appropriate for young deaf readers, discovering what motivates them may provide entry into a world where reading and writing are self-motivating. The result may be not only greater academic success but personal and economic opportunities that better allow deaf students to achieve their potentials.

Language and Literacy

Before leaving the topic of reading and writing, it will be useful to consider the link between language fluency and the acquisition of literacy skills. The importance of language fluency to all domains of development has been emphasized in earlier chapters, and the link to literacy is an essential one, even if the language of early communication and the language of the reading–writing domain are different (e.g., ASL and English).

A 1995 report from the National Institutes of Health reported that deaf children of deaf parents, in general, are better readers than deaf children of hearing parents. This common assumption typically is ascribed to the early availability and access to language. Findings supporting that suggestion have been reported by several authors, but many of those studies remain unpublished (but see Padden & Ramsey, 1998; Singleton et al., 1998). In fact, the relationship between parental hearing status and reading ability is not a particularly strong one, the evidence is inconsistent, and even when that finding has been obtained, the causes have been unclear (Akamatsu et al., 2000; Brasel & Quigley, 1977; Calderon & Greenberg, 1997; Strong & Prinz, 1997). Overall, the generalization should be taken as tentative and its basis explored.

Regardless of whether their parents are deaf or hearing, deaf children who are better readers are those who had their hearing losses diagnosed earlier, had early access to language (usually via sign language), and were exposed to English. Together, these factors give them the advantage both of early exposure to language and English-relevant experience. Similarly, having a mother who is a good signer has been found to be more important than whether she is deaf or hearing and more important than the precise age at which a child learns to sign. Deaf children of deaf parents therefore may read better than deaf children of hearing parents if their parents read with them more regularly and are able to ensure their understanding and elaborate on various topics through sign language (Andrews et al., 1994). Hearing parents who learn to sign well also can have a powerful impact (and perhaps an equivalent one to deaf parents) on their children's reading abilities. Anecdotal evidence aside, however, we do not yet have empirical studies of the link between deaf children's reading skills and specific, reading-related parental behaviors.

Clearly, the factors that influence reading development are complex, and we should not expect to find a single predictor of reading that applies to all children, deaf or hearing. It may be that different environments lead to different strengths and weaknesses in literacy skills depending on when, where, and from whom children learn their first and second languages. For example, deaf children of hearing parents tend to have better speech and speechreading abilities than peers who have deaf parents, but those abilities do not seem to predict better reading (Wilbur, 2000). There also have been suggestions that English gloss of ASL might be helpful in supporting reading (see Singleton 1998, for a review). This potential advantage may be offset, however, by the fact that ASL vocabulary and syntax do not parallel those of printed English.

Theoretically, exposing deaf children to some form of English-based signing as well as ASL could provide a bridge to written English, albeit with a stronger language base than when children are exposed only to simultaneous communication (see chapters 5 and 7). Too often, however, educators have assumed that English–based signing is sufficient, in itself, to provide the language necessary for social and academic functioning. A complete discussion of this issue would require more space than is available here, but a variety of findings indicate that the assumption is far from accurate (see Mayer & Akamatsu, 1999; Musselman, 2000; Singleton et al., 1998; Wilbur, 2000).

For students with fluency in ASL, it may be most effective to sign a passage of text first and then deal with the English in some form of English-based signing or directly in print. When focusing on decoding, spelling, and grammar, it may be appropriate to fingerspell, to use cued speech, or to use invented signs for English grammatical markers (e.g., from Signed English) (Fischer, 1998; Grushkin, 1998; Mayer & Moskos, 1998; Padden, 1991). Teachers may substitute fingerspelling for a sign if they want to draw attention to a different meaning of a word: for example, fingerspelling P-R-O-B-L-E-M in a mathematics class to differentiate the concept from the sign PROBLEM, meaning "a difficult situation." Several investigators also have pointed out that in fluent ASL discourse, some signs (e.g., HAVE, LARGE, and MOTHER) and borrowed words or acronyms (e.g., B-E-E-F [bif:], P-H-D [fd], U-F-O [ufo]) are accompanied by facial gestures or mouth movements that can provide clues for reading (Johnson, 1994; Marschark et al., 1998).

Chapter 7 described the recent development of bilingual–bicultural education, a model that (in the United States) incorporates ASL as the language of instruction, but emphasizes the importance of reading and writing in English. There is currently great variability among bilingual–bicultural programs in their approaches to fostering language fluency and literacy in deaf children. "Pure" ASL is used in some programs, while others report using simultaneous communication in some contexts (McCutcheon, 2000).

Summary

Data from a variety of sources indicate that hearing American students read and write better today than at any other time in history (Kibby, 1993, 1995). Studies that would allow us to evaluate the parallel claim with regard to deaf students are not available, but it appears that, overall, they have shown at least modest improvements in their literacy skills. Examination of scores on standardized reading tests, for example, show that, as a group, deaf 10 year olds in 1994 were reading at the level achieved by deaf 12 year olds in 1974 (Dossetor, 2000). Nevertheless, a large and perhaps increasing discrepancy between hearing and deaf peers of the same age remains, and many deaf students graduating from high school today are still reading at levels comparable to hearing students who are five to nine years younger. As society becomes more dependent on technology and information exchange, the literacy demands in school and in the workplace will increase. If deaf individuals are to succeed in this brave new world, we will need to learn how to do a better job of teaching them the literacy skills they need.

This chapter described the various components of reading and writing, demonstrating that they are complex tasks that involve the interplay of skills ranging from word decoding to the application of content knowledge. Less skilled deaf readers differ from more skilled (deaf and hearing) peers on a variety of dimensions, but their primary challenges appear to lie in phonological processing—the decoding of words that allow automatic retrieval of meaning—and the integration of information across grammatical units of text (Banks et al., 1990; Kelly, 1995; Marschark et al., 1993; Oakhill & Cain, 2000). Contrary to earlier reports, however, young deaf learners do understand discourse rules and use them in structuring the meanings of their writing.

Literacy thus can be considered at a variety of different levels, and the challenges and successes of deaf students' pursuit of literacy skills have been examined by investigators in several domains. Regardless of perspective, reading and writing are complementary processes both in theory and in practice, and, on average, good writers tend to be avid readers. If instruction is to mirror reality, the connection between reading and writing has to be implicit throughout all teaching. In the teaching of particular subjects and in the workplace, the distinction between reading and writing is irrelevant; both are considered necessary tools.

Taking a narrower approach to literacy, it also is important to consider the ways in which it is related to language development. Bilingual ASL–English programs have developed in part because of the belief that early acquisition of sign language can contribute to literacy skills. In fact, the assumption that deaf children of deaf parents generally read better than deaf children of hearing parents is not strongly supported by existing research. There are consistent findings, however, indicating that early exposure to both ASL and English provides the strongest support for the acquisition of literacy skills. Hearing children and deaf children of deaf parents or deaf children of hearing parents may differ in the component skills underlying reading, even when their overall reading levels are the same. Alternatively, they may be similar on particular dimensions that create overall differences in reading level. In any case, without broad evaluations of bilingual education programs and their influences on literacy and academic achievement, it is too soon to evaluate their potential impact in any particular area.

Several alternatives to straightforward ASL–English bilingual programs also have been suggested. Beyond the possible use of English gloss (Singleton et al., 1998), ASL might be combined with either simultaneous communication or cued speech to provide a more effective bridge from early language (via ASL) to literacy (via English) (Marschark, 1997). Several programs in England recently have adopted such an approach to education, combining British Sign Language and *sign-supported English*, but it is too early to determine the extent of their success. Alternatively, ASL might be used initially to provide early access to language, to be followed by a combination of ASL and written English to promote literacy (Wilbur, 2000). Either of these possibilities would fit with recent theoretical perspectives on literacy acquisition by deaf learners, but only time and evaluation will determine whether they work.

Strategies used by deaf adults in reading to children should also be used by hearing teachers, even if deaf teachers and deaf teacher aides are available.

Recent methods for teaching, assessing, and evaluating the literacy skills of deaf students have focused on understanding students' skills and having them understand the processes of reading and writing in the larger context of their lives. Literacy instruction that includes this perspective appears to have a better chance to motivate students to achieve and yield more valid assessments of their abilities. Early exposure to reading and writing in the home, the availability of fluent role models, and access to well-written materials also provide a natural context for literacy and appear to have advantages over the use of simplified and artificial materials. The latter may be appropriate for some remedial purposes, but integrating reading and writing into content areas (writing across the curriculum) provides a more naturalistic alternative.

The limited improvement in literacy skills of deaf students of the past several decades is disheartening to some. From the perspective of most researchers and teachers, however, this is not necessarily the case. More progress has been made in this domain during the last 15 years than in the previous 150. As we better understand how deaf children learn, we can more appropriately tailor our educational methods with regard to literacy and other domains. Reading programs in which stories are presented in both sign language and spoken language, where young children all have copies of the same story book, and where parents share with their children stories first presented at school, for example, all appear to have a positive impact on both language growth and literacy.

Having children retell stories at home, collect or draw relevant pictures, and act out portions of the stories all help to establish links between the written word, meaning, and the language used in one-on-one communication. Strategies used by deaf adults in reading to children should also be used by hearing teachers, even if deaf teachers and deaf teacher aides are available.

While some educators and educational administrators lament the fact that we have not yet solved the literacy problem, it is unlikely that there is

Learning to Read

Thomas Holcomb is reading a bedtime story to his daughter, Tara. He is lying on her bed, knees up, a book propped up on his chest facing Tara. She is sitting on his lap, facing him, and using his legs as a backrest. In this comfortable position, Tara can see both the book and her father as he signs the story to her.

going to be a single solution. Educators, parents, and researchers alike thus continue to seek a balance between the provision of effective early communication skills, usually best achieved through sign language, and the provision of English skills needed for academic success. Evaluation of new alternatives requires careful and consistent monitoring to ensure that they are being used in quality instructional environments that provide fair tests of their utility. It may well be that the apparent failure of some educational methods results primarily from poor implementation.

What constitutes effective curriculum development and teaching for deaf students?

How well are our schools following national standards?

How do characteristics of deaf students influence the teaching-learning process?

9

NINE

Teaching and the Curriculum

We have discussed how the education of deaf children depends on their characteristics as well as on the characteristics of parents, teachers, and school programs that serve those children. We have summarized a variety of studies that have implications for parents, teachers, and educational administrators with regard to fostering communication skills, cognitive growth, and social interaction by deaf children. The available evidence supports the need for strong early intervention programs that provide the experiential diversity critical for development across the life span and for achievement in a variety of educational settings. Chapter 8 dealt with the specific educational challenges confronting deaf students in reading and writing. The message there was that English literacy needs to be considered broadly, as it affects both learning and success in a variety of areas, both academic and nonacademic. In chapter 8, we also discussed implications for curriculum materials and particular teaching emphases. Now, we turn to some best practices for teaching and curriculum development in content areas such as science, mathematics, and social studies and show how information in the previous chapters comes together in the day-to-day activities of students and teachers.

Understanding Deaf Students in Diverse Settings

As we have seen, available research findings indicate the need to exercise caution when deaf learners are placed in inclusive academic environments. Deaf students have specific needs that may not be met adequately if it is assumed that, aside from communication differences, deaf students and hearing students are the same. This is not a point to be raised only with regard to mainstream classrooms; it is a complex issue that needs to be addressed throughout the educational system. To set the stage for the remainder of this chapter, let us review some salient points which emerged from earlier chapters and were seen as key in understanding the teaching and learning of deaf students:

- Deaf students have different experiences that may influence how they view and interact with the world.
- A diversity of both object-oriented and person-oriented experiences is crucial to normal development.
- Deaf students depend more on visual information, but they also may be more prone to distraction than hearing peers in the visual domain.
- Deaf students are often unfamiliar with the multiple meanings of words, even if they know their primary meanings.
- During memory retrieval, problem solving, or reading, the activation of information in long-term memory may not be as directed or focused for deaf students as for their hearing peers.
- In retaining a list of items in working (or short-term) memory, speech-based memory appears more efficient than sign-based memory for deaf students.
- There may be differences between deaf and hearing learners in terms of the way they organize knowledge and the strategies they use to access stored information. Some expectations, interactions, and educational methods appropriate for hearing children thus may not always generalize to deaf children.
- Attending to two or more sources of information simultaneously (e.g., a teacher, a computer screen, and an overhead projector) requires constant attention switching and makes communication and learning more challenging for deaf students.
- Learning/problem-solving situations that involve two or more dimensions that have to be considered simultaneously present greater difficulty for deaf than for hearing students.

These findings from empirical studies clearly have implications for formal teaching-learning situations, but they also relate to the informal activities that constitute the majority of children's learning contexts. We have seen, for example, that the essentials of language and communication support other aspects of learning and development as well. Normal language acquisition requires early access to language models, and both the diversity of those models and social reinforcement facilitate vocabulary growth. Moreover, effective shared communication enhances language development, and mode of communication is not as important as consistency and full accessibility.

Although the above findings present some challenges for educators, our review of available research also showed that the notion of deaf children as concrete thinkers who struggle with abstract concepts and interpret everything literally is an outdated perspective. Parents and teachers need to raise and educate deaf children with careful thought given to the interactions among language, social, and intellectual development. When fostered appropriately, deaf children are able to reach their full potential as readily as hearing children. Providing deaf children with the necessary contexts for normal development is the important goal, and we need to expend our energies and resources in that direction.

Content Knowledge and the Broadening of Literacy

The original meaning of the word "literacy" related exclusively to reading and writing. After acquiring a sense linked to dealing with economics and commerce ("economic literacy"), around the time of the Second World War, literacy came to be applied more broadly to the understanding of the ability to deal with a variety of content areas. We thus now see references to "computer literacy," "mathematics literacy," and "general academic literacy." The latter phrase, for example, refers to the global competencies required to function effectively in academic environments, a concept clearly including the traditional notion of being well-versed in reading and writing but involving both automatic and strategic applications of other skills as well.

As with cognitive and linguistic development, general academic competency or literacy is likely to be affected by the communication barriers that frequently confront deaf children. Let us examine how communication can impact a child's general literacy and preparation for learning a subject such as history. Learning about history during childhood usually comes through stories from parents, grandparents, or peers. Sometimes these stories are initiated through pictures or particular descriptions in reading materials. A child may ask a variety of questions, expressing curiosity about unusual clothes, a coonskin cap, or a horse-drawn cart. Other times, history may be learned through family-related stories: "Uncle Bill was at Iwo Jima during World War II" (an opportunity for an early geography lesson as well).

Such communicative interactions also can be stimulated by television or through the use of other technologies. During the early years of TTY technology, for example, various news services were established where deaf people could call a telephone number and receive a printout of local news and weather. These were the days before captioned television, when small networks of deaf people found their own ways to gain access to local and national news. One ingenious rabbi in New York City set up a system for

sharing "Jewish tales," which provided families with deaf children the opportunity to receive such stories through the TTY and to discuss Jewish heritage and religious concepts together. Providing children with such personalized information makes it both relevant and interesting.

Such storytelling is less likely to happen in hearing families with deaf children, at least when those children are involved, because of the lack of comfortable communication. This situation is compounded by the general problems that deaf children often have in reading, so that they also are less likely than hearing children to obtain such information on their own. Consequently, teachers in the early grades will have difficulty building a foundation of general background knowledge when children lack a sense of history. The implications will certainly be felt in the history classroom, but also in other subjects including geography, biology, literature, and physics, where memorizing might take place of the more natural, gradual accumulation of relevant information.

When parents struggle to communicate effectively, deaf children are likely to miss opportunities to discuss their experiences and construct knowledge. How does a big, heavy airplane stay in the sky? What makes a rainbow? The seemingly trivial number and language games parents play with hearing family members, such as "twenty questions" or "I spy" play an important role in providing children with background knowledge and skills that serve as a knowledge structure or scaffolding in the school setting. These are general issues critical to academic achievement across the curriculum and to everyday functioning in society. With this in mind, let us consider three primary areas of the curriculum: science, mathematics, and social studies.

Science

The relative lack of basic knowledge and skills in science and technology has become a serious concern for educators in the United States. The Third

International Mathematics and Science Study (TIMSS), conducted in 1995, was a series of international assessments of student performance. According to that assessment (and the 1999 "TIMSS-Repeat"), high school seniors in the United States performed near the bottom of the rankings in general science competency relative to students in most other technologically advanced countries. Analyses of the TIMSS and other international assessments have included discussions of sampling bias, test bias, and the educational quality of those tests. The harsh reality is that no matter how we look at the findings, the problem is not with the students, but with the educational system.

Beyond the content of the TIMSS assessment, lower test scores in the United States have been attributed, in part, to students avoiding math and science courses, low learning expectations on the part of parents and teachers, and weak teaching (Stedman, 1994). Recognizing that students in some age groups have excelled in some subjects on international assessments, the continuing disappointing results from such surveys have generated educational concerns related to the decline in America's scientific and technological leadership. Clearly, reform is needed.

A variety of science education reforms introduced over the years have attempted to address the persistent concerns over science literacy (see Yager, 1997, for a summary). There have been efforts to teach science as used by scientists, rather than as lists of facts to be remembered. Other approaches tried to apply science to students' lives and make it personally meaningful. Science educators have delved into research on cognition, discovery approaches, and ways to relate science, technology, and society. The most recent reforms focus on functional scientific literacy, the ability to read and write passages with scientific and technological vocabulary, and conceptual scientific literacy, understanding the major ideas that form the disciplines of physical, life, and earth sciences.

Mathematics

The National Council of Teachers of Mathematics (NCTM) has provided an excellent framework for educational planning in mathematics through their *Professional Standards for Teaching Mathematics* (1991). This important curriculum guide for educators refers to the need to develop *mathematical power* in all students, which is defined as "the ability to explore, conjecture, and reason logically; to solve nonroutine problems; to communicate about and through mathematics; and to connect ideas within mathematics and between mathematics and other intellectual activity" (NCTM, 1991, p. 1). Mathematical power leads to the development of self-confidence in seeking, evaluating, and using quantitative and spatial information in solving problems and making decisions. Students' flexibility, perseverance, interest, curiosity, and inventiveness also affect the realization of mathematical power.

Being quantitatively literate means having a broad range of skills that allows one to deal with quantitative concepts in a variety of settings. It is not intended to imply mastery of a specific list of mathematical skills or concepts deemed important by educators or some accrediting body. As one educator of deaf students noted, "by limiting the manner in which mathematics literacy is viewed, educators limit what students are expected to know and do, and in turn limit the career options and possibilities available to them" (Daniele, 1993, p. 76).

Social Studies

Competency in social studies draws on several aspects of the curriculum, consistent with its place in society. In the U.S. educational system, social studies involves more than just the development of civic competence, it draws on disciplines such as anthropology, archaeology, economics, geography, history, law, philosophy, political science, psychology, religion, and sociology. Social studies also involves the ability to apply multidisciplinary knowledge to complex societal issues such as health care, crime, and foreign policy.

Thomas Jefferson called the knowledge, skills, and attitudes needed for civic competence in our democratic republic "the office of citizen." This notion fits well with the idea of being competent in social studies and is a worthy goal of education in the United States for the twenty-first century (National Council for the Social Studies, [NCSS], 1994). After all, the purpose of social studies is to help students develop the ability to make informed and reasoned decisions for the public good as citizens of a culturally diverse, democratic society (NCSS, 1994).

Curriculum Reform and the Education of Deaf Students

Efforts to incorporate reforms into curricula designed for classrooms of deaf students have been sporadic and ill defined. In many cases, "reform" has meant using materials that have been developed in the context of particular schools or classrooms rather than being based on sound educational theories or models. Meanwhile, there have been a number of curriculum reform efforts in public schools, particularly in science, mathematics, and social studies. In the 1960s and 1970s, the National Science Foundation sponsored a number of "alphabet curricula," emphasizing science processes (e.g., observing, predicting, and classifying) and the nature of scientific inquiry.[1] These programs proved to be effective with hearing students; but they never took hold in schools serving deaf students, apparently because

"The History of the Act of Instructing the Deaf and Dumb" (Harvey Prindle Peet, 1851)

Thus it happened that, in almost every country, the early teachers of the deaf . . . were obliged each to grope his own way, and invent his own processes."

of lack of resources and teacher training (Lang & Propp, 1982; Shymansky et al., 1983; Sunal & Burch, 1982).

There is little reason to doubt that, given the chance, deaf students can achieve better when curriculum materials emphasize active learning, discovery, and hands-on activities. One investigation, for example, evaluated the feasibility of using an alphabet curricula, the Biological Sciences Curriculum Study (BSCS) "Me Now" program, with deaf students who had low reading abilities. The BSCS materials are characterized by low verbal content and an emphasis on hands-on activities (they were originally developed for mentally handicapped students). The study resulted in substantial gains and retention of content for six deaf students participating in the study (Grant et al., 1975). Another study using materials from the Science Curriculum Improvement Study and Science: A Process Approach alphabet curriculum, resulted in increased scores for deaf students who used the hands-on materials (Boyd & George, 1973). Although these studies showed promise for materials with reduced reading demands, the curricula apparently were never instituted on a larger scale in programs serving deaf students.

There also have been several curricula reform movements in mathematics education over the past decades. Before the 1950s, the emphasis was on performing routine computations. That was followed by "new math," which focused on set theory and other theoretical approaches to understanding mathematical concepts. The new math efforts did not involve elementary and secondary teachers of deaf students in any significant way, however, and the reform benefited college-bound hearing students the most.

Public dissatisfaction with mathematics education, exemplified in Morris Kline's 1973 book *Why Johnny Can't Add: The Failure of New Math*, led to calls for reform again. The mathematics curriculum movement in the 1970s was characterized by the "back to basics" approach, which was expected to address the needs of slower students. Unfortunately, many schools attempted to fit a single syllabus or textbook series to all students, without considering different levels of prior knowledge and ability. Educators of deaf students were heavily dependent on textbooks distributed by commercial publishers for decades, while teacher-developed supplementary materials were most often of a drill-and-practice nature. The use of "math lab" techniques were infrequent, owing to lack of teacher experience and lack of materials.

In 1982, mathematics teachers of deaf students met at a mathematics symposium in Austin, Texas, and established a set of national educational priorities (Williams & Kubis, 1982). These called for an emphasis on the development of thinking skills, improved teacher preparation in the area of mathematics, and a *mathematics-across-the-curriculum* approach. One of their more radical suggestions was a call for investigating possible uses of calculators in the mathematics classroom, but the NCTM has now endorsed the use of calculators at all school levels.[2]

As in mathematics and science, the social studies curriculum also has undergone reform efforts. Historically, the focus of the social studies curriculum has been on contemporary social problems, their place in the school, and their relationship to history (Hertzberg, 1982). The dominant pattern of elementary (K-6) social studies has been the study of "expanding environments," ranging from self and home to communities and geographic regions. In secondary education, the focus has been on U.S. and world history, civics and government, and what was essentially social psychology. But articulation of the social studies curriculum across grade levels is seen as weak (Weiss, 1978). One reason for this problem is that in most cases the elementary and secondary programs occur in separate schools, making it difficult for teachers to communicate with one another. A second factor may be the role and use of textbooks, which are often developed separately for different courses or are purchased from different publishers (Patrick & Hawke, 1982).

Whether in social studies, mathematics, or science, one problem for students in public schools in this country is that curricula touch upon too many subjects (see following discussion on standards). More important, they tend to encourage memorization of facts rather than showing students how to see the patterns, relationships, and big ideas (probability, great theorems, immigration, and so on) that make up the fabric of the world. Mathematics, for example, should be treated as a science, with complex, real-world problems to solve, not just a process of computation. Similarly, science and technology influence society, and the relations between them and their impact on individuals and groups are important. These academic subjects are like strands of a rope, intertwined as integral components of literacy. They should not be seen as distinct.

National Standards

Routine teaching remains predominant in school programs serving deaf students, and there is a dire need to apply national standards in mathematics, science, and social studies to enhance both curriculum and instruction. We therefore consider the standards in each area separately.

Science

National content standards for science now are being widely promoted in the United States by various organizations, including the American Association for the Advancement of Science's *Science for All Americans* and *Benchmarks for Science Literacy*, and the National Research Council's *National Science Education Standards*. The clear and well-planned guides included in the standards help teachers prepare children with both specific skills and knowledge and general scientific and mathematics literacy needed for living in a complex world.

Such standards largely agree on what is important for students to know. They recommend excluding the clutter and focusing on fewer topics by teaching fundamental concepts in more depth. Standards cannot reform education. Educators reform education by teaching the core ideas and helping students to learn them well (Rhoten & Bowers, 1997). Science education standards can provide educators with valuable information on student achievement, curriculum and instruction, and teacher qualifications, however, all of which are needed to bring about more widespread, meaningful reform of K-12 education. State and local curriculum developers thus should use these credible, widely accepted national guidelines to direct and build support for their efforts. The standards help to promote articulation across grade levels and bring the big pictures of science and science education into better focus. Further, although curriculum and teaching standards are intended to ensure that students are literate in science, they also encourage a more diverse pool of students to consider scientific fields for their careers.

Mathematics

In introducing *Curriculum and Evaluation Standards for School Mathematics* in 1989, the NCTM sought to prepare students to become mathematically literate. In establishing broad goals for K-12 education, the NCTM (1989, p. 5) states that students should

- Learn to value mathematics
- Become confident in their ability to do mathematics
- Become mathematical problem solvers
- Learn to communicate mathematically, and
- Learn to reason mathematically.

To the NCTM, the classroom is a setting where problems are explored and students use mathematical ideas to collect information, describe properties, and examine graphical representations. Students should do as well as know mathematics. In a sense, mathematics becomes a science rather than a drill-and-practice exercise.

The NCTM (1989, p. 1) summarizes the components of a high-quality mathematics education for K-12 students in the United States, emphasizing the development of "mathematical power" for all students, as follows:

> A curriculum is an operational plan for instruction that details what mathematics students need to know, how students are to achieve the identified curricular goals, what teachers are to do to help students develop their mathematical knowledge, and the context in which learning and teaching occur. . . . the term describes what many would label as the "intended curriculum" or the "plan for a curriculum."

Mathematics experts further recommend a basic shift from current practices toward an emphasis on deepening student understanding of mathematics and its applications, encouraging classroom discourse to promote the growth of mathematical ideas, and using technology and other tools to investigate mathematics. These changes would have the added benefit of using real-world mathematics problems, incorporating more visual materials into instruction, expanding laboratory activities, and emphasizing concepts underlying mathematics—all of which we have seen to be important for deaf students.

The *Curriculum and Evaluation Standards for School Mathematics* promotes mathematical reasoning, problem solving, communication, and connections. It is divided into categories of tasks, environment, discourse, and analysis. Both new and experienced teachers will benefit from the years of analysis that went into the formation of these standards. For example, under "environment" the NCTM presents issues associated with the intellectual, social, and physical characteristics of the learning context and how the context is not only the materials and space, but also the setting for embedding tasks and discourse. The NCTM does not believe that teaching can be reduced to prescriptions. The standards highlight issues important to creating an effective curriculum and good teaching practices.

Social Studies

Educators interested in developing a meaningful curriculum have as a resource the NCSS's *Expectations of Excellence: Curriculum Standards for Social Studies*, which include 10 thematic strands:

- Culture
- Time, continuity, and change

- People, places, and environment
- Individual development and identity
- Individuals, groups, and institutions
- Power, authority, and governance
- Production, distribution, and consumption
- Science, technology, and society
- Global connections, and
- Civic ideals and practices.

Within each thematic strand, applications are provided for the early grades, middle grades, and high school. These standards are intended for use by different audiences responsible for assuring the competence of social studies teaching professionals, including institutions of higher education and their teacher preparation units, state agencies that approve teacher education programs, state licensure (or certification) offices, and prospective social studies teachers.

The subject matter standards help guide social studies teachers in obtaining the knowledge and skills associated with the concepts and methods of inquiry in related disciplines. There are three types of subject matter standards: thematic standards, disciplinary standards, and programmatic standards for initial licensure. The thematic standards describe NCSS expectations of what students should know and be able to do. The disciplinary standards are based on documents that have been compiled by various expert groups that have identified what learners should know and be able to do as a result of instruction in subjects such as history, geography, civics and government, economics, and psychology.

Applying National Standards to Deaf Learners

National standards can be important resources for educators of deaf students. They were developed with careful consideration for all students, regardless of age, gender, cultural or ethnic background, or disability. As far as the authors of the standards were able, they recognized the fact that students achieve in different ways. In effect, the standards not only enable teachers to address issues related to competency in various subject areas, but they also assist them in enhancing their own knowledge of science, math, technology, social studies and relationships among them.

Specific suggestions in the national standards for addressing the needs of deaf learners are scarce. In a 1998 national study, mathematics reform in school programs serving deaf students in the United States was examined to determine whether educators are keeping up with the national standards (Pagliaro, 1998). (No similar study has been attempted recently in science and social studies.) Based on program and teacher questionnaires, the study found that some areas of reform, such as encouraging problem solving and using concrete materials, have been partially addressed. Despite the NCTM standards, however, the mathematics curriculum for deaf students remains largely traditional in terms of its emphasis on drill and practice and rote memorization, especially in the higher grades. Teaching strategies that encouraged more conceptual thinking among deaf students (e.g., justification of answers, integration of mathematics content across the curriculum) were used frequently by less than half of survey respondents (Pagliaro, 1998). Recommendations from the study for mathematics teachers included additional familiarization with the standards and commitment to continuous improvement of school programs, including the use of technology to expand instruction and enhance learning. These same broad recommendations would be appropriate for science and social studies educators as well.

Effective Teaching and Curriculum Development

Characteristics of Effective Teachers

Research indicates that deaf adolescents generally value the same characteristics in teachers as do hearing students. Both groups highly rate teachers who have extensive knowledge of course material, who use visual materials, who present materials in an organized manner, and who provide clear explanations. Like hearing students, deaf students also believe that it is important for teachers to be warm, friendly, and caring. Deaf students who use sign language have a preference for teachers who can communicate directly and clearly with them (Lang et al., 1993, 1994).

   With regard to their learning styles, deaf and hearing college students alike are dependent learners, meaning that they need teachers who provide structure and organization to the presentation of material, a characteristic which seems likely to generalize across other age groups. In addition, the more deaf students participate in classroom activities (as compared to passive reception of lectures), the better they appear to achieve academically in terms of course grades (Lang et al., 1998). Thus, regardless of the teaching strategies and curriculum materials teachers use, one important goal should be to encourage each student to participate in the class activities as much as possible. Findings like these suggest some general directions we should take, most noticeably avoiding traditional lectures and physically involving the students more.

General Classroom Strategies

Current research findings support many of the perspectives that teachers of deaf children develop through years of classroom experience. This is, in effect, *action research*—systematically experimenting with instructional techniques and modifying them according to how well they work. Such strategies can be followed up with formal research, allowing us to understand what it is that makes the strategies effective (and for whom), testing them for generality in other contexts, and disseminating them to other educators. In some cases, new discoveries relating to the education of deaf children have been around for decades but have been lost.

How might a teacher present a history lesson effectively to deaf children? One teacher's reflections, offered many years ago, exhibit several elements now known to be essential to good instruction (Adams, 1920, p. 555):

> Perhaps I have taught the deaf so long that I underestimate what the hearing can do; that is a common fault with us; but for the deaf I am pretty sure that fairly straight narratives of events, stories of great men and women taught as units, with lessons of patience, perseverance, faithfulness, personal bravery, and patriotism drawn from them—all lightened up by constant impromptu dramatization and copiously illustrated by pictures—pictures drawn by the pupils as well as furnished by the teacher— these, if based upon a carefully developed historical sense of time, will result in a better general knowledge of history by the time pupils reach the eighth grade than a much more ambitious course, covering much more ground and dealing too largely with the philosophical aspects of history.

Being aware of the attitudes of students can be a helpful adjunct to evaluating knowledge and skills. There are many nonverbal behaviors that may indicate motivation and enjoyment of learning, including attention and eye contact, note-taking, manipulation of objects, and leaning forward in their seats. One of the most important indicators is the student's willingness to interact with the teacher. . . . Knowing how students feel will help the teacher plan motivating lessons.

This particular teacher was focusing on elementary-level teaching, and thus she placed less emphasis on the philosophical dimensions of history one might include in later grades. Instead, she stressed the important ingredients of hands-on activities, visual media, participative learning, organization and structure, and working through the affective domain. She recognized the importance of bringing in human qualities and values and portraying historical figures in a context that distinguishes the relation between time was and time is.

Similarly, in 1926 a geography teacher published an article encouraging use of "the three I's"—initiative, intensity, and incentive—and writing-to-learn. In her early use of writing across the curriculum, the teacher suggested various activities associated with an imaginary trip through the southern and western states. The children first were asked to identify which states to visit. They were encouraged to develop an itinerary, and each child wrote a letter to a different city, seeking information. Pictures were collected from magazines and other sources, a diary of the trip was kept, and the children wrote short essays such as "The Change in Temperature Between Cincinnati and Richmond," and attempted to identify the natural resources and chief industries of various locales. As the teacher summarized, "Until some plan similar to the above is attempted, one cannot realize the vast amount of material that can be collected for use in the schoolroom, nor conceive of the wealth of imagination that is stored in the brain of the child" (Fisher, 1926, p. 347).

> "Tell me, and I will forget.
> Show me, and I will remember.
> Involve me, and I will understand."

An instructor's suggestions for teaching geography in 1901 provides another example, clearly appropriate in terms of the structure and organization needed for students with a highly dependent learning style: "The teacher cannot afford to roam at random in any part of the work. Each move on her part must be actuated by a purpose to be consummated at some future step. Hence the great necessity of the teacher's knowledge of what she means to cover in a given length of time as well as forethought of how it is best to be presented" (Smith, 1901, p. 397). This teacher went on to provide a clear sequence of steps for teaching young children geography, emphasizing relative distances (training the eye to quickly grasp positions and changes); directions (using experiential learning and compasses); and fundamentals of map reading (by relating the class work to the school, its campus, and surrounding town). From there she led the students to mental excursions across the state, bringing in other aspects of geography such as industry and commerce, relating to each child's family locale, and mapping rivers and mountain ranges. Expanding this concept, using a printed map, she helped the children map other states and surround them with an outline of the country. Canada and Mexico came next, and this continued across the globe, introducing dimensions of culture, imports and exports, and other concepts critical to the subject.

Such examples provide teachers today with a rich menu of fundamental teaching techniques that are consistent with contemporary national standards. Some of the tips from teachers are also strongly supported by the social constructivist approach to learning. Identifying a child's current thinking in regard to a topic, for example, is a basic element of a social constructivist approach to education. Through interaction with the teacher and peers in such activities, children may be led to develop new conceptions. "The study of history," wrote a teacher in 1892, "not only increases one's ability to entertain apparently conflicting ideas, but the ideas themselves which she presents, considered as food for the mind from which we may justly expect intellectual growth, are at least of equal value with the ideas offered by science" (Fletcher, 1892, p. 180). We might add that the metacognitive skills this educator described are critical to good reading and mathematical problem solving as well.[3]

Motivation and Self-Efficacy

In addition to the characteristics of teachers, another important factor in the instruction of deaf students is the affective attributes that students bring to the learning context. Motivation, interest, and a positive attitude may not be required for learning, but they are certainly helpful qualities. Similarly, *self-efficacy*, the ability to engage in a task and successfully complete it, can be reinforcing in itself, while contributing to *self-esteem* and a sense of *mastery* (Bandura, 1997).

There is a large body of literature on the attitudes of hearing students toward the subjects they are learning, but few studies have examined the attitudes of deaf learners. Years of working in different school environments have shown us that deaf students (and their teachers) have remarkably positive attitudes toward learning, despite all of the hurdles they have faced. As with most students, the teaching-learning process flows more smoothly when deaf students are interested in the subject area. In one investigation with more than 300 junior and senior high school students from nine school programs, more than 80 percent of deaf students reported enjoying studying science (Lang & Meath-Lang, 1985). The most common reasons offered for liking science, accounting for nearly 50 percent of the responses, related to students' personal interests in the science principles and concepts they were learning. The study indicated that students were motivated to learn; it is up to the teacher to find ways to take advantage of the context to maintain interest and enjoyment. As we have seen, hands-on experiences or laboratory work can be instrumental in this regard, and comments from students in all of the schools involved in the above study showed that they valued activities that involved scientific techniques such as observing, classifying, interpreting data, and so on.

If deaf students enjoy science, one wonders why so few of them go on to professional careers related to science. The answer to this question is complex and is at least partly due to a lack of information. Few educators, parents, and counselors are aware of the many significant contributions made by deaf people in the history of science, or the potential of many deaf role models in these fields today. *Silence of the Spheres: The Deaf*

Experience in the History of Science tells the success stories of hundreds of deaf men and women in fields of science, mathematics, engineering, and medicine, as well as the barriers they faced in acquiring education and employment (Lang, 1994). *Deaf Persons in the Arts and Sciences: A Biographical Dictionary* similarly presents biographies of deaf and hard-of-hearing people who have founded new fields of science, discovered scientific principles, chemical elements, stars and comets, received Nobel Prizes, and helped to develop the Internet (Lang & Meath-Lang, 1995). Many more deaf women and men chemists, biologists, mathematicians, engineers, medical doctors, dentists, and physicists are listed in the American Association for the Advancement of Science's *Resource Directory of Scientists and Engineers with Disabilities* (Stern & Summers, 1995). Many of the individuals included in these resource books were either born deaf or became deaf early in life and succeeded despite the challenges they may have had in overcoming lags in reading and writing skills.

> "To me I like to do something active, not just stand around and listen to something boring. I have to do something in action to keep me busy learn more. I like to do something with my hands and thinking how to get the right answer by doing the experiments. I like to find the answer why it appears like this, etc . . . it makes me to think more harder and want to get the right answer by myself."

Books about successful deaf people can foster positive self-esteem and motivation to learn in young deaf students. Increased awareness and the development of self-efficacy can also be found in the writings of students who have read the biographies of deaf scientists and done reports about them as classroom assignments. Yet, even with a proven track record of deaf men and women over the years, the percentage of deaf students pursuing science and math careers today is low in comparison to the proportion of their hearing peers entering these fields. This situation is complicated by the difficulty many deaf students have in developing English reading and writing skills, by shortages of qualified science and mathematics teachers, and by low expectations for deaf student performance by teachers and parents. When deaf students are successful in reaching post-secondary programs, they often face additional problems of gaining access to quality support services such as interpreting, notetaking, and tutoring (see chapter 7).

Social studies is another area in which "the deaf experience" can be used to motivate students' interest and make it personally relevant. Students are understandably more interested in history when they learn that

Thomas Jefferson's deaf great nephew taught at the New York School for the Deaf, that General George Armstrong Custer had learned sign language at the Texas School for the Deaf, or that the Civil War song of the Missouri Unionists, "Belle Missouri," was penned by the deaf poet Laura Redden Searing. In geography, such diverse locations as Deaf Smith County, Texas, and Glyndon, Minnesota, have been named for deaf people who made important contributions to their communities. Such tidbits can spark interest in history, geography, and other areas of social studies, motivate a deaf student to learn more, and build self-esteem.

According to the NCSS curriculum standards, it is expected that the social studies students be able to understand and apply to personal and public experiences the content they learn from several academic fields of the social studies. To accomplish this, the curriculum should emphasize authentic activities that call for using course content in day-to-day activities. The National Commission on Social Studies in the Schools, for example, argued that good teaching requires spontaneity, creativity, and the ability to respond to the "specialness" of each new classroom experience (NCSS, 1989, p. 49):

> Like the individual students themselves, each class has its own
> personality and might require a different approach to learning.
> The vitality and effectiveness of a course depends on what both
> students and teacher bring to the classroom. It is their ability to
> adjust and respond to what they find in the classroom that wins
> teachers the status of professionals as opposed to assembly line
> functionaries.

Teachers of the middle grades can assist learners in exploring and asking questions about the nature of culture, questions that reveal cultural universals as well as unique aspects of particular cultures in various places, times, and contexts. High school teachers can assist learners in increasing the breadth and depth of their comprehension and the ability to apply cultural concepts such as cultural assimilation, accommodation, and the impact of traditions on thought and action within social groups to new situations. They also can introduce new concepts such as the function and interactions of language, literature, and the arts in terms of traditions, beliefs, and values; and the transmitting of culture in the face of environmental, technical, and social change. Some scholars believe that for real change to happen for deaf people, educators need to redefine their roles in the classroom, examining assimilation, pluralism, and power relationships with their students, learning the relative degrees of membership in Deaf society, its lack of homogeneity, forces that pull multicultural deaf people in different directions, and a melange of related issues relevant to the social studies curriculum (Fischgrund & Akamatsu, 1993).

Social Constructivism and Learning

Throughout this book, we have emphasized two principles of constructivism as essential in effective instruction of deaf students: (1) learning as an act of construction, and (2) learning as a dialogical, two-way process. Much of the research cited thus far supports a theoretical perspective in which the learner has an active role in building understanding and creating meaning (see also Marschark & Lukomski, 2001). Applying these principles meaningfully and extensively, however, will require careful planning by educators in various school programs and collaborations among teachers, administrators, and researchers. Fostering the development of thinking skills and introducing students to the discipline and content being taught have to be balanced in ways that allow different learning strategies to interact and enhance each other.

Until the 1970s, the view of knowledge as a commodity to be transmitted from teacher to student dominated public school teaching in the United States. Students were expected to learn in a way that adhered to the notion of learner as a passive recipient of knowledge. Following the work in developmental psychology by Piaget and Vygotsky, many preschool and primary programs were modeled on their theories. Discovery learning and supporting the developing interests of the child were two primary instructional techniques, and parents and teachers were encouraged to use a variety of objects and toys to challenge a child's abilities without going too far beyond his or her level of "knowing." These approaches emphasized a continuous process of construction and reconstruction of knowledge, as children were encouraged to make hypotheses about the outcomes of activities or events and modify them, as necessary, if results were different than expected. In more recent, neo-Piagetian and neo-Vygotskyian approaches to education, the individual learner is viewed as constructing knowledge from personal experience, an active process that can be reinforced by instruction. Although constructivists have continued the active learning tradition begun by Piaget, they place less emphasis on the procession of developmental stages and more on the content of student thinking.

When learning and cognition are considered in the context of the society in which they occur, education is seen as involving a community-sharing process (hence, *social construction*). Knowledge is the sum of our direct and indirect experiences, which may vary widely among deaf children as well as between deaf and hearing children. Children are seen as problem solvers, and their learning as "active construction," applying knowledge to novel information and events. Educators interested in constructivism also have tapped the work of Jerome Bruner (1966, 1990), who argued that the questions that guide the discovery learning process should be relevant personally as well as societally, and David Ausubel (1968), who

"Straight Language Discusses Arithmetic" (Marie Kennard & Edith Fitzgerald, Georgia School for the Deaf, 1939)

"There are few ordinary mathematical principles that cannot be presented in the language of situations with which our children come in contact. These situations furnish material for problems that mean something to them. Such problems will be more enthusiastically faced than those dealing with situations they have not met—and which they may never meet."

focused on meaningful learning and how students relate new information to conceptual structures already established. ⌡

Active construction is a principle that can guide us in educating deaf children of all ages. In chapters 4 and 7, we discussed the importance of early intervention and how multisensory stimuli and constant interaction with parents were critical for both neurological and cognitive development. Although the rate of neural development is much faster in infancy and early childhood than in later years, the brain continues to develop, and it is never too late to provide a variety of stimuli. Planning more opportunities for critical thinking and reflection should be a high priority for teachers of deaf children in the elementary and middle-school years. We should also take a cue from educators in other countries such as Japan and Germany and increase time on task and make more efficient use of allotted classroom time.

Classrooms that encourage the active construction of knowledge allow deaf students to have a variety of personal, concrete experiences that assist in the construction of abstract concepts, categories, and inferences. Such an approach encourages students to adopt a flexible, curious approach to the world and promotes critical thinking. Activities involving problem solving, the manipulation of objects in play or in laboratories, concept mapping, and writing also encourage communication, especially when compared to passive, rote learning (see chapter 6).

Activity per se, however, should not be the exclusive focus of a teacher's approach. Although meaningful activity provides a context for leading the student to extract meaning, teachers need to learn how to focus on students' understanding and to question them about their thinking. Thus, a second important principle in viewing learning from a constructivist perspective is the *dialogical process*. In this process, the teacher learns what the student already knows and determines with the student how best to represent and communicate this knowledge (e.g., through writing, drawings, symbols, and interpersonal exchanges).

The dialogical process leads students to combine personal experiences with theory, especially through the collaboration of teachers and other students. Theory is assimilated as part of individualized acts of meaning construction. When a student is confronted with new knowledge in an environment based on active construction and the dialogical process, his or her intentions and previous experiences, preferred learning styles, and teaching strategies are all elements in determining what is done with the knowledge. Written conversations with a teacher and other students can promote inquiry and reflection. Written responses validate one's ideas and motivate further inquiry. When a student uses writing independently to develop ideas, the process is still dialogic, but it is now internal and personal (Albertini et al., 1994).

The social-constructivist view of literacy instruction—that it should be interactive, involve meaningful exchange, and involve authentic materials and purpose—parallels a theory of second language teaching called the natural approach (Krashen, 1981; see also Meath-Lang & Albertini, 1984; Meath-Lang et al., 1982). Because many deaf students are learning a signed language, a spoken language, and literacy skills simultaneously—while relying on reading and writing to learn English—literacy instruction has to be viewed in a more unified way than we have in the past. Within the social-constructivist framework, classroom activities are linked to reading, writing, and thought, and classroom dialogue is linked to internal dialogue, questioning, and reflection—all useful techniques for teaching academic subjects to deaf students which also contribute to their development of language fluencies.

The emphases of the social-constructivist framework are not new to our field. Rather, they have been reformulated in the context of modern theory. More than a century ago, educators of deaf students recognized the value of frequent writing experiences aimed at enhancing understanding of the world through meaningful exchanges with teachers and peers. In advocating that skill in writing comes from writing, one educator argued as follows (Pettengill, 1874, p. 237):

> In most of our school-rooms there are at least twenty large
> slates arranged around the room, in view of all the pupils of the
> class, and those slates for a large part of the day are not in use
> for the regular exercises of the class. Why should they not be
> continually employed by the teacher and pupils as a means of
> social communication by writing?

To date, however, literacy instruction for deaf students has dealt with writing on a very limited basis.

Throughout the history of formal instruction of deaf students, educators have become preoccupied with English literacy and the development of speech-language skills to such an extent that students usually have had to give up classroom time that should have been devoted to content area instruction. This monopolization of time, together with inadequate resources and the lack of qualified teachers, led to some schools having no courses at all in science and other content areas. In one study, for example, 21 percent of the schools surveyed were found to offer no elementary science classes to deaf children (Sunal & Burch, 1982). Such thinking fails to recognize the important fact that content courses can provide motivating contexts for learning language.

Today, the relationships among reading, writing, and content areas in science are being carefully studied by many educators; and claims that reading and writing in science inhibit students' creativity, curiosity, and interest have been shown to be unfounded (Holliday, 1992). Some educators believe that authentic language uses and practices should be part of an interactive-constructive process. But one of the most challenging issues involved in explicit reading instruction and writing-to-learn activities is to "convince science teachers and professors who did not receive such instruction or experience that such activities are valuable and to be subtle and creative enough not to embarrass or alienate bright, successful science students" (Yore, 2000, p. 119).

We noted earlier that little is known about teaching deaf students through the use of interpreters and other support services in mainstream settings. It thus also is unclear whether deaf students in mainstream settings have appropriate classroom support for reading activities inside or outside of school. The reading interests of deaf children, however, appear to be at least as broad as those of hearing peers (Stoefen-Fisher, 1985). Given a choice of books, teachers should select those which will help the child better understand the environment. Reading is a wonderful way to foster interest in other subject areas, and children who read more become better readers. Encouraging teachers and parents to read regularly to and with deaf children implies that there is effective communication with the child (see chapter 8).

Because deaf students frequently perform better in areas with fewer linguistic demands, teachers may be led to the erroneous assumption that materials should be developed that minimize the need for English language skills or that deaf children should not be asked to write as much as their hearing peers. This conception can be harmful to student progress (not to mention self-esteem). Reading and writing are essential processes in western countries, and deaf children, like hearing children, need to master them. Instead of avoiding reading and writing assignments, teachers should develop curriculum materials that capitalize on the students' strengths and interests and progressively challenge the deaf students in terms of gaining and demonstrating fluency in English.

Activities of this sort can be conducted in virtually all content areas, from word problems in mathematics to writing historically based fictional stories. Creative stories also can be elicited in other domains. In one action research study involving 12 science teachers in middle and high schools, informal (not graded) writing activities were combined with hands-on, structured activities (Lang & Albertini, 2001). One teacher, for example, asked her students to write a paragraph titled "Chocolate Chip Cookie Adventure," to determine how well they had learned class material concerning the human digestive system. Another teacher used *guided-free writing* as follows: she asked her students to write down one sentence predicting what would happen when sealed cans of diet and regular Coca Cola™ were placed in a large beaker of water. After the demonstration, students wrote a brief summary describing what happened and why. Teachers in this study reported that such activities helped students develop English literacy skills over time, but they also provided the teachers with a means to evaluate student conceptions and misconceptions concerning class material on an ongoing basis.

Consider, for example, "Beauty Pink," written by a deaf eighth-grade student whose teacher participated in the above study. This student's writing reveals that she has a basic understanding of volcanoes, lava, temperature change, and mixed colors in an igneous rock sample. Although she did not use the term "igneous," she demonstrates in her writing how the heat from the volcano produced lava which solidified when cooled. Such writing assignments provides us with an opportunity to enhance both science and English literacy.

Informal writing is also an effective strategy for the social construction of meaning. In a follow-up dialogue with the author of "Beauty Pink," we might ask her whether it were really possible for the rock to travel in the air

---

"Beauty Pink," Written by a Deaf Eighth-grade Student

I live in Italy. then by name is beauty pink. the heat and hot thing keeps pressure me I don't like it! then the volcano eupt I poped out! I flew all over to other country and I land in California of Hollywood. then I was so hot so I land in a water finally I'm so cool not hot anymore! Whew! then I was flowing in a beach some cute guy found me he picked me up and brought me to a new home it was his place a guy Who named a [boy's name]. I was dull but later on for days [boy's name] took me to a rock store. asked the man to make me look beautiful now I look beautiful I'm color of pink, white, dark pink mixed together! So now I'm a beautiful crstayal now I'm so happy that [boy's name] found me and kept me forever!

from Italy to California. Along with checking for possible misconceptions, we also might suggest the insertion of more technical vocabulary such as "igneous." Regardless of the follow-up, it is important that the student not be discouraged with too many corrections of spelling and grammar.

Effective teachers shape the curriculum with national standards in mind (sometimes including state and local standards as well) and a thorough understanding of how to translate course content into meaningful, active learning. Recognizing that communication barriers and different backgrounds might influence the dialogical process, such teachers will modify instructional materials and content activities to optimize communication and student learning outcomes from the activity. Regardless of whether reading, writing, signing, or other forms of communication are used, a key focus in the dialogue is the student's understanding of their experiences and the context in which they occur.

It may seem difficult to emphasize written dialogue when working with deaf students who have poor reading and writing skills. This is, indeed, a challenge that can be addressed through professional development. Many teachers simply do not know how to have meaningful dialogue with a deaf student using written materials. Deaf students often will not have much experience with such interactions either; writing may be seen as a laborious process done only when necessary for a grade (but see Albertini & Shannon, 1996). Viewing literacy and learning at large as social processes, with language development as a critical but unobtrusive component, may be part of the solution to the challenges of developing literacy in deaf learners.

When an instructional environment includes the appropriate resources, every effort should be made to apply them in the active, dialogical learning process taking place in the classroom. If these communicative resources are not available, teachers need to recognize the impact this may have on the deaf child's construction of knowledge. Without effective communication, learning will suffer, and teachers, parents, and other professionals involved in the child's educational program will need to explore alternatives. In every way possible, teachers should encourage the deaf child's interaction with the world. Whether through English, American Sign Language, or English-based signing (depending on the child's most effective mode of communication) it is essential that students and teachers carry out meaningful dialogue about these interactions.

Technology in the Teaching-Learning Process

Another important consideration in planning classroom activities involving deaf students is the use of instructional technology. As we teach in the twenty-first century, our educational tools are a far cry from the chalk and slates of our grandparents. For that matter, they seem equally distant from the fat pencils, slide rules, and filmstrips that the three authors of this book remember.

Schools in the United States and in other countries are making substantial investments in computer technology for Internet access and are moving forward with classroom activities and interactive, collaborative academic projects that utilize the Internet. Although there is not yet substantive scientific evidence in support of the assumption that student learning is enhanced by these resources, there is no doubt that these technologies have provided new opportunities for accessing information and have brought more resources into classrooms (Owston, 1997). The graphics and animation capabilities of computers, multimedia presentations, and the World Wide Web provide the opportunity to develop educational materials especially oriented toward the visuospatial strengths of deaf students. At present, however, these are heavily text dependent, placing even greater demands on the reading skills of deaf students who may be unable to access available information.

Computers and related technology offer opportunities for us to transform the education of students who are deaf and hard of hearing and, along with captioning, may help to rectify the long-standing reading difficulties of deaf children. A successful technological revolution for deaf people in computers thus may be within our grasp. Caution must be taken, however, to avoid repeating history. Invention of the telephone and talking movies, hailed as important achievements for hearing people, immediately excluded deaf people. At this time, it is important that teachers, parents, researchers, and manufacturers/developers work together to ensure that future technologies will be accessible to students who are deaf and those with other disabilities (e.g., captioning on CD-ROMs and teleconferencing). Such technologies do not have to be designed specifically with deaf individuals in mind, but they do have to be produced in ways that ensure the possibility of either flexible manufacture or inexpensive post-manufacture modification.

We know, for example, that when captions are adjusted to the linguistic level and reading rate of deaf viewers, the amount of information obtained increases significantly (Boyd &Vader, 1972; Hertzog et al., 1989). Adjusting the language level of captions has its own difficulties, however, as slower rates of captioning necessitate either simplification or reduction in the amount of information communicated. Clearly, these variables are related. The optimum captioning rate suggested for children's television is 60 words per minute, but the average rate on available programming is often more than 140 words per minute, with speeds greater than 200 words per minute in programming for adults and greater than 120 words per minute in programming for children (Baker, 1985; Jensema et al., 1996). Varying captioning speed (at least within the range of 60 to 120 words per minute) does not always affect comprehension, but the language level of the captions usually does. Further, recent findings indicate that comprehension of captions is higher for hearing than for deaf students, even when reading ability is controlled (Braverman & Hertzog, 1980; Jelinek Lewis & Jackson, 2001). These findings could indicate the influence of background knowledge on comprehension or the fact that deaf students have to divide their attention between two sources of visual information in such situations. In any case, the needs of deaf students (and others) should be considered in producing audiovisual materials or when selecting them for the classroom.[4]

Although these technologies have increased the quantity of reading among deaf learners, the implications for comprehension and broader literacy skills are not yet clear. Deaf students may be overwhelmed by the volume of text found on the Internet and skip over many resources in favor of simpler materials. They might find it difficult to process closed captioning as fast as it is projected on the screen, especially when verbatim roll-up captioning is used. Further, in the case of both real-time captioning and TTYs, language production frequently is elliptical and truncated, presenting the language learner with considerable inconsistency (and poor models). This is not to say that these technologies will not facilitate literacy, only that the issues are complex, and further investigation is needed to understand their interaction with literacy skills.

Early studies with computer-assisted mathematics instruction have shown that deaf students can achieve gains in mathematics computation. But, again, the performance of deaf students is affected by the demand on verbal ability (Suppes, 1974). Such gains may not necessarily have been a result of the technology as much as the increased time on task, for example, by freeing students and teachers from tedious computational tasks and repetitive numerical and geometric manipulations (Cooney & Hirsch, 1990). Technologies can help teachers plan additional time to foster problem solving and problem posing, which will promote the metacognitive skills so valuable to reading comprehension and critical thinking.

The World Wide Web now offers a gateway to countless sources of information. The challenge for the student is to avoid distractions and extraneous material while evaluating the quality of the resources that are so readily available. The Web provides a rich opportunity to learn new skills and knowledge in the comfort of one's own home, to network with others, and to take advantage of multimedia aids to enhance reading comprehension. Educators interested in examining the issues presented in this chapter in greater detail or identifying specific strategies, materials, or opportunities for networking and skills development can consult World Wide Web sites devoted to the content and teaching strategies for science, math, and social studies instructors. Grant projects and web sites come and go, and the specific web site addresses change over time. Casting a broad net on the World Wide Web, searching for "deaf" and "science," "mathematics," or "social studies" will turn up some valuable resources. Surfing for information on specific topics, such as crossing "Pythagorean theorem" and "lesson," will yield numerous ideas for teachers preparing a hands-on activity for a geometry class. Some sites include "frequently asked questions" (FAQs), lesson plans teachers have found successful with deaf learners and are willing to share with others, hotlines for requesting assistance or information, and samples of student writing. Many school programs serving deaf students also have Web pages summarizing their school science or math projects.

The value of the Internet lies in its user. The computer environment offers equal and sometimes greater control and flexibility to young children compared to a library or other resources (Clements et al., 1993). Computer-based telecommunications through the Internet and online services afford a tremendous potential for social studies classrooms now and in the future for students to become active learners. By providing this hands-on classroom experience with technology, students gain skills and knowledge necessary for personal, professional, and civic productivity. Using the Internet stimulates curiosity and eagerness to learn through immediate availability to infinite resources. The Internet also provides unique opportunities for teachers and educators to collaborate and learn from one another. Teachers can use the Internet to find resources for a thematic unit, explore the possibilities for Internet resources of lesson plans, primary sources, virtual field trips, documents, and data collection. Internet materials and activities can be integrated into classroom activities, encouraging students to expand the breadth and depth of their knowledge.

The use of technology thus should be viewed not as an end in itself, but as a means for helping deaf students become aware of their own ideas and to engage in activities that will lead them to search for answers, make connections, see patterns, and become independent learners.

The Dilemma in Teacher Education

As we have seen, research evidence clearly supports activity-based learning throughout life. So why do we continue to use the traditional lecture approach as a primary method of instruction? One reason concerns the depth and breadth of teachers' content knowledge. Teachers are often asked to teach outside of their primary area of expertise. In that situation, lecturing provides more control over the material and makes class preparation more manageable, in contrast to activity-based learning, which requires teachers to be continuously ready to answer questions on almost any relevant topic. Lecturing also makes classes more predictable, allowing the teacher who is not fully comfortable with material to direct questions toward the students and ensure that most important topics are covered.

Another reason that active learning emphases frequently are not incorporated into learning activities is that effective strategies and rationales for their use often have not been well represented in teacher preparation or professional development programs. Many teachers are expected to teach multiple subjects, making it difficult to find time to prepare both activities and materials. Because they only have a part-time commitment to a particular content area, those teachers tend to participate in professional meetings of educators of deaf students rather than meetings involving science teachers, math teachers, or history teachers. In addition, many schools do not have the necessary budgets for equipment, materials, and supplies to support active learning strategies. Although common, inexpensive materials often can be helpful in teaching content subjects more effectively, appropriate resource books and in-service training about the usefulness of such resources are rare.

Summary

This chapter has provided an overview of some important issues in teaching science, mathematics, and social studies to deaf students. We began by reiterating some characteristics of deaf learners that were discussed in earlier chapters such as the need for diverse, hands-on experiences; lesser familiarity with multiple meanings of words; and the challenge of balancing multiple, visual inputs. We emphasized the importance of active learning and effective dialogue as priorities for enhancing academic competencies among deaf learners, while suggesting that didactic lectures and traditional paper-and-pencil instruction should be replaced by strategies that encourage interaction and critical thinking. The more teachers of deaf students promote such interactions with appropriate curriculum materials, the better they will be able to deal with the wide range of abilities and communication needs they encounter in the classroom.

The extent to which instruction is effective will depend on various factors, chief among them the ease of communication between the deaf student and teacher. Linguistically and culturally, even with the best of interpreters, dialogue and active learning will be most effective when teachers understand deaf students and when students feel accepted in the classroom. In studies of the perceived characteristics of effective teachers, deaf adolescents valued the same characteristics that hearing students do, especially knowledge of course content. But it is no surprise that these studies reveal several unique teacher characteristics desired by deaf learners. One is the ability to communicate clearly (in sign language, for signing deaf students, for example); the other is the ability to understand deaf people, deafness, and its impact on learning.

Many resources are available to teachers searching for assistance. Published materials and the Internet provide strategies, methods, research findings, and support for preservice and in-service teacher preparation programs as well as for the individual teacher in search of excellence. The regional and national conventions of organizations such as the National Science Teachers Association, the National Council of Teachers of Mathematics, and the National Council for the Social Studies offer workshops, presentations, and the most current materials for effective teaching. The periodicals published by these organizations also include practical ideas for enhancing instruction, and teachers of deaf students have disseminated some excellent reports on innovative curriculum efforts (e.g., Laporta-Hupper et al., 2000). The curriculum and teaching standards available outline what students need to know, understand, and be able to do at different grade levels. The standards are usually organized for teaching, professional development, assessment, and content. They are both challenging and attainable and embody excellence and equity, applying to all students.

But we cannot expect students to achieve high levels of performance without effective educational practices. Teachers need to be supported with professional development programs, adequate classroom and preparation time, availability of learning materials, and information specifically regarding the needs and strengths of deaf students. Many of the strategies and techniques that have been shown to be effective in teaching deaf students are of general utility and would improve the academic environments of hearing students as well. Involving students in the *contextualization* of learning, both in terms of integrating material and understanding the social-cultural bases of knowledge, will help teachers move away from traditional methods of teaching deaf students that have often focused on the concrete and the literal. The social-constructivist approach to education described here encourages active participation of deaf students in the academic enterprise, supporting their personal and social development as well as the acquisition of content knowledge and skills.

The discussions of national standards for academic programming, curriculum reform, and the role of technology in the classroom should not be seen as unrelated topics. Throughout this book, we have seen that learning is best viewed from the perspective of the child as an active participant in a complex social mosaic. Adults, peers, and physical characteristics of learning environments all combine with children's backgrounds and early experiences to make learning attractive and enjoyable. Language serves as the essential underpinning throughout, and early access to interpersonal communication supports the acquisition of learning strategies and their eventual application to curricular and extracurricular school activities.

Research in a variety of areas has contributed to our understanding of the teaching-learning process and can enhance matching educational methods with the needs of deaf learners. Both educational research and basic research concerning language, cognition, and social processes help give us a better understanding of the foundations of learning and attributes that deaf and hearing students bring to the learning context. Educators are constantly experimenting, elaborating and extending what works, and modifying or abandoning what does not. Our challenge for the future is to bring together formal investigations with research *in situ*, making the best use of all available information to optimize the educational opportunities for deaf students.

PART III

Conclusion

What are the implications of research for parents, teachers, and others involved in educating deaf students?

What have we learned about teaching deaf students in inclusive environments?

10

TEN

Looking Ahead While Glancing Back

In the preceding chapters, we have seen that a remarkable amount of progress has been made over the past 30 years toward understanding the impact of deafness on learning and development. Bringing together educational and research findings from diverse disciplines, we have endeavored to explain the current state of the art with regard to raising and educating deaf children, as well as some historical bases for contemporary approaches to deaf education. In describing research relating to educational foundations and teaching-learning processes, we have seen that providing parents with balanced and accurate information, continued research efforts, and professional development for teachers are vital parts of the educational futures of deaf students.

At the end of each chapter, we have summarized significant findings and developments. Rather than attempting to provide an additional summary here, we reiterate some of the general themes of this book and the major implications for parents, teachers, and others involved in educating deaf students.

Educational Foundations

Probably the most general and salient theme of this book is that the deaf learner should not be viewed as a hearing learner who cannot hear. It is often tempting, for reasons of either perceived equity or for expedience in the classroom, to assume that deaf and hearing children are the same. As we have seen, deaf and hearing children have different backgrounds, experiences, communication histories, and knowledge. To optimize the educational opportunities of deaf learners, we need to develop instructional materials, teaching strategies, and learning environments that take advantage of their strengths while compensating for their special needs. This means that treating deaf children the same as hearing children may be doing them a great disservice. At a minimum, we should resist superficial modifications to educational settings so that deaf children can share classrooms with hearing children when the fundamental needs of all involved have not been considered.

A recurring finding across language, social, and academic domains is that early intervention for deaf children and their families is critical. Such programs do more than just support the development of communication and language—they provide deaf children with similar peers, role models, and contexts that promote early development. Early intervention programs also offer parents support that can help them understand the needs of their deaf children in order to make informed decisions about issues that will influence their children's futures. The more we work toward improving such programs, the greater the likelihood that deaf students will begin schooling on an even footing with hearing peers.

We have emphasized repeatedly our belief that the education and development of deaf children can be enhanced if parents and educators provide them with early access to language, a rich environment of meaningful social interactions, and a wide diversity of person-oriented experiences (Marschark, 2000). Throughout history, parents have played critical roles as advocates in their children's education, and the new millennium, as well as recent federal legislation, provide an exciting venue for building on this tradition. Having seen the progress parents have made in establishing new schools and innovative educational programs, calling for new educational policies, and collaborating with teachers and researchers, one cannot help but be impressed by their successes in raising their deaf children with so few resources available. The research reviewed here provides a strong argument in support of programs where parents and educators work together in planning rich home and school environments.

Deaf and Hearing Learners May Have Different Characteristics and Needs

In considering the variety of research related to educating deaf students and ensuring that they are ready for academic instruction, we found a variety of gaps in the existing literature relating to both basic research and, especially, applied research. For us, this book became a guide to our research agenda as well as our approach to teaching.[1] We have seen, for example, the ways in which visual materials, technology, and alternative teaching techniques seem likely to contribute to providing deaf learners with better access to information in the classroom. At the same time, we have been disappointed by how many such assumptions have not been evaluated empirically. Deafness influences many aspects of learning, and it behooves both teachers and researchers to go that extra critical step in learning more about the best ways to match the classroom to the student.

One of the authors, who is profoundly deaf, was reminded of this formidable challenge through a personal experience while writing this book. Together with the other two (hearing) authors, he was enrolled in a two-day workshop to learn how to use a new statistical software package. Superficially, the learning context seemed ideal: The lecturer from the software company was a sensitive individual who went to great lengths to ensure full access by deaf individuals participating in the workshop. He had a high-quality projection of his own computer display on a large screen behind him, and each participant had their own, high-quality computer for hands-on activities throughout the course. The sign language interpreters were the best that could be found, all experienced in interpreting under such conditions. The two deaf participants had strong backgrounds in the use of computers, research, and statistics. Yet, both quickly became lost in the workshop, viewing the two days as a waste of their time. What went wrong?

Whether or not educators or parents accept deafness as a cultural phenomenon, viewing deafness as a disability tends to stigmatize and marginalize deaf children. The message we need to present to deaf children, their hearing peers, and their gatekeepers, should be that it is okay to be different.

Primarily, the problem was one of multiple, visual tasks placing too many demands on the processing of information in the learning situation. While the hearing participants were able to look at the computer screens on their desks and listen to the presenter, the deaf participants had to look away from the interpreter to see the instructor's screen or to try a procedure on their own computer. Missing one sentence of the instructions was enough to slow down or even derail learning. Watching the interpreter made it difficult to catch each action of the presenter on the terminal keyboard, as presented on the projected screen.

The author was later asked by the workshop planner for strategies to make the environment more inclusive. As a first step toward improving the participation of the deaf learners, a simple, no-cost procedure was suggested: Each person could be asked to place a pencil or other marker on top of the individual computer terminals, on the left side. When an instruction is given, each learner moves the marker to the right side when the task has been successfully completed. Once all of the markers have been moved, the next instruction can be given, and the markers moved back to the left side of the computer. In addition to keeping the instructor informed as to individual progress, this strategy encourages cooperative learning among the participants, as they notice who is lagging behind and assist one another when necessary.

Examples like this one show in a powerful way the need for educating teachers and continued research on adjusting learning contexts for the special needs of diverse students. We know of little research, however, that has been conducted on the issue of how to best accommodate the visual needs of deaf students in classrooms (although we suspect there is likely a considerable body of relevant research on human factors and military uses of computers). More generally, it shows the need for training educators and informing parents and others about the complex ways deafness influences learning.

Another message derived from this example is that high technology, extensive use of media, and quality support services are alone not sufficient to level the educational playing field. Technology can certainly help, but we do not yet have empirical evidence concerning the best ways to take advantage of computers in the classroom. We therefore continue to expend scarce resources on regular upgrades of instructional technology without any idea as to whether the expense is worthwhile.

Education Is Part of Life

Recognition that deaf learners have some distinctly different needs from hearing learners is critical for placing the uniqueness of deaf students in a positive and supportive context. This is true not only for classroom structure and management, but also with regard to the attitudes we bring to our interactions with deaf learners. Whether or not educators or parents accept deafness as a cultural phenomenon, viewing deafness as a disability tends to stigmatize and marginalize deaf children. The message we need to present to deaf children, their hearing peers, and their gatekeepers, should be that it is okay to be different.

While preparing this chapter, one of the authors had an opportunity to spend some time with a hard-of-hearing woman who was working on a doctoral dissertation related to educating deaf students. In describing her background, the woman explained that she had been raised entirely with spoken language and attended mainstream schools through college. Although her parents might have thought that her considerable residual hearing and excellent speech allowed her to fit in with other children, she told of an entire school career in which she was never really accepted by hearing peers. She never felt a part of the class or the playground and was always an outsider, the recipient of hurled rocks as well as taunts.

Thinking that things would be better if she socialized with deaf people, she began working on a master's degree in a program that primarily served deaf students. She learned to sign so that she could communicate effectively in the classroom, where American Sign Language was the language of instruction. Still, she was not accepted, but now it was because of her oral background and her unwillingness to give up hearing friends and her use of speech.

Is there some solution that was missed? Probably not. A more balanced bilingual–bicultural upbringing might have helped her to fit in better with deaf classmates, but she remarked that parents are fooling themselves if they think that children will be generally accepting of those who are different. Let's face facts: Most children tease those who are perceived as different and "less desirable" than they are and rarely accept those who are different into dominant social groups. Research concerning the integration of deaf children into mainstream classrooms (see chapter 7) fails to inspire great confidence for the social-emotional well-being of deaf children in such settings. This does not mean that mainstreaming cannot work. It means that we have to make some fundamental changes to the educational system (assuming that we cannot change human nature) if it is to serve deaf children and others with special needs.

Cognizant of this need, educators who are involved in developing national curricula and teaching standards have attempted to set an inclusive tone with emphases such as "science for all students" and "mathematics for all students." The national social studies standards speak to this need as well, emphasizing that each content area and class has its own personality in which the effectiveness of a course depends on what both students and teacher bring to the classroom.

In addition to such curriculum-based movements, philosophical and theoretical views such as social constructivism address the distinct differences learners bring to the classroom and the need to promote learning within the nexus of authentic activity and collaborative social interaction. Educational theorists, for example, have been exploring a process of *enculturation,* in which the activities of a domain are viewed as being framed by its culture (Brown et al., 1989). In this way, the meaning and purpose of learning activities are socially constructed and, it is hoped, made intrinsically motivating to all members of culture.

As educators and parents, we are responsible for understanding that the psychological and academic framework deaf children bring to a learning situation may indeed be different from that of hearing children. If authentic activities are defined as the ordinary practices of the culture, we must recognize that what is ordinary to a hearing child may not be ordinary a deaf child.

The implications of situated cognition are different from those of the "hydraulic" or information processing model popular since the 1960s, in which knowledge was viewed as a commodity to be transferred from teacher to student. Learning is instead viewed as a trajectory of increasing participation that needs to be constantly changing.[2] This view includes the deinstitutionalization of learning to encompass home and community experiences. It involves the incorporation of the children's life experiences and respect for differences in experiences. To incorporate children's viewpoints and experience into ongoing activities, parents and teachers must find ways to elicit their participation and attend carefully to their contributions.

Education Is a Many-Splendored Thing

Another theme that has emerged from our study of research and practice in educating deaf children is the need to consider the whole child. In recognizing diversity and flexibility in learning styles and adapting our styles accordingly, we need to tap each child's strengths by building upon what is known. Take, for example, a physical science class focusing on the Doppler effect. Nine out of ten textbooks begin a section on the Doppler effect with a sentence such as, "Everyone has heard the changing pitch of a fire truck passing by." Yet, "pitch" is as foreign to a deaf learner who has never heard sounds as "mauve" is to a blind learner who has never seen colors. Although the physical concept "frequency" can be taught both visually and tactually (for example, by plucking a plastic ruler on the edge of a table top with different lengths of the ruler allowed to vibrate), "pitch" as a psychological interpretation of "frequency" may be more difficult.

Research has shown that individuals who have been completely blind since birth report having visual imagery and, in most laboratory tasks, their imagery leads to the same kind of performance as it does in sighted individuals. Similarly, deaf students have an understanding of the loudness of things (e.g., a rocket versus a rock), such that their ratings of relative loudness correlate almost perfectly with those of hearing students, and they provide valid explanations for their ratings (Marschark, 1996). Certainly there are differences: Deaf students rate parrots and uncles, for example, as being considerably less loud than do hearing students; but they know where each fits on a "loudness continuum" with other things. Further, in laboratory tasks, their mental representation of sound information leads to the same kind of performance as it does in hearing individuals (perhaps giving some clue as to how deaf readers can assemble phonological codes; Leybaert, 1993).

Experience plays a critical role in understanding many concepts. What does "heavy metal music" mean to a deaf person who has never heard it? How is it different from jazz or rock and roll? Will that individual ever understand the meaning of these types of music as well as a hearing person does? If science is truly for all students, then the science teacher needs to find ways to relate new knowledge to each child's experiences as effectively as possible. The critical concept underlying the Doppler effect, for example, is the change of frequency (pitch) resulting from relative motion between the source of sound waves and the observer who receives them. Imagine standing in a pond where the source of waves causes regular ripples to pass your body. Counting the number of waves that pass your body in a given time is a measure of frequency. If the source of the waves moves toward you (or, if you move toward the source) and count the waves, the frequency will increase. Similarly, if you move away from the source (or the source moves away from you), there will be a decrease in observed frequency. This effect occurs even though the frequency of the source remains the same.

Using a visual example may not only help the deaf learner in the classroom, but also provide a multisensory (or *cross-modal*) learning experience for the whole class, including deaf and hearing students. These extra efforts made by teachers of children with disabilities have often been recognized as potentially enhancing the learning of all students. The teacher of a blind child who passes a rose around in order for the children to feel the texture of the petals and smell the flower introduces a multisensory experience that all students will appreciate. Similarly, providing sighted children with the opportunity to try to read Braille while blindfolded or providing hearing children with experience using a vibrotactile assistive listening device while wearing earplugs can be informative with regard to physics as well as interpersonal diversity.

Clearly, much more research is needed to help us deal effectively with the special learning needs of deaf children, and it is critical that we adopt a positive perspective that will develop self-efficacy, empowerment, and motivation to learn. Although the extent to which particular research findings can be utilized in educating deaf students is not yet clear, we now know that deaf and hearing learners are not strictly comparable in many respects. This means that expectations, interactions, and educational methods appropriate for hearing children may not generalize to deaf children, and it is in no way deprecating to say so.

The Twenty-first Century—What Does It Hold?

In many ways, the new millennium has provided the world with a psychological sense of new beginnings. In educating deaf children, as in the pursuit of health services and education for children worldwide, there is a renewed sense of vigor and dedication. Can we take advantage of this window of opportunity?

The educational scenarios we have presented throughout this book reinforce the critical need for information sharing and professional development opportunities for teachers and parents. The more we know, the better we will be in our roles in raising and educating deaf children. We cannot take a superficial view of mainstreaming or separate school programs and assume learning will be optimized by placement alone. Nor can we expect that technology will be a panacea. There is a paramount need to have well-informed and well-trained educators as well as the resources necessary to provide deaf children with fair and appropriate public educations. Sensitive also to the need to avoid generalities without providing either justification or guidance for implementation, we have tried throughout this book to draw specific conclusions from existing practices and predictions from research. To drive these points home, let us briefly reconsider some specific implications of our findings for educational practice and policy change that seem beyond debate and which could be implemented immediately.

Some Recommendations for Practice

Chronologically, one of the first important recommendations to be drawn from this book is better education for hearing parents concerning strategies to enhance communication with their deaf and hard-of-hearing children, regardless of whether they use spoken or sign language. Getting and maintaining attention, labeling and commenting on objects, and explaining events are essential components of early language, social, and cognitive development. Parents and teachers of deaf children need to learn to use effective visual communication techniques of the sort typically used by deaf parents. Parent training programs have been implemented in other countries, and several investigators and practitioners are seeking to do the same in the United States. Early results suggest that parents find these programs to be positive experiences and helpful for communication with their children, even if longer-term implications for development have not yet been determined.

Parents also should be advised concerning the importance of reading and writing with their young children and instructed on methods by which they can combine sign language with either a spoken language or alternative communication systems. Early reading and writing experience not only will directly facilitate language development and literacy in children with hearing loss, but it also should demonstrate the value placed on such skills by parents, thus increasing motivation and self-directed learning. At the same time, the blending of sign language, reading, and writing helps to communicate to all involved that we need to "do what works" and that usually means providing deaf children with the opportunity to use both signed and spoken language.

Beyond the use of reading and writing at home for pleasure and communication, these activities should be given high priority in the classroom. Programs in which stories have been presented in both sign language and spoken language, where young children all have copies of the same story book, and where parents share with their children stories first presented at school appear to have a positive impact on literacy and language growth. As we noted earlier, having children retell stories at home, collect or draw relevant pictures, and act out portions of the stories all help to establish links between the written word and meaning. Strategies used by deaf adults in reading to children should also be used by hearing teachers, even if deaf teachers and deaf teacher aides are available.

To foster thinking skills as well as language development and literacy, greater attention should be given to hands-on experiences, relations among concepts, and multiple meanings of words (including nonliteral meanings). All of these represent areas in which children with hearing loss appear to lag behind their hearing peers in terms of both expressive and receptive language. Visual aids should be used in establishing links between words and their superordinate and subordinate categories (animal, dog, collie), as well as coordinating relations among concepts. Problem solving, analogies, and dealing with ambiguity also deserve greater attention and can be integrated with activities in the preceding areas.

Finally, parents and teachers should take advantage of opportunities for interaction among children and diverse language models. Whether in school settings, social settings, or at home, interactions with language models whose communication is accessible, either other children or adults, will provide broad-based support for language and social growth. We have seen that, in general, adults make better language models than children, but peer influences increase through the school years, and it is essential to expose children to competent, accessible communicators who are valued (Nelson, 1973).

Some Recommendations for Policy Change

The research reviewed in the preceding chapters has several important implications for policymakers regarding the kinds of programs, staff, and resources that might be most effective in enhancing educational achievement in deaf children. Administrators and policymakers can have immediate and direct impact on the development and education of deaf children by supporting universal hearing screening for newborns and infants, early intervention programs for families with deaf or hard-of-hearing children, and establishing parent training programs in specific areas like those described above (e.g., early visual communication strategies, foundations of literacy). There is a need for greater numbers of deaf language models in the classroom, and such models should demonstrate bilingual fluencies. Hearing individuals in the classroom also need to demonstrate bilingual fluencies, and higher expectations for sign language skill can only enhance access to information in the classroom and language abilities of children with hearing loss.

With regard to research policy, several areas in which there is support (and pressure) for research have already been described. Teachers and researchers agree on the need to implement evaluation procedures for early intervention and bilingual education programs already in place, something already overdue. These groups are joined by educational administrators in advocating for more research concerning the potential impact of new technologies (and especially cochlear implants) (Marschark, 2001). Currently, there is a rush toward technology, with less attention devoted to evaluating its cost effectiveness and long-term impact on either literacy or academic achievement in particular content areas. Educational administrators are faced with implicit and explicit demands for newer and more sophisticated equipment, with increasing costs. Greater consideration needs to be given to which technologies offer benefits in which domains, ensuring that limited resources are not committed to high-profile hardware that offers little by way of increased educational efficacy. Only specifically directed research and comparisons with baseline (pre-technology) performance can provide such information.

Research also should be directed toward determining methods for improving access to language and the richness of language available to young deaf children to facilitate development as well as comprehension. Research on captioning and interpreting preferences of adults, for example, may be useful in their own right but will have little influence on the knowledge base in the area of language development. Research with older children and young adults can be informative with regard to their language processing strategies and variables affecting their comprehension of interpreting and text, but the sources of observed effects must then be traced backward, with younger children. Finally, longitudinal studies concerning the impact of exposure to different early interventions and alternative educational programs are essential, even if they are expensive.

The research and educational practices reviewed in this book offer one other important recommendation concerning who should be involved in decision making that affects the education of deaf children. Legally and morally, parents have the right to make decisions about educational programming for their children. Unfortunately, these decisions often are made with only limited access to pertinent information. Parents and children sometimes seem to be channeled into programming determined more by convenience and political expediency than individual and family needs. A broad range of alternative services is necessary to be able to provide optimal support for the heterogeneous needs of children with hearing loss. Understanding that school systems and other agencies are limited in their resources, care must be taken to ensure that those resources are well spent. Policymakers therefore need to establish some means of ensuring that parental involvement, utilization of resources, and children's needs are balanced without having the process collapse. Clearly, changes need to be made in this regard, but unfortunately, no research is available that offers enlightenment on how to go about it.

Moving Ahead

As we pursue improving the level of academic achievement of deaf learners, it is essential that we not only examine the characteristics of the child and the school program, but also our own attitudes. If we are serious about providing deaf children with all of the opportunities available to hearing children, we must accommodate schooling to meet their needs and perhaps adjust our own perceptions and priorities.

With regard to the contemporary education movement toward inclusive environments, our review of research on learning and development is conclusive: Deaf learners are different from hearing learners as a result of having had different experiences than their hearing peers. Such differences do not in any way make them less able than hearing learners, but they do add to the responsibility of those involved in educating deaf students. In some cases, the quality or mode of children's experience may have little discernible impact on the course or long-term outcomes of development. In other cases, specific interventions may be necessary to ensure that deaf children receive the kinds of experiences necessary for them to build on in other developmental and educational domains. The key is to be able to tell the difference.

Notes

Chapter 2

1. One very thorough analysis of the work of Augustine, Jerome, and the Venerable Bede is provided in King (1996). The writings of Augustine and Jerome have shed some light on how deaf people and communication through signs and gestures were perceived within Western society in the era of the Dark Ages. Unfortunately, Augustine has also been unfairly victimized by historians. In discussing a passage in the Bible by the apostle Paul, "Faith comes by hearing" (Romans 10:17), Augustine saw deafness as possibly hindering the development of faith, but he never directly spoke to the exclusion of deaf people from the church. As in the case of Aristotle, however, the writing of Augustine was misinterpreted and for a long time the view persisted that deaf people could not be taught the Christian faith.
2. Another popular text of this period was Gilbert the Englishman's *Compendium Medicinae* (about 1250), printed in 1510 in Lyons, which included a chapter on deafness.

Chapter 3

1. Some individuals describe themselves as "profoundly hard-of-hearing," meaning that they have severe to profound hearing losses but still function as hard-of-hearing people, relying fully on spoken communication.
2. Sound also can be carried through the bones of the body via bone conduction just as it can through solid materials outside of the body (remember Indians in old westerns putting their ear

to the ground to listen for oncoming horses?). Most fetuses thus are able to hear their mothers' but not fathers' voices during the last part of pregnancy, when their heads are resting on their mothers' pelvises (see chapter 4). To demonstrate bone conduction of sound for yourself (unless you are deaf), tap on your teeth with the soft end of a finger.

3. This discussion focuses on school-age deaf learners, not late-deafened and adults. For individuals in the latter group, implantation can be useful in showing quick gains in speech perception.

4. The primary goal of the law was to eliminate discrimination in education by preventing the exclusion of children with disabilities from programs in which they could favorably compete with non-disabled peers. The law was not clear, however, on the extent to which putting children into mainstream, public school environments was a requirement or only an option, and differences of interpretation still exist.

Chapter 4

1. While we are strong supporters of parents who involve themselves in their deaf (or hearing) children's educations, we believe that parents should not try to be teachers or turn their homes into schools-away-from-school (unless they are home-schooling their children). Situations can be structured in order to promote language and literacy in ways that emphasize enjoyment, discovery, and creativity. Focusing on sentence practice, object labeling, and speech skills, in contrast, should be left for formal school and therapy situations. Children need play time and they need their parents to act like parents.

2. Of course, human speech is not recognized as such from within the womb; it is merely a sound in the environment.

3. By mid-2001, more than 35 states had mandated universal newborn hearing screening, and the goal is to have such screening nationally as quickly as possible. This intervention will greatly reduce the frequency with which parents are unaware of their newborns' hearing losses.

4. To help parents and their deaf children establish mutually enjoyable, meaning-ful communication, Dr. Heather Mohay and her colleagues at Queensland University of Technology have assembled these strategies into a home-based tutorial. The goal of the program is to foster communication-based interactions regardless of the mode of communication used (e.g., spoken language, sign language), but as the following strategies indicate, they appear likely to have broader social and cognitive implications (see Mohay et al., 1998).

5. See Koester et al. 2000a for a comprehensive review of the effects of touch during parent-child interactions for both deaf and hearing children.

6. The sign LOOK-FOR, for example, is made with two C-hands, from the French *chercher*, and YEAR is made with two A-hands, from the French *annee*.

7. Saying that signs are arbitrary means that, like words, they bear no relation to the things they represent. A few words do sound like what they represent (*onomatopoetic* words like *gurgle* and *swish*) and a few signs look like what they represent (*iconic* signs like CAMERA or FISHING). Even these examples are arbitrary, however, in the sense that the speakers and signers of

different languages will choose other words and signs to represent similar concepts. The units of language acquire meanings by social agreement, and therefore they are different in each language.

8. Nonmanual markers in ASL such as eyebrow raising and head tilting indicate sentence structure (relative clauses) and pragmatic function (question type). See Marschark et al. (1998) and Metzger (1998) for examples.

9. *Contact sign* is the more general term when other languages are involved; see Lucas and Valli (1989).

10. Of course, for those who believe that the fundamentals of language are innate (e.g., Lillo-Martin, 1997), the age of 3 is simply when we see most of them expressed.

11. *Instrumental* support (or instrumental dependence) refers to obtaining help from others, rather than *emotional* support.

Chapter 5

1. Although it may be easier for children than adults to learn a second language, adolescents and adults also can reach high levels of proficiency in a second language (Lightbown & Spada, 1993).

2. Marschark and Everhart (1997) and others have argued that "carving up" the world in terms of the functional meaning is a basic (innate) information processing ability in infants. While there are arguments suggesting that language-related abilities have a separate, perhaps preeminent status, the issue has not been resolved and is irrelevant to the present discussion (see Marschark, Siple, Lillo-Martin, Campbell, & Everhart, 1997, for discussion).

3. Note that "verbal" is used throughout this book to refer to both signed and spoken language, where "vocal" is reserved for the latter.

4. It is frequently stated that only 20 percent of speech is visible on the lips. This estimate is based on speech sounds in isolation. With context, clear enunciation, and appropriate lighting, experienced adult speechreaders can do much better.

5. Overgeneralization of grammatical rules represent one source of evidence, along with the fact that children learn the various structures (patterns) of negation and question formation in predictable sequences. Further, children do not produce many possible errors, leading linguists to posit the existence of a universal grammar (e.g., Chomsky, 1986). Because children seem to know more about language than their experience could have possibly supplied, it is assumed that there must be a predisposition in the brain to guide acquisition and set parameters for what are acceptable and unacceptable utterances in the language, regardless of whether it is spoken or signed (see Emmorey, 2001, Lillo-Martin, 1997, for discussion).

6. See Gregory and Hindley (1996) and Marschark (1997), among others, who have emphasized the need for the availability of communication alternatives for young deaf children.

7. Note that all of the children had been implanted at an average of 5;6 years of age, already past the most critical years for language development, so no strong generalizations should be drawn from this study. The same data were

reported by Miyamoto et al. (1997), although citations by other investigators in the literature might suggest that these are two independent confirmations of the value of cochlear implants.

8. Note that the hearing aid group in this study was composed of implant candidates, 12 of whom served in both hearing aid and implant groups.

9. Children with implants produced an average of 23 percent of the words with voice only and 6 percent of the words with sign only. Children with hearing aids, in contrast, produced 5 percent of the words with voice only and 23 percent of their words with sign only.

Chapter 6

1. Capirci et al. (1998) have also demonstrated that the acquisition of sign language can improve the cognitive performance of hearing children.

2. Because language is normally localized in the left hemisphere and visuospatial abilities are located in the right hemisphere (at least for right-handers), one might wonder what happens when language is visual-spatial, as in sign language. The observed differences in *hemispheric specialization* of deaf individuals is not at issue here, and readers are referred to Neville et al. (1997) for a review. In general, greater left-hemisphere specialization for language is linked to better speech abilities in deaf children and better language skills, in general, for hearing children (Gottlieb et al. 1964; Tomlinson-Keasey et al. 1978). It is still unclear however, whether there are other academic implications of deaf children's having relatively less hemispheric dominance than hearing peers or whether such differences are overshadowed by behavioral and experiential factors.

3. Caution should be taken not to introduce too many novel situations. Positive responses to novelty follow the "inverted U function" shown in figure 6.1, and too much novelty can be frightening or frustrating to young children.

Chapter 7

1. This school-related advantage in motor development was seen in skills like catching and kicking, on which the children had practice, but not general locomotor skills.

2. The remaining students were schooled at home or in "other" programs. In addition, 10 percent of the mainstream students were reported to receive part of their education in resource rooms.

Chapter 8

1. In this chapter, as throughout the book, "English" is used generically to refer to any spoken/written national language. Specific examples may be more or less appropriate across languages (gender-specific articles, flexibility of subject–verb–object ordering, etc.), but it is assumed that the principles of

literacy and its acquisition are the same. American Sign Language also is used generically to refer to all natural sign languages.

2. Wilbur (1977) and others have found deaf students using fewer devices to signal cohesion (see also Maxwell & Falick 1992). Marschark, Mouradian and Halas (1994), in contrast, found deaf and hearing students equally competent in their use of cohesive discourse structures in written and signed/spoken stories.

3. See also Stuckless and Marks's (1966) national study of 1,350 compositions written by deaf students attending residential schools.

Chapter 9

1. Examples of alphabet curricula include Science Curriculum Improvement Study (SCIS), Science: A Process Approach (SAPA), Elementary Science Study (ESS), Biological Sciences Curriculum Study (BSCS), and CHEMStudy.

2. Some parents and teachers continue to resist the use of calculators in school, arguing that children should learn how to do arithmetic by hand before using calculators.

3. Similar, contemporary references to effective practices by teachers of deaf students can be found in periodicals for professionals in deaf education.

4. It is frequently suggested that captioning would have a positive impact on language development and literacy in young deaf children, but that assumption still is in need of empirical evaluation.

Chapter 10

1. See Marschark (2001a) for consideration of a research agenda suggested by teachers, researchers, and educational administrators serving deaf children.

2. See Marschark (2000) for discussion of the hydraulic model and others with regard to deaf children.

References

Ackerman, J., Kyle, J., Woll, B., & Ezra, M. (1990). Lexical acquisition in sign and speech: Evidence from a longitudinal study of infants in deaf families. In C. Lucas (Ed.), *Sign language research: Theoretical issues* (pp. 337–345). Washington, DC: Gallaudet University Press.

Acredolo, L., & Goodwyn, S. (1988). Symbolic gesturing in normal infants. *Child Development, 59,* 450–466.

Adams, M. E. (1920). In reaction to J. Schuyler Long's paper "The Teaching of History." *Volta Review, 22,* 550–557.

Adelman, C. (1999). Answers in the tool box: Academic intensity, attendance patterns, and bachelor's degree attainment. Washington DC: U.S. Department of Education. (Publication PLLI 1999–8021.)

Ainsworth, M. D. (1973). The development of infant-mother attachment. In B.M. Caldwell and H.N. Ricciuti (Eds.), *Review of Child Development Research* (pp. 1–94). Chicago: University of Chicago Press.

Akamatsu, C. T., Musselman, C., & Zweibel, A. (2000). Nature vs. nurture in the development of cognition in deaf people. In P. Spencer, C. Erting, & M. Marschark (Eds.), *Development in context: The deaf child in the family and at school* (pp. 255–274). Mahwah, NJ: Lawrence Erlbaum Associates.

Albertini, J. (1990). Coherence in deaf students' writing. In J. Peyton, (Ed.), *Students and teachers writing together: Perspectives on journal writing* (pp. 127–136). Alexandria, VA: Teachers of English to Speakers of Other Languages.

Albertini, J. (1993). Critical literacy, whole language, and the teaching of writing to deaf students: Who should dictate to whom? *TESOL Quarterly, 27,* 59–73.

Albertini, J., Meath-Lang, B., & Harris, D. (1994). Voice as muse, message, and medium: The views of deaf college students. In K. Yancey (Ed.), *Voices on voice: Perspectives, definitions, inquiry* (pp. 172–190). Urbana, IL: National Council of Teachers of English.

Albertini, J., & Samar, V. (1983). Early instruction of object complements to hearing-impaired college students. *Applied Psycholinguistics, 4,* 345–357.

Albertini, J., & Shannon, N. (1996). Kitchen notes, "the Grapevine," and other writing in childhood. *Journal of Deaf Studies and Deaf Education, 1,* 64–74.

Als, H., Lester, B. M., & Brazelton, T. B. (1979). Dynamics of the behavioral organization of the premature infant: A theoretical perspective. In T. M. Field, A. M. Sostek, S. Goldberg, & H. H. Shuman (Eds.), *Infants born at risk* (pp. 173–192). New York: Spectrum Press.

American Annals of the Deaf (1870), *15,* 189. Deaf-mutes in the time of Queen Elizabeth.

American Association for the Advancement of Science. (1993). *Benchmarks for science literacy.* Washington, DC: National Academy Press.

American Association for the Advancement of Science. (1997). *Resources for science literacy.* New York: Oxford University Press.

American Association for the Advancement of Science. (1997). *Science for all Americans.* New York: Oxford University Press.

Andrews, J. F., Winograd, P., & DeVille, G. (1994). Deaf children reading fables: Using ASL summaries to improve reading comprehension. *American Annals of the Deaf, 139,* 378–386.

Antia, S. (1982). Social interaction of partially mainstreamed hearing-impaired children. *American Annals of the Deaf, 127,* 18–25.

Armstrong, D. F., Stokoe, W. C., & Wilcox, S. E. (1995). *Gesture and the nature of language.* New York: Cambridge University Press.

The Association Review (1900), *5,* 527–533. Discovery of an early instance of instruction of a deaf-mute in America.

Ausubel, D. (1968). *Educational psychology: A cognitive view.* New York: Holt, Rinehart, and Winston.

Baddeley, A. (1986). *Working memory.* Oxford: Clarendon Press.

Baker, R. (1985). Subtitling television for deaf children. *Media in Education Research Series, 3,* 1–46.

Ballmann, R.E. (1995). *The how and why of home schooling.* Wheaton, IL: Crossway Books.

Bandura, A. (1997). *Self-efficacy: The exercise of control.* New York: W.H. Freeman and Company.

Banks, J., Gray, C., & Fyfe, R. (1990). The written recall of printed stories by severely deaf children. *British Journal of Educational Psychology, 60,* 192–206.

Bates, E., Thal, D., Whitesell, K., Fenson, L., & Oakes, L. (1989). Integrating language and gesture in infancy. *Developmental Psychology, 25,* 1004–1019.

Bateson, M. C. (1975). Mother-infant exchanges: The epigenesis of conversational interaction. In D. Aaronson & R. W. Rieber (Eds.), *Developmental psycholinguistics and communication disorders* (pp. 101–113). New York: New York Academy of Sciences.

Battacchi, M. W. & Montanini-Manfredi, M. (1986). Recent research trends in Italy: Cognitive and communicative development of deaf children. *Sign Language Studies, 52,* 201–218.

Bebko, J. M., & McKinnon, E. E. (1990). The language experience of deaf children: Its relation to spontaneous rehearsal in a memory task. *Child Development, 61,* 1744–1752.

Bebko, J. M., & McKinnon, E. E. (1998). Assessing pragmatic language skills in deaf children: The Language Proficiency Profile. In M. Marschark & M. D. Clark (Eds.), *Psychological perspectives on deafness, Volume 2* (pp. 243–263). Mahwah, NJ: Lawrence Erlbaum Associates.

Bebko, J. M., & Metcalfe-Haggert, A. (1997). Deafness, language skills, and rehearsal: A model for the development of a memory strategy. *Journal of Deaf Studies and Deaf Education, 2,* 131–139.

Belanoff, P. & Dickson, M. (Eds.)(1991). *Portfolios: Process and product.* Portsmouth, NH: Boynton/Cook.

Bell, S. M., & Ainsworth, M. D. (1972). Infant crying and maternal responsiveness. *Child Development, 43,* 1171–1190.

Bellugi, U., Klima, E., & Siple, P. (1975). Remembering in sign. *Cognition, 3,* 93–125.

Berent, G. P., Samar, V. J., Kelly, R. R., Berent, K., Bochner, J., Albertini, J., & Sacken, J. (1996). Validity of direct assessment of writing competency for deaf and hard-of-hearing college students. *Journal of Deaf Studies and Deaf Education, 1,* 167–178.

Best, H. (1943). *Deafness and the deaf in the United States.* New York: Macmillan.

Bettger, J. G., Emmorey, K., McCullough, S. H., & Bellugi, U. (1997). Enhanced facial discrimination: Effects of experience with American Sign Language. *Journal of Deaf Studies and Deaf Education, 2,* 223–233.

Bézagu-Deluy, M. (1993). Personalities in the world of deaf mutes in 18th century Paris. In R. Fischer & H. Lane (Eds.), *Looking back: A reader on the history of deaf communities and their sign languages.* Hamburg: SIGNUM Press.

Blackwell, P., Engen, E., Fischgrund, J., & Zarcadoolas, C. (1978). *Sentences and other systems: A language and learning curriculum for hearing-impaired children.* Washington, DC: National Association of the Deaf.

Bloom, A. (1987). *The closing of the American mind: How higher education has failed democracy and impoverished the souls of today's students.* New York: Simon & Schuster.

Boatner, M. T. (1959). *Voice of the deaf: A biography of Edward Miner Gallaudet.* Washington, DC: Public Affairs Press.

Bonvillian, J. D. (1983). Effects of signability and imagery on word recall of deaf and hearing students. *Perceptual and Motor Skills, 56,* 775–791.

Bowe, F. (1998). Language development in deaf children. *Journal of Deaf Studies and Deaf Education, 3,* 73–77.

Boyd, E., & George, K. (1973). The effect of science inquiry on the abstract categorization behavior of deaf children. *Journal of Research in Science Teaching, 10,* 91–99.

Boyd, J., & Vader, E. A. (1972). Captioned television for the deaf. *American Annals of the Deaf, 117,* 34–37.

Boyes-Braem, P. (1990). Acquisition of the handshape in American Sign Language: A preliminary analysis. In V. Volterra and C. J. Erting (Eds.), *From gesture to language in hearing and deaf children* (pp. 107–127). Berlin: Springer-Verlag.

Braden, J. P. (1994). *Deafness, deprivation, and IQ.* New York: Plenum Press.

Braden, J. (2001). The clinical assessment of deaf people's cognitive abilities. In M. D. Clark, M. Marschark, & M. Karchmer (Eds.), *Context, cognition, and deafness* (pp. 14–37). Washington, DC: Gallaudet University Press.

Brasel, K., & Quigley, S. P. (1977). Influence of certain language and communicative environments in early childhood on the development of language in deaf individuals. *Journal of Speech and Hearing Research, 20,* 95–107.

Brazelton, T. B. (1982). Joint regulation of neonate-parent behavior. In E. Z. Tronick (Ed.), *Social interchange in infancy* (pp. 7–22). Baltimore, MD: University Park Press.

Braverman, B. B., & Hertzog, M. (1980). The effects of caption rate and language level on comprehension of a captioned video presentation. *American Annals of the Deaf, 125,* 943–948.

Brown, J. S., Collins, A., & Duguid, P. (1989). Situated cognition and the culture of learning. *Educational Researcher, 18,* 32–42.

Bruner, J. S. (1966). *Toward a theory of instruction.* Cambridge, MA: The Belknap Press.

Bruner, J. (1990). *Acts of meaning.* Cambridge, MA: Harvard University Press.

Buchanan, R. (1991). The Silent Worker newspaper and the building of a deaf community, 1887–1929. In J. Van Cleve (Ed.), *Deaf history unveiled* (pp. 172–197). Washington, DC: Gallaudet University Press.

Caccamise, F., Hatfield, N., & Brewer, L. (1978). Manual/simultaneous communication research: Results and implications. *American Annals of the Deaf, 123,* 803–823.

Calderon, R., Bargones, J., & Sidman, S. (1998). Characteristics of hearing families and their young deaf and hard of hearing children: Early intervention follow-up. *American Annals of the Deaf, 143,* 347–362.

Calderon, R., & Greenberg, M. T. (1993). Considerations in the adaptation of families with school-aged deaf children. In M. Marschark and D. Clark (Eds.), *Psychological perspectives on deafness* (pp. 27–48). Hillsdale, NJ: Lawrence Erlbaum Associates.

Calderon, R., & Greenberg, M. (1997). The effectiveness of early intervention for deaf children and children with hearing loss. In M.J. Guralnik (Ed.), *The effectiveness of early intervention* (pp. 455–482). Baltimore, MD: Paul H. Brookes.

Campbell, R. (1992). Speech in the head? Rhyme skill, reading, and immediate memory in the deaf. In D. Reisberg (Ed.), *Auditory imagery* (pp. 73–94). Hillsdale, NJ: Lawrence Erlbaum Associates.

Campbell, R., & Wright, H. (1990). Deafness and immediate memory for pictures: Dissociation between "inner speech" and "inner ear." *Journal of Experimental Child Psychology, 50,* 259–286.

Capirci, O., Cattani, A., Rossini, & Volterra, V. (1998). Teaching sign language to hearing children as a possible factor in cognitive enhancement. *Journal of Deaf Studies and Deaf Education, 3,* 135–142.

Carney, A. E., & Moeller, M. P. (1988). Treatment efficacy: Hearing loss in children. *Journal of Speech, Language, and Hearing Research, 41*, S61–S84.

Caselli, M. C., & Volterra, V. (1990). From communication to language in hearing and deaf children. In V. Volterra and C.J. Erting (Eds.), *From gesture to language in hearing and deaf children* (pp. 261–277). Berlin: Springer-Verlag.

Cawthon, S. W. (2001). Teaching strategies in inclusive classrooms with deaf students. *Journal of Deaf Studies and Deaf Education, 6*, 212–224.

Charrow, V. (1976). A psycholinguistic analysis of "deaf English." *Sign Language Studies, 1*, 139–150.

Chomsky, N. (1986). *Knowledge of language: Its nature, origin, and use.* New York: Praeger.

Ciocci, S. R., & Baran, J. A. (1998). The use of conversational repair strategies for children who are deaf. *American Annals of the Deaf, 143*, 235–245.

Clay, R. A. (1997). Do hearing devices impair deaf children? *APA Monitor, 28*, July.

Clements, D., Nastasi, B., & Swaminathan, S. (1993). Young children and computers: Crossroads and directions from research. *Young Children, 48*, 56–64.

Cohen, S. (1967). Predictability of deaf and hearing story paraphrasing. *Journal of Verbal Learning and Verbal Behavior, 6*, 916–921.

Cole, E., & Paterson, M. M. (1984). Assessment and treatment of phonologic disorders in the hearing-impaired. In J. Castello (Ed.), *Speech disorders in children* (pp. 93–127). San Diego, CA: College-Hill Press.

Commmission on Education of the Deaf. (1988). *Toward equality: Education of the deaf.* Washington, DC: U.S. Government Printing Office.

Commission on Reading, National Council of Teachers of English. (1989). Basal readers and the state of American reading instruction: A call for action. *Language Arts, 66*, 896–898.

Conlin, D., & Paivio (1975). The associative learning of the deaf: The effects of word imagery and signability. *Memory and Cognition, 3*, 333–340.

Conrad, R. (1972). Short-term memory in the deaf: A test for speech coding. *British Journal of Psychology, 63*, 173–180.

Conrad, R. (1979). *The deaf school child.* London: Harper & Row.

Cook, J. H., & Harrison, M. (1995). Private sign & literacy development and preschoolers with hearing loss. *Sign Language Studies, 88*, 201–226.

Cooley, J. (1981). Use of grammatical constraints in reading by young deaf adults as reflected in eye-voice span. *Language and Speech, 24*, 349–362.

Cooney, T., & Hirsch, C. (Eds.). (1990). *Teaching and learning mathematics in the 1990s, 1990 yearbook.* Reston, VA: National Council of Teachers of Mathematics.

Corina, D. P., Kritchevsky, M., & Bellugi, U. (1992). Linguistic permeability of unilateral neglect: Evidence from American Sign Language. In *Proceedings of the 14th Annual Conference of the Cognitive Science Society* (pp. 384–389). Hillsdale, NJ: Lawrence Erlbaum Associates.

Cornelius, G., & Hornett, D. (1990). The play behavior of hearing-impaired kindergarten children. *American Annals of the Deaf, 135*, 316–321.

Cornett, O. R., & Daisey, M. E. (1992). *The cued speech resource book.* Raleigh, NC: National Cued Speech Association.

Craig, W. & Craig, H. (1986). Schools and classes for the deaf in the United States. *American Annals of the Deaf, 131*, 93–135.

Crystal, D. (1987). *The Cambridge encyclopedia of language.* New York: Cambridge University Press.

Dalgarno, G. (1680). *Didascalocophus.* Oxford.

Daniele, V. (1993). Quantitative literacy. *American Annals of the Deaf, 138,* 76–81.

Daniels, M. (1993). ASL as a factor in acquiring *English. Sign Language Studies, 75,* 23–29.

Dawson, P. W., Blamey, P. J., Dettman, S. J., Barker, E. J., & Clark, G. M. (1995). A clinical report on receptive vocabulary skills in cochlear implant users. *Ear and Hearing, 16,* 287–294.

DeCasper, A. J., & Fifer, W. P. (1980). Of human bonding: Newborns prefer their mothers' voices. *Science, 208,* 1174–1176.

DeCasper, A. J., & Prescott, P. A. (1984). Human newborns' perception of male vices: Preference, discrimination, and reinforcing value. *Developmental Psychobiology, 17,* 481–491.

DeCasper, A. J., & Sigafoos, A. D. (1983). The intrauterine heartbeat: A potent reinforcer for newborns. *Infant Behavior and Development, 6,* 19–25.

Deland, F. (1931). *The story of lipreading.* Washington, DC: The Volta Bureau.

Desselle, D. D. (1994). Self-esteem, family climate, and communication patterns in relation to deafness. *American Annals of the Deaf, 139,* 322–328.

Dodd, B. (1980). The spelling abilities of profoundly pre-lingually deaf children. In U. Frith (Ed.), *Cognitive processes in spelling* (pp. 423–440). New York: Academic Press.

Dodd, B., McIntosh, B., & Woodhouse, L. (1998). Early lipreading ability and speech and language development of hearing-impaired pre-schoolers. In R. Campbell & B. Dodd (Eds.), *Hearing by eye II: Advances in the psychology of speechreading and auditory-visual speech,* (pp. 229–242). Hove, England: Psychology Press.

Dolman, D. (1992). Some concerns about using whole language approaches with deaf children. *American Annals of the Deaf, 137,* 278–282.

Dossetor, D. (2000). Deafness, autism, and the neurobiology of social development. Paper presented at the International Symposium on Mental Health—Deaf Children and Youth. Sydney, Australia (July).

Dowaliby, F., & Lang, H. (1999). Adjunct aids in instructional prose: A multimedia study with deaf college students. *Journal of Deaf Studies and Deaf Education, 4,* 270–282.

Drasgow, E. (1998). American Sign Language as a pathway to linguistic competence. *Exceptional Children, 64,* 329–342.

Dummer, G. M., Haubenstricker, J. L., & Stewart, D. A. (1996). Motor skill performances of children who are deaf. *Adapted Physical Activity Quarterly, 13,* 400–414.

Edelsky, C., Altwerger, B., & Flores, B. (1991). *Whole language: What's the difference?* Portsmouth, NH: Heinemann.

Emmorey, K. (1998). The impact of sign language use on visuospatial cognition. In M. Marschark & M. D. Clark, (Eds.), *Psychological perspectives on deafness, Volume 2* (pp. 19–52). Mahwah, N.J.: LEA.

Emmorey, K. (2001). *Language, cognition, and the brain: Insights from sign language research.* Mahwah, NJ: Lawrence Erlbaum and Associates.

Erting, C., Prezioso, C., & Hynes, M. (1990). The interactional context of deaf mother-infant interaction. In V. Volterra & C. Erting (Eds.), *From gesture to language in hearing and deaf children.* Berlin: Springer-Verlag.

Evelyn, J. (1955). *The diary of John Evelyn.* Oxford: Clarendon Press.

Everhart, V., & Marschark, M. (1988). Linguistic flexibility in signed and written language productions of deaf children. *Journal of Experimental Child Psychology, 46,* 174–193.

Ewoldt, C. (1985). A descriptive study of the developing literacy of young hearing impaired children. *Volta Review, 87,* 109–126.

Fabbretti, D., Volterra, V., & Pontecorvo, C. (1998). Written language abilities in deaf Italians. *Journal of Deaf Studies and Deaf Education, 3,* 231–244.

Farrar, A. (1926). The deaf in medieval times. *Volta Review, 28,* 389–393.

Farstrup, A. E. & Myers, M. (Eds.) (1996). *Standards for the English language arts.* Urbana, IL: National Council of Teachers of English.

Fay, P. B. (1923). A miracle of the thirteenth century. *American Annals of the Deaf, 67,* 121–128.

Fischer, R., & Lane, H. (Eds.). (1993). *Looking back: A reader on the history of deaf communities and their sign languages.* Hamburg: SIGNUM Press.

Fischer, S. (1998). Critical periods for language acquisiton: Consequences for deaf education. In A. Weisel (Ed.), *Issues unresolved: New perspectives on language and deaf education* (pp. 9–26). Washington, DC: Gallaudet University Press.

Fischgrund, J. E., & Akamatsu, T. (1993). Rethinking the education of ethnic/ multicultural deaf people: Stretching the boundaries. In K. M. Christensen and G. L Delgado (Eds.), *Multicultural issues in deafness* (pp. 169–178). White Plains, NY: Longman.

Fischler, I. (1985). Word recognition, use of context, and reading skill among deaf college studetns. *Reading Research Quarterly, 20,* 203–218.

Fisher, J. G. (1926). The three "I's" in geography and composition. *Volta Review, 28,* 346–347.

Fletcher, K. (1892). Some reasons for teaching history. *American Annals of the Deaf, 37,* 177–182.

Foster, S. B. (1992). *Working with deaf people.* Springfield IL: Charles C. Thomas.

Francis, H. W., Koch, M. E., Wyatt, J. R., & Niparko, J. K.(1999). Trends in educational placement and cost-benefit considerations in children with cochlear implants. *Archives of Otolaryngology and Head and Neck Surgery, 125,* 499–505.

Freire, P. (1970). *Pedagogy of the oppressed.* New York: Seabury Press.

Frith, U. (1985). Beneath the surface of developmental dyslexia. In K. Patterson, J. Marshall, & M. Coltheart (Eds.), *Surface dyslexia: Neuropsychological and cognitve studies of phonological reading* (pp. 301–330). London: Lawrence Erlbaum Associates.

Furstenberg, K. & Doyal, G. (1994). The relationship between emotional-behav-ioral functioning and personal characteristics on performance outcomes of hearing impaired students. *American Annals of the Deaf, 139,* 410–414.

Furth, H. G. (1964). Reasearch with the deaf: Implications for language and cognition. *Psychological Bulletin, 62,* 145–164.

Furth, H. G. (1966). *Thinking without language.* New York: Free Press.

Gallaudet, E. M. (1983). *History of the college for the deaf: 1857–1907* (L. J. Fischer & D. L. deLorenzo, Editors). Washington, DC: Gallaudet College Press.

Gallaway, C., & Woll, B. (1994). Interaction and childhood deafness. In C. Gallaway & B. J. Richards (Eds.), *Input and interaction in language acquisition* (pp. 197–218). Cambridge: Cambridge University Press.

Geers, A. E., & Moog, J. S. (1978). Syntactic maturity and spontaneous speech and elicited indications of hearing impaired children. *Journal of Speech and Hearing Disorders, 43,* 380–391.

Geers, A. E., & Moog, J. S. (1992). Speech perception and production skills of students with impaired hearing from oral and Total Communication education settings. *Journal of Speech and Hearing Research, 35,* 1384–1393.

Geers, A. E., & Moog, J. S. (Eds.). (1994). Effectiveness of cochlear implants and tactile aids for deaf children: The sensory aids study at Central Institute for the Deaf. *Volta Review, 96,* 1–231.

Geers, A., Moog, J., & Schick, B. (1984). Acquisition of spoken and signed English by profoundly deaf children. *Journal of Speech and Hearing Disorders, 49,* 378–388.

Geers, A. E., & Schick, B. (1988). Acquisition of spoken and signed English by hearing-impaired children of hearing-impaired or hearing parents. *Journal of Speech and Hearing Disorders, 53,* 136–143.

Gershkoff-Stowe, L., Thal, D. J., Smith, L. B., & Namy, L. L. (1997). Categorization and its development relation to early language. *Child Development, 68,* 843–859.

Golinkoff, R. M., & Hirsh-Pasek, K. (1999). *How babies talk.* New York: Plume.

Goodman, K. S., Smith, E. B., Meredith, R. & Goodman, Y. M. (1987). *Language and thinking in school.* (3rd ed.). New York: Richard Owen.

Gottlieb, G., Doran, C., & Whitley, S. (1964). Cerebral dominance and speech acquisition in deaf children. *Journal of Abnormal and Social Psychology, 69,* 182–189.

Grant, B. (Ed.) (1988). *The quiet ear: Deafness in literature.* London: Faber and Faber.

Grant, W. D., Rosenstein, J., & Knight, D. L. (1975). A project to determine the feasibility of BSCS's Me Now for hearing impaired students. *American Annals of the Deaf, 120,* 63–69.

Greenberg, M. T., & Marvin, R. S. (1979). Attachment patterns in profoundly deaf preschool children. *Merrill-Palmer Quarterly, 25,* 265–279.

Greenberg, M. T., Calderon, R., & Kusché, C. (1984). Early intervention using simultaneous communication with deaf infants: The effect on communication development. *Child Development, 55,* 607–616.

Greenberg, M. T. & Kusché, C. A. (1987). Cognitive, personal, and social development of deaf children and adolescents. In M. C. Wang, M. C. Reynolds, & H. J. Walberg (Eds.), *Handbook of special education: Research and practice. Vol. 3: Low incidence conditions* (pp. 95–129). New York: Pergamon Press.

Gregory, S. (1995). *Deaf children and their families.* Cambridge: Cambridge University Press.

Gregory, S. (1998). *Issues in deaf education.* London: D. Fulton.

Gregory, S., & Barlow, S. (1989). Interaction between deaf babies and their deaf and hearing mothers. In B. Woll (Ed.), *Language development and sign language, Monograph 1* (pp. 23–35). Bristol, England: International Sign Language Association.

Gregory, S., & Hindley, P. (1996). Communication strategies for deaf children. *Journal of Child Psychology and Psychiatry, 37*, 895–905.

Gregory, S., Smith, S., & Wells, A. (1997). Language and identity in sign bilingual deaf children. *Journal of the British Association of Teachers of the Deaf, 21*, 31–38.

Griswold, L. E., & Commings, J. (1974). The expressive vocabulary of preschool deaf children. *American Annals of the Deaf, 119*, 16–28.

Groce, N. E. (1985). *Everyone here spoke sign language: Hereditary deafness at Martha's Vineyard.* Cambridge, MA: Harvard University Press.

Grushkin, D. (1998). Why shouldn't Sam read? Toward a new paradigm for literacy and the deaf. *Journal of Deaf Studies and Deaf Education, 3*, 179–204.

Hairston, M. (1982) The winds of change: Thomas Kuhn and the revolution in the teaching of writing. *College composition and communication, 33*, 76–88.

Halbertstam, L. (1938). The father of the Activity School. *Volta Review, 40*, 757–759

Hanson, V. (1982). Short-term recall by deaf signers of American sign language: Implications of encoding strategy for order recall. *Journal of Experimental Psychology: Learning, Memory, and Cognition, 8*, 572–583.

Hanson, V. L. (1986). Access to spoken language and the acquisition of orthographic structure: Evidence from deaf readers. *Quarterly Journal of Experimental Psychology, 38A*, 193–212.

Hanson, V., & Fowler, C. (1987). Phonological coding in word reading: Evidence from hearing and deaf readers. *Memory & Cognition, 15*, 199–207.

Hanson, V. L., & Lichtenstein, E. H. (1990). Short-term memory coding by deaf signers: The primary language coding hypothesis reconsidered. *Cognitive Psychology, 22*, 211–224.

Hanson, V., & McGarr, N. (1989). Rhyme generation by deaf adults. *Journal of Speech and Hearing Research, 32*, 2–11.

Hanson, V. L., Shankweiler, D., & Fischer, F. W. (1983). Determinants of spelling ability in deaf and hearing adults: Access to linguistic structure. *Cognition, 14*, 323–344.

Harris, M., & Beech, J. R. (1998). Implicit phonological awareness and early reading development in prelingually deaf children. *Journal of Deaf Studies and Deaf Education, 3*, 205–216.

Harris, M., & Mohay, H. (1997). Learning how to see signs: A comparison of attentional behaviour in eighteen month old deaf children with deaf and hearing mothers. *Journal of Deaf Studies and Deaf Education, 2*, 95–103.

Harris, R. I. (1978). The relationship of impulse control parent hearing status, manual communication, and academic achievement. *American Annals of the Deaf, 123*, 52–67.

Hart, B., & Risley, T. (1995). *Meaningful differences in the everyday experience of young American children.* Baltimore, MD: Paul H. Brookes.

Hart, D. (1994). *Authentic assessment: a handbook for educators.* New York: Addison-Wesley.

Hay, J. (1996). Deaf history: Extracts from the Parish book of St. Martin's, Leicester, 1576, February the 5th day. *British Deaf News*, November, p. 7.

Heider, F., & Heider, G. (1940). A comparison of sentence structure of deaf and hearing children. *Psychological Monographs 52*, 42–103.

Herodotus. *The Persian Wars*. New York: Random House Modern Library, 1947.

Hertzberg, H. W. (1982). Social studies reform: The lessons of history. In I. Morrissett (Ed.), *Social studies in the 1980s*. Alexandria, VA: Association for Supervision and Curriculum Development.

Hertzog, M., Stinson, M. S., & Keiffer, R. (1989). Effects of caption modification and instructor intervention on comprehension of a technical film. *Educational Technology Research and Development, 37*, 59–68.

Hirsch, E. D. Jr. (1987). *Cultural literacy: What every American needs to know.* Boston: Houghton Mifflin.

Hirshoren, A., Hurley, O. L., & Kavale, K. (1979). Psychometric characteristics of the WISC-R Performance Scale with deaf children. *Journal of Speech and Hearing Disorders, 44*, 73–79.

Hockett, C. (1958). *A course in modern linguistics.* New York: Macmillan.

Hoemann, H., Andrews, C., & DeRosa, D. (1974). Categorical encoding in short-term memory by deaf and hearing children. *Journal of Speech and Hearing Research, 17*, 426–431.

Holliday, W. G. (1992). Helping college science students read and write. *Journal of College Science Teaching, 21*, 58–61.

Holliday, W. G., Yore, L. D., & Alvermann, D. E. (1994). The reading-science-learning-writing connection: Breakthroughs, barriers, and promises. *Journal of Research in Science Teaching, 31*, 877–893.

Holt, J. A. (1997). *Stanford Achievement Test—8th Edition for Deaf and Hard of Hearing Students: Reading Comprehension Subgroup Results.* URL: gri.gallaudet.edu/Assessment/sat-read.html.

Hutton, J. S. (1888). The teaching of language. *Proceedings of the sixth national conference of superintendents and principles of institutions for deaf mutes.* Held at Mississippi Institution, Jackson Mississippi, April 14–17, 1888. Jackson, MS: Clarion-Ledger Printing Establishment.

Iran-Nejad, A., Ortony, A., & Rittenhouse, R. K. (1981). The comprehension of metaphorical uses of English by deaf children. *Journal of Speech and Hearing Research, 24*, 551–556.

Israelite, N., & Helfrich, M. (1988). Improving text coherence in basal readers: Effects of revisions on the comprehension of hearing-impaired and normal-hearing readers, *Volta Review, 90*, 261–276.

Jamieson, J. R. (1994). Instructional discourse strategies: Differences between hearing in deaf mothers of deaf children. *First Language, 14*, 153–171.

Jamieson, J. R. (1995). Visible fault: deaf children's use of signed & spoken private speech. *Sign Language Studies, 86*, 63–80.

Janos, L. M. & Robinson, N. M. (1985). Psychological development in intellectually gifted children. In F. D. Horowitz & M. O'Brien (Eds.), *The gifted and talented: Developmental perspectives* (pp. 145–195). Washington, D.C.: American Psychological Association.

Jeanes, R. C., Nienhuys, T. G. W. M., & Rickards, F. W. (2000). The pragmatic skills of profoundly deaf children. *Journal of Deaf Studies and Deaf Education, 5*, 237–247.

Jelinek Lewis, M. S., & Jackson, D. W. (2001). Television literacy: Comprehension of program content using closed-captions for the deaf. *Journal of Deaf Studies and Deaf Education, 6*, 43–53.

Jensema, C., McCann, R., & Ramsey, S. (1996). Closed-captioned television presentation speed and vocabulary. *American Annals of the Deaf, 141*, 284–292.

Johnson, D. L., Swank, P. R., Owen, M. J., Baldwin, C. D., Howie, V. M., & McCormick, D.P. (2000). Effects of early middle ear effusion on child intelligence at three, five, and seven years of age. *Journal of Pediatric Psychology, 25*, 5–13.

Johnson, R. E., Liddell, S., & Erting, C. (1989). *Unlocking the curriculum: Principles for achieving access in deaf education* (working paper 89–3). Washington, DC: Gallaudet University, Gallaudet Research Institute.

Johnson, R. E. (1994). Possible influences on bilingualism in early ASL acquisition. *Teaching English to Deaf and Second Language Students, 10*, 9–17.

Johnson, S. (1912). A journey to the Hebrides. In *Works of Samuel Johnson, Volume 8*, New Cambridge Edition. Cambridge, MA: Harvard Cooperative Society.

Jones, M. L. & Quigley, S. P. (1979). The acquisition of question formation in spoken English and American Sign Language by two hearing children of deaf parents. *Journal of Speech and Hearing Disorders, 44*, 196–208.

Kampfe, C. M., Harrison, M., Oettinger, T., Ludington, J., McDonald-Bell, C., & Pillsbury, H.C. III (1993). Parental expectations as a factor in evaluating children for the multichannel cochlear implant. *American Annals of the Deaf, 138*, 297–303.

Kauffman, J. M. (1993). How we might achieve the radical reform of special education. *Exceptional Children, 60*, 6–16.

Kelly, L. (1995). Processing of bottom-up and top-down information by skilled and average deaf readers and implications for whole language instruction. *Exceptional Children, 61*, 318–334.

Kelly, L. (1996). The interaction of syntactic competence and vocabulary during reading by deaf students. *Journal of Deaf Studies and Deaf Education, 1*, 75–90.

Kelly, R. R., & Mousley, K. (2001). Solving word problems: More than a reading issue for deaf students. *American Annals of the Deaf, 146*, 253–264.

Kibby, M. W. (1993). What reading teachers should know about reading proficiency. *U.S. Journal of Reading, 37*, 28–40.

Kibby, M. W. (1995). *Student literacy: Myths and realities (Fastback 381)*. Bloomington, IN: Phi Delta Kappa Educational Foundation.

Kindig, J. S., & Richards, H. C. (2000). Otitis media: Precursor of delayed reading. *Journal of Pediatric Psychology, 25*, 15–18.

King, L. A. (1996). *Surditas: The Understandings of the Deaf and Deafness in the Writings of Augustine, Jerome, and Bede*. Unpublished doctoral dissertation, Boston University.

Kirkwood, D. H. (1999). In '98, hearing aid market hit new highs, but growth slowed. *The Hearing Journal, 52*, 21–31.

Kline, M. (1973). *Why Johnny can't add: The failure of the new math.* New York: St. Martin's Press.

Kluwin, T. N. (1993). Cumulative effects of mainstreaming on the achievement of deaf adolescents. *Exceptional Children, 60*, 73–81.

Kluwin, T., & Gaustad, M. G. (1994). The role of adaptability and communication in fostering cohesion in families with deaf adolescents. *American Annals of the Deaf, 139*, 329–335.

Kluwin T., & Kelly, A. (1991). The effectiveness of dialogue journal writing in improving the writing skills of young deaf writers. *American Annals of the Deaf, 136*, 284–291.

Kluwin, T. N., & Stinson, M. S. (1993). *Deaf students in local public high schools: Background, experiences, and outcomes.* Springfield, IL: Charles C. Thomas.

Koester, L. S. (1994). Early interactions and the socioemotional development of deaf infants. *Early Development and Parenting, 3*, 51–60.

Koester, L. S., Brooks, L., & Traci, M. A. (2000a). Tactile contact by deaf and hearing mothers during face-to-face interactions with their infants. *Journal of Deaf Studies and Deaf Education, 5*, 127–139.

Koester, L. S., Papoušek H., & Smith-Gray, S. (2000b). Intuitive parenting, communication, and interaction with deaf infants. In P. Spencer, C. Erting, & M. Marschark (Eds.), *Development in context: The deaf child in the family and at school* (pp. 55–72). Mahwah, NJ: Lawrence Erlbaum Associates.

Koester, L. S., & Trimm, V. M. (1991). Face-to-face interactions with deaf and hearing infants: Do maternal or infant behaviors differ? Paper presented at biennial meetings of Society for Research in Child Development. Seattle, April 18–20.

Koh, S. D., Vernon, M., & Bailey, W. (1971). Free-recall learning of word lists by prelingual deaf subjects. *Journal of Verbal Learning and Verbal Behavior, 10*, 542–547.

Kolb, B., & Wishaw, I. Q. (1996). *Fundamentals of human neuropsychology* Fourth Edition. New York: W.H. Freeman.

Konigsmark, B. W. (1972). Genetic hearing loss with no associated abnormatlities. *Journal of Speech and Hearing Disorders, 37*, 89–99.

Krashen, S. D. (1981). Bilingual education and second language acquisition theory. *Schooling and language minority students: Theoretical framework.* Sacramento: Office of Bilingual Bicultural Education.

Kusché, C. A., Greenberg, M. T., & Garfield, T. S. (1983). Nonverbal intelligence and verbal achievement in deaf adolescents: An examination of heredity and environment. *American Annals of the Deaf, 128*, 458–466.

Kyle, J. (1990). The Deaf community: Custom, culture and tradition. In S. Prillwitz & T. Vollhaber (Eds.), *Sign language research and application* (pp. 175–186). Hamburg: SIGNUM Press.

Kyle, J., Ackerman, J., & Woll, B. (1987). Early mother-infant interactions: Language and pre-language in deaf families. In P. Griffiths, A. Mills, & J. Local (Eds.), *Proceedings of the Child Language Seminar*, University of York.

Kyle, J., Woll, B., & Ackerman, J. (1989). *Gesture to sign and speech: Final report* to ESRC (Project no. CC00232327). Bristol, UK: Centre for Deaf Studies, University of Bristol.

Lane, H. (1984). *When the mind hears: A history of the deaf.* New York: Random House.

Lang, H. G. (1994). *Silence of the spheres: The deaf experience in the history of science.* Westport, CT: Bergin & Garvey.

Lang, H. G. (2000). *A phone of our own: The deaf insurrection against Ma Bell.* Washington, DC: Gallaudet University Press.

Lang, H. G., & Albertini, J. A. (2001). The construction of meaning in the authentic science writing of deaf students. *Journal of Deaf Studies and Deaf Education, 6,* 258–284.

Lang, H. G., & Conner, K. (2001). *From dream to reality: The history and first 30 years of the National Technical Institute for the Deaf at Rochester Institute of Technology.* Rochester, NY: National Technical Institute for the Deaf.

Lang, H. G., Dowaliby, F. J., & Anderson, H. (1994). Critical teaching incidents: Recollections of deaf college students. *American Annals of the Deaf, 139,* 119–127.

Lang, H. G., McKee, B. G., & Conner, K. N. (1993). Characteristics of effective teachers: A descriptive study of perceptions of faculty and deaf college students. *American Annals of the Deaf, 138,* 252–259.

Lang, H. G., & Meath-Lang, B. (1985). The attitudes of hearing-impaired students toward science: Implications for teachers. Presentation at the Convention of American Instructors of the Deaf, St. Augustine, FL, June.

Lang, H. G., & Meath-Lang, B. (1995). *Deaf persons in the arts and sciences: A biographical dictionary.* Westport, CT: Greenwood Press.

Lang, H. G., & Propp, G. (1982). Science education for hearing impaired students: State of the art. *American Annals of the Deaf, 127,* 860–869.

Lang, H. G., & Stokoe, W. (2000). A treatise on signed and spoken language in early 19th century deaf education in America. *Journal of Deaf Studies and Deaf Education, 5,* 196–216.

Lang, H. G., Stinson, M. S., Kavanagh, F., Liu, Y, & Basile, M.. (1998). Learning styles of deaf college students and teaching behaviors of their instructors. *Journal of Deaf Studies and Deaf Education, 4,* 16–27.

Laporta-Hupper, M., Monte, D., & Scheifele, P. (2000). Classroom of the sea. *The Science Teacher, 67,* 44–47.

LaSasso, C. (1999). Test-taking skills: A missing component of deaf students' curriculum. *American Annals of the Deaf, 144,* 35–43.

LaSasso, C. J., & Metzger, M. A. (1998). An alternative route for preparing deaf children for BiBi programs: The home language as L1 and cued speech for conveying traditionally-spoken languages. *Journal of Deaf Studies and Deaf Education, 3,* 265–289.

LaSasso, C. J., & Mobley, R. T. (1997). National survey of reading instruction for deaf or hard-of-hearing students in the U.S. *Volta Review, 99,* 31–58.

Lederberg, A. R. (1991). Social interaction among deaf preschoolers: The effects of language ability and age. *American Annals of the Deaf, 136,* 35–59.

Lederberg, A. R. (1993). The impact of deafness on mother-child and peer relationships. In M. Marschark & M. D. Clark (Eds.), *Psychological perspectives on deafness* (pp. 93–119). Hillsdale, NJ: Lawrence Erlbaum Associates.

Lederberg, A. & Mobley, C. (1990). The effect of hearing impairment on the quality of attachment and mother-toddler interaction. *Child Development*, *61*, 1596–1604.

Lederberg, A. R., Rosenblatt, V., Vandell, D. L., & Chapin, S. L., (1987). Temporary and long-term friendships in hearing and deaf preschoolers. *Merrill-Palmer Quarterly*, *33*, 515–533.

Lederberg, A. R., Ryan, H. B., & Robbins, B. L. (1986). Peer interaction in young deaf children: The effect of partner hearing status and familiarity. *Developmental Psychology*, *22*, 691–700.

Lederberg, A. R., & Spencer, P. E. (2001). Vocabulary development of deaf and hard of hearing children. In M. D. Clark, M. Marschark, & M. Karchmer (Eds.), *Context, cognition, and deafness* (pp. 88–112). Washington, DC: Gallaudet University Press.

Leigh, G. R. (1995). *Teachers' use of the Australasian Signed English system for simultaneous communication with their hearing-impaired students*. Unpublished doctoral dissertation, Monash University, Melbourne, Australia.

Lenneberg, E. (1967). *Biological foundations of language*. New York: Wiley.

Levy, Y. (1997). Autonomous linguistic systems in the language of young children. *Journal of Child Language*, *24*, 651–671.

Leybaert, J. (1993). Reading in the deaf: The roles of phonological codes. In M. Marschark & M. D. Clark (Eds.), *Psychological perspectives on deafness* (pp. 269–310). Hillsdale, NJ: Lawrence Earlbaum Associates.

Leybaert, J. (1998). Effects of phonologically augmented lipspeech on the development of phonological representations and deaf children. In M. Marschark & M. D. Clark (Eds.), *Psychological perspectives on deafness*, *Volume 2* (pp. 103–130). Hillsdale, NJ: Lawrence Earlbaum Associates.

Liben, L. S. (1978). Developmental perspectives on experiential deficiencies of deaf children. In L. Liben (Ed.), *Deaf children: Developmental perspectives* (pp. 195–215). New York: Academic Press.

Liben, L. S. (1979). Free recall by deaf and hearing children: Semantic clustering and recall in trained and untrained groups. *Journal of Experimental Child Psychology*, *27*, 105–119.

Lichtenstein, E. (1998). The relationships between reading processes and English skills of deaf college students. *Journal of Deaf Studies and Deaf Education*, *3*, 80–134.

Lightbown, P., & Spada, N. (1993). *How languages are learned*. New York: Oxford University Press.

Lillo-Martin, D. (1993). Deaf readers and universal grammar. In M. Marschark, & M. D. Clark (Eds.), *Psychological perspectives on deafness* (pp. 311–337). Hillsdale, NJ: Lawrence Earlbaum Associates.

Lillo-Martin, D. (1997). The modular effects of sign language acquisition. In M. Marschark, P. Siple, D. Lillo-Martin, R. Campbell & V. Everhart (Eds.), *Relations of language and thought: The view from sign language and deaf children* (pp. 62–109). New York: Oxford University Press.

Lillo-Martin, D., Hanson, V., & Smith, S. (1992). Deaf readers' comprehension of relative clause structures. *Applied Psycholinguistics*, *13*, 13–30.

Livingston, S. (1997). *Rethinking the education of deaf students*. Portsmouth, NH: Hineman.

Lowenbraun, S., & Thompson, M. (1987). Environments and strategies for learning and teaching. In M. C. Wang, M. C. Reynolds, & H. J. Walberg (Eds.), *Handbook of special education: Research and practice, Volume 3: Low incidence conditions* (pp. 47–70). New York: Pergamon Press.

Lucas, C., & Valli, C. (1989). Language contact in the American Deaf community. In C. Lucas (Ed.), *The sociolinguistics of the Deaf community* (pp. 11–39). San Diego, CA: Academic Press.

Luetke-Stahlman, B. (1990). Types of instructional input as predictors of reading achievement for hearing-impaired students. In C. Lucas (Ed.), *Sign language research*. Washington, DC: Gallaudet University.

Luetke-Stahlman, B., & Luckner, J. (1991). *Effectively educating students with hearing impairments*. New York: Longman.

Luterman, D. (1987). *Deafness in the family*. Boston, MA: College-Hill Press.

MacKay-Soroka, S., Trehub, S. E., & Thorpe, L. A. (1987). Referential communication between mothers and their deaf children. *Child Development, 58*, 986–992.

MacLeod-Gallinger, J. (1992). Employment attainments of deaf adults one and ten years after graduation from high school. *Journal of the American Deafness anad Rehabilitation Association, 25*, 1–10.

Maestas y Moores, J. (1980). Early linguistic environment: Interactions of deaf parents with their infants. *Sign Language Studies, 26*, 1–13.

Marmor, G., & Petitto, L. (1979). Simultaneous communication in the classroom: How well is English grammar represented? *Sign Language Studies, 23*, 99–136.

Marschark, M. (1993). *Psychological development of deaf children*. New York: Oxford University Press.

Marschark, M. (1994). Gesture and sign. *Applied Psycholinguistics, 15*, 209–236.

Marschark, M. (1997). *Raising and educating a deaf child*. New York: Oxford University Press.

Marschark, M. (1996). What's an image? Invited paper in "Imageless thought or thoughtless images" symposium. European Society for Cognitive Psychology, Wuerzburg, Germany, September.

Marschark, M. (2000). Education and development of deaf children—or is it development and education? In P. Spencer, C. Erting, & M. Marschark (Eds.), *Development in context: The deaf child in the family and at school* (pp. 275–292). Mahwah, NJ: Lawrence Earlbaum Associates.

Marschark, M. (2001a). Context, cognition, and deafness: Planning the research agenda. In M. D. Clark, M. Marschark, & M. Karchmer (Eds.), *Cognition, context, and deafness* (pp. 179–198). Washington, DC: Gallaudet University Press.

Marschark, M. (2001b). *Language development in children who are deaf and hard of hearing: A research synthesis*. Washington DC: National Association of State Directors of Special Education.

Marschark, M., & Clark, D. (1987). Linguistic and nonlinguistic creativity of deaf children. *Developmental Review, 7*, 22–38.

Marschark, M., De Beni, R., Polazzo, M. G., & Cornoldi, C. (1993). Deaf and hearing-impaired adolescents' memory for concrete and abstract prose: Effects of relational and distinctive information. *American Annals of the Deaf, 138*, 31–39.

Marschark, M., & Everhart, V.S. (1995). Understanding problem solving by deaf children. In T. Helstrup, G. Kaufmann, & K. H. Teigen (Eds.), *Problem solving and cognitive processes* (pp. 315–338). Bergen, Norway: Fagbokforlaget.

Marschark, M., & Everhart, V. S. (1997). Relations of language and cognition: What do deaf children tell us? In M. Marschark, P. Siple, D. Lillo-Martin, R. Campbell, & V. S. Everhart, *Relations of language and thought: The view from sign language and deaf children* (pp. 3–23). New York: Oxford University Press.

Marschark, M. & Everhart, V. S. (1999). Problem solving by deaf and hearing children: Twenty questions. *Deafness and Education International, 1,* 63–79.

Marschark, M., & Harris, M. (1996). Success and failure in learning to read: The special (?) case of deaf children. In C. Cornoldi & J. Oakhill (Eds.), *Reading comprehension difficulties: Processes and intervention* (pp. 279–300). Hillsdale, NJ: Lawrence Erlbaum Associates.

Marschark, M., LePoutre, D., & Bement, L. (1998). Mouth movement and signed communication. In R. Campbell & B. Dodd (Eds.), *Hearing by eye: The psychology of lipreading and audiovisual speech* (pp. 243–264). London: Taylor & Francis.

Marschark, M., & Lukomski, J. (2001). Cognition, literacy, and education. In M. D. Clark, M. Marschark, & M. Karchmer (Eds.), *Context, cognition, and deafness* (pp. 71–86). Washington, DC: Gallaudet University Press.

Marschark, M., & Mayer, T. (1998). Mental representation and memory in deaf adults and children. In M. Marschark & M. D. Clark (Eds.), *Psychological perspectives on deafness, Volume 2* (pp. 53–77). Hillsdale, NJ: Lawrence Erlbaum Associates.

Marschark, M., Mouradian, V., & Halas, M. (1994). Discourse rules in the language processing of deaf and hearing children. *Journal of Experimental Child Psychology, 57,* 89–107.

Marschark, M., Siple, P., Lillo-Martin, D., Campbell, R., & Everhart, V. (1997). *Relations of language and thought: The view from sign language and deaf children.* New York: Oxford University Press.

Maxwell, M. (1985). Some functions and uses of literacy in the deaf community. *Language in Society, 14,* 205–221.

Maxwell, M., & Falick, T. G. (1992). Cohesion & quality in deaf & hearing children's written English. *Sign Language Studies, 77,* 345–372.

Mayberry, R. I., & Eichen, E. B. (1991). The long-lasting advantage of learning sign language in childhood: Another look at the critical period for language acquisition. *Journal of Memory and Language, 30,* 486–512.

Mayer, C. (1999). Shaping at the point of utterance: An investigation of the composing processes of the deaf student writer. *Journal of Deaf Studies and Deaf Education, 4,* 37–49.

Mayer, C., & Akamatsu, C. T. (1999). Bilingual-bicultural models of literacy education for deaf students: Considering the claims. *Journal of Deaf Studies and Deaf Education, 4,* 1–8.

Mayer, C., & Moskos, E. (1998). Deaf children learning to spell. *Research in the teaching of English, 33,* 158–180.

Mayer, C., & Wells, G. (1996). Can the linguistic interdependence theory support a bilingual-bicultural model of literacy education for deaf students? *Journal of Deaf Studies and Deaf Education, 1,* 93–107.

McCullough, S. & Emmorey, K. (1997). Face processing by deaf ASL signers: Evidence for expertise in distinguishing local features. *Journal of Deaf Studies and Deaf Education, 2,* 212–233.

McCutcheon, C. (2000). *The bilingual-bicultural education of deaf children in the United States.* Rochester, NY: School Psychology Program, Rochester Institute of Technology.

McEvoy, C., Marschark, M., & Nelson, D. L. (1999). Comparing the mental lexicons of deaf and hearing individuals. *Journal of Educational Psychology, 91,* 1–9.

McLaren, P. (1988). Culture or canon? Critical pedagogy and the politics of literacy. *Harvard Educational Review, 58,* 213–234.

McNeill, D. (1992). *Hand and mind.* Chicago: University of Chicago Press.

Meadow, K. P. (1976). Personality and social development of deaf people. *Journal of Rehabilitation of the Deaf, 9,* 1–12.

Meadow, K. P., Greenberg, M. T., Erting, C., & Carmichael, H. (1981). Interactions of deaf mothers and deaf preschool children: Comparisons with three other groups of deaf and hearing dyads. *American Annals of the Deaf, 126,* 454–468.

Meadow-Orlans, K. P., MacTurk R. H., Prezioso, C. T., Erting C. J., & Day P. S. (1987). Interactions of deaf and hearing mothers with three and six month old infants. Paper at the Biennial meeting of the Society for Research in child Development, Baltimore, MD, April.

Meadow-Orlans, K. P., & Steinberg, A. G. (1993). Effects of infant hearing loss and maternal support on mother infant interactions at 18 months. *Journal of Applied Developmental Psychology, 14,* 407–426.

Meath-Lang, B., & Albertini, J. (1984). Keeping the purpose before the learner: A notional-functional curriculum framework for deaf students. *Teaching English to Deaf and Second-Language Students, 2,* 4–11.

Meath-Lang, B., Caccamise, F., & Albertini, J. (1982). Deaf students' views on English language learning: Educational and sociolinguistic implications. In H. Hoemann & R. Wilbur (Eds.), *Social aspects of deafness, Volume 5* (pp. 295–329). Washington, DC: Gallaudet University.

Meier, R. P., & Newport, E. L. (1990). Out of the hands of babes: On a possible sign advantage in language acquisition. *Language, 66,* 1–23.

Meier, R. P., & Willerman, R. (1995). Prelinguistic gesture in deaf and hearing infants. In K. Emmorey & J. Snitzer Reilly (Eds.), *Language, gesture, and space* (pp. 391–409). Hillsdale, NJ: Lawrence Erlbaum Associates.

Metzger, M. (1998). Eye gaze and pronomial reference in American Sign Language. In C. Lucas (Ed.), *Pinky extension & eye gaze.* Washington, DC: Gallaudet University Press.

Meyer, T. A., Svirsky, M. A., Kirk, K. I., & Miyamoto, R. T. (1998). Improvements in speech perception by children with profound prelingual hearing loss: Effects of device, communication mode, and chronological age. *Journal of Speech, Language, and Hearing Research, 41,* 846–858.

Miller, P. (1997). The effect of communication mode on the development of phonemic awareness in prelingually deaf students. *Journal of Speech, Language, and Hearing Research, 40,* 1151–1163.

Miyamato, R. T., Svirksy, M. A., & Robbins, A. M. (1997). Enhancement of expressive language in prelingually deaf children with cochlear implants. *Advances in Oto-Rhino-Laryngology, 50,* 160–165.

Mohay, H., Milton, L., Hindmarsh, G., & Ganley, K. (1998). Deaf mothers as communication models for hearing families with deaf children. In A. Weisel (Ed.), *Issues unresolved: New perspectives on language and deaf education* (pp. 76–87). Washington, DC: Gallaudet University Press.

Moores, D. F. (1996). *Educating the deaf: Psychology, principles, and practices, Fourth edition.* Boston: Houghton Mifflin.

Moores, D., & Meadow-Orlans, K. P. (1990). *Education and developmental aspects of deafness.* Washington, DC: Gallaudet University Press.

Morris, P., & Tchudi, S. (1996). *The new literacy: Moving beyond the 3Rs.* San Francisco, CA: Josey-Bass.

Musselman, C. (2000). How do children who can't hear learn to read an alphabetic script? A review of the literature on reading and deafness. *Journal of Deaf Studies and Deaf Education, 5,* 9–31.

Musselman, C., & Churchill, A. (1993). Maternal conversational control and the development of deaf children: A test of the stage hypothesis. *First Language, 13,* 271–290.

Musselman, C. & Mootilal, A. (1996). The social adjustment of deaf adolescents in segregated, partially integrated, and mainstreamed settings. *Journal of Deaf Studies and Deaf Education, 1,* 52–63.

Musselman, C., & Szanto, G. (1998). The written language of deaf adolescents: Patterns of performance. *Journal of Deaf Studies and Deaf Education, 3,* 245–257.

Myklebust, H. (1964). *The psychology of deafness.* New York: Grune & Stratton.

National Center for Educational Statistics (1995). *Approaching kindergarten: A look at preschoolers in the united states.* National Household Education Survey. Washington, DC: U.S. Department of Education, Office of Educational Research and Improvement.

National Center for Health Statistics (1994). *Vital and Health Statistics.* Series 3, No. 30. Beltsville, MD: NCHS.

National Center for Health Statistics (1999). *Vital and health statistics.* Series 10, No. 194. Beltsville, MD: NCHS.

National Commission on Social Studies in the Schools (1989). *Charting a course: Social studies for the 21st century.* Washington, DC: National Commission of Social Studies in the Schools.

National Council for the Social Studies (1994). *Expectations of excellence: Curriculum standards for social studies.* Washington, DC: National Council for the Social Studies.

National Council of Teachers of Mathematics. (1989). *Curriculum and Evaluation Standards for School Mathematics.* Reston VA: NCTM.

National Council of Teachers of Mathematics (1991). *Professional standards for teaching mathematics.* Reston, VA: NCTM.

National Institutes of Health (1995). *Cochlear implants in adults and children.* Online NIH Consensus Statement, 13(2), 1–30. Bethesda, MD: NIH.

National Research Council. (1996). *National Science Education Standards.* Washington, DC: National Academy Press.

Nelson, K. (1973). Structure and strategy in learning to talk. *Monographs of the Society for Research and Child Development, 38,* (149), no. 1–2.

Nelson, K. E., Loncke, F., & Camarata, S. (1993). Implications of research on deaf and hearing children's language learning. In M. Marschark & M. D. Clark (Eds.), *Psychological perspectives on deafness* (pp. 123–152). Hillsdale, NJ: Lawrence Erlbaum Associates.

Neville, H. J., Coffey, S. A., Lawson, D., Fischer, A., Emmorey, K., & Bellugi, U. (1997). Neural systems mediation American Sign Language: Effects of sensory experience and age of acquisition. *Brain and Language, 57,* 285–308.

Nevins, M. E. & Chute, P. M. (1995). Success of children with cochlear implants in mainstream educational settings. *Annals of Otolaryngology, Rhinology, and Laryngology Supplement, 166,* 100–102.

Newport, E. L. (1988). Constraints on learning and their role in language acquisition: Studies of the acquisition of American Sign Language. *Language Sciences, 10,* 147–172.

Newton, L. (1985). Linguistic environment of the deaf child: A focus on teachers' use of nonliteral language. *Journal of Speech and Hearing Research, 28,* 336–344.

Notoya, M., Suzuki, S., & Furukawa, M. (1994). Effects of early manual instruction on the low-language development of deaf children. *American Annals of the Deaf, 139,* 348–351.

Oakhill, J., & Cain, K. (2000). Children's difficulties in text comprehension: Assessing causal issues. *Journal of Deaf Studies and Deaf Education, 5,* 51–59.

O'Connor, N., & Hermelin, B. M. (1976). Backward and forward recall by deaf and hearing children. *Quarterly Journal of Experimental Psychology, 28,* 83–92.

O'Donoghue, G. M. (1996). Cochlear implants in children: Principles, practice, and predictions. *Journal of the Royal Society of Medicine, 89,* 345P–347P.

Oléron, P. (1953). Conceptual thinking of the deaf. *American Annals of the Deaf, 98,* 304–310.

Oller, D. K., & Eilers, R. E. (1988). The role of audition in infant babbling. *Child Development, 59,* 441–449.

Oller, D. K., Eilers, R. E., Bull, D. H., & Carney, A. E. (1985). Prespeech vocalizations of a deaf infant: A comparison with normal metaphonological development. *Journal of Speech and Hearing Research, 28,* 47–63.

Ottem, E. (1980). An analysis of cognitive studies with deaf subjects. *American Annals of the Deaf, 125,* 564–575.

Owston, R. D. (1997). The World Wide Web: A technology to enhance teaching and learning? *Educational Researcher, 27,* 27–33.

Paatsch, L. E., Blamey, P. J., & Sarant, J. Z. (2001). The effects of articulation training on the production of trained and untrained phonemes in conversations and formal tests. *Journal of Deaf Studies and Deaf Education. 6,* 32–42.

Padden, C. (1991). The acquisition of fingerspelling by deaf children. In P. Siple & S. Fischer (Eds.), *Theoretical issues in language for search, Volume 2: Psychology* (pp. 191–210). Chicago: University of Chicago Press.

Padden, C. A., & Hanson, V. L. (2000). Search for the missing link: The development of skilled reading in deaf children. In K. Emmorey and H. Lane (Eds.), *The signs of language revisited* (pp. 435–448). Mahwah, NJ: Lawrence Erlbaum Associates.

Padden, C., & Humphries, T. (1988). *Deaf in America: Voices from a culture.* Cambridge, MA: Harvard University Press.

Padden, C. & Ramsey, C. (1998). Reading ability in signing deaf children? *Topics in Language Disorders, 18,* (4), 30–46.

Pagliaro, C. M. (1998). Mathematics reform in the education of deaf and hard of hearing students. *American Annals of the Deaf, 143,* 22–28.

Panara, R. F., Denis, T. B., & McFarlane, J. H. (1960). *The silent muse: An anthology of prose and poetry by the deaf.* Washington, DC : Gallaudet College Alumni Association.

Parasnis, I., & Samar, V. J. (1985). Parafoveal attention in congenitally deaf and hearing young adults. *Brain and Cognition, 4,* 313–327.

Parasnis, I., Samar, V. J., Bettger, J. G., & Sathe, K. (1996). Does deafness lead to enhancement of visual spatial cognition in children? Negative evidence from deaf nonsigners. *Journal of Deaf Studies and Deaf Education, 1,* 145–152.

Patrick, J. J., & Hawke, S. D. (1982). Curriculum materials. In I. Morrissett (Ed.), *Social studies in the 1980s* (pp. 39–50). Alexandria, VA: Association for Supervision and Curriculum Development.

Paul, P. (1998). *Literacy and deafness: The development of reading, writing, and literate thought.* Boston: Allyn and Bacon.

Perfetti, C., & Sendak, R. (2000). Reading optimally builds on spoken language: Implications for deaf readers. *Journal of Deaf Studies and Deaf Education, 5,* 32–50.

Petitto, L. A. (1987). On the autonomy of language and gesture: Evidence from the acquisition of personal pronouns in American Sign Language. *Cognition, 27,* 1–52.

Petitto, L. A., & Marentette, P. (1991). Babbling in the manual mode: Evidence for the ontogeny of language. *Science, 251,* 1493–1496

Pettingill, B. D. (1874). The acquisition of written language by deaf-mutes. *American Annals of the Deaf, 19,* 230–237.

Pickersgill, M. & Gregory, S. (1998). *Sign Bilingualism: A Model.* Wembley, Middlesex, A LASER publication. (Publication No. 004239)

Pintner, R. & Patterson, D. (1917). A comparison of deaf and hearing children in visual memory for digits. *Journal of Experimental Psychology, 2,* 76–88.

Poizner, H., Bellugi, U., & Tweney, R. D. (1981). Processing of formational, semantic and iconic information in American Sign Language. *Journal of Experimental Psychology: Human Perception and Performance, 7,* 1146–1159.

Pollard, R. Q. Jr. (1996). Conceptualizing and conducting the pre-operative psychological assessments of cochlear implant candidates. *Journal of Deaf Studies and Deaf Education, 1,* 16–28.

Pollard, R. Q. Jr. (1998). Psychpathology. In M. Marschark & M. D. Clark (Eds.), *Psychological perspectives on deafness, Volume 2* (pp. 171–197). Mahwah, NJ: Lawrence Erlbaum Associates.

Pollard, R. Q., & Rendon, M. (1999). Mixed deaf-hearing families: Maximizing benefits and minimizing risks. *Journal of Deaf Studies and Deaf Education, 4,* 156–161.

Power, D. J., & Hyde, M. B. (1997). Multisensory and unisensory approaches to communicating with deaf children. *European Journal of Psychology and Education, 12,* 449–464.

Power, D., & Leigh, G. (2000). Principles and practices of literacy development for deaf learners: A historical overview. *Journal of Deaf Studies and Deaf Education, 5*, 3–8.

Powers, G. W., & Saskiewicz, J. (1998). A comparison study of educational involvement of hearing parents of deaf and hearing children of elementary school age. *American Annals of the Deaf, 143*, 35–39.

Preisler, G. M., & Ahlstroem, M. (1997). Sign language for hard of hearing children—A hindrance or a benefit for their development? *European Journal of Psychology of Education, 2*, 465–477.

Pressley, M. (1998). *Reading instruction that works: The case for balanced teaching.* New York: Guildford Press.

Pressman, L. J., Pipp-Siegel, S., Yoshinaga-Itano, C., & Deas, A. (1999). Maternal sensitivity predicts language gained in preschool children who are deaf and hard of hearing. *Journal of Deaf Studies and Deaf Education, 4*, 294–304.

Quigley, S., & King, C. (Eds.). (1982). *Reading milestones.* Beaverton, OR: Dormac.

Quigley, S. P., & Paul, P. V. (1984). *Language and deafness.* San Diego, CA: College Hill Press.

Quigley, S., Wilbur, R., Power, D., Montanelli, D., & Steinkamp, M. (1976). *Syntactic structure in the language of deaf children.* Urbana, IL: University of Illinois, Institute for Child Behavior and Development.

Quittner, A. L., Smith, L. B., Osberger, M. J., Mitchell, T. V., & Katz, D. B. (1994). The impact of audition on the development of visual attention. *Psychological Science, 5*, 347–353.

Rawlings, B. W., & Jensema, C. J. (1977). *Two studies of the families of hearing impaired children.* Washington, DC: Office of Demographic Studies, Gallaudet College.

Rea, C. A., Bonvillian, J. D., & Richards, H. C. (1988). Mother-infant interactive behaviors: Impact of maternal deafness. *American Annals of the Deaf, 133*, 317–324.

Rhoton, J., & Bowers, P. (Eds.). (1997). *Issues in science education.* Arlington, VA: National Science Teachers Association.

Richardson, J. T. E., McLeod-Gallinger, J., McKee, B. G., & Long, G. L. (1999). Approaches to studying in deaf and hearing students in higher education. *Journal of Deaf Studies and Deaf Education, 5*, 156–173.

Robbins, A. M., Osberger, M. J., Miyamoto, R. T., & Kessler, K. S. (1995). Language development in young children with cochlear implants. *Advances in Oto-Rhino-Laryngology, 50*, 161–166.

Rodda, M., & Grove, C. (1987). *Language, cognition, and deafness.* Hillsdale, NJ: Lawrence Erlbaum Associates.

Rupp, R. (1998). *The complete home learning sourcebook. The essential resource guide for homeschoolers, parents, and educators covering every subject from arithmetic to zoology.* New York: Three Rivers Press.

Scarr, S. (1998). American child care today. *American Psychologist, 53*, 95–108.

Schein, J. D., & Delk, M. T. (1974). *The deaf population of the United States.* Silver Spring, MD: National Association of the Deaf.

Schick, B. (1997). The effects of discourse genre on English language complexity in school-age deaf students. *Journal of Deaf Studies and Deaf Education, 2*, 234–251.

Schiff, N. B., & Ventry, I. M. (1976). Communication problems in hearing children of deaf parents. *Journal of Speech and Hearing Disorders, 41,* 348–358.

Schildroth, A. N. (1986). Residential schools for deaf students: A decade in review. In A. N. Schildroth & M. A. Karchmer (Eds.), *Deaf children in America* (pp. 83–104). San Diego, CA: College-Hill Press.

Schirmer, B. (2000). *Language and literacy development in children who are deaf,* Second edition. New York: Merrill.

Schlesinger, H. S., & Meadow, K. P. (1972). Development of maturity in deaf children. *Exceptional Children,* 461–467.

Schley, S. (1991). Infant discrimination of gestural classes: Precursors of ASL acquisition. *Sign Language Studies, 72,* 77–296.

Scruggs, T., & Mastropeiri, M. (1996). Teacher perceptions of mainstreaming/ inclusion. *Exceptional Children, 63,* 59–72.

Seal, B. C. (1998). *Best practices in educational interpreting.* Boston: Allyn and Bacon.

Serry, T., & Blamey, P. (1999). A 4-year investigation into phonetic inventory development in young cochlear implant users. *Journal of Speech, Language, and Hearing Research, 42,* 141–154.

Shaughnessy, M. (1977). *Errors and expectations: A guide for the teacher of basic writing.* New York: Oxford University Press.

Sheridan, L. C. (1875). The higher education of deaf-mute women. *American Annals of the Deaf and Dumb, 20,* 248–252.

Shymansky, J., Kyle, W., & Alport, J. (1983). The effects of the new science curricula on student performance. *Journal of Research in Science Teaching, 20,* 397–404.

Siedlecki, T. Jr., & Bonvillian, J. (1993). Location, handshape & movement: Young children's acquisition of the formational aspects of American Sign Language. *Sign Language Studies, 78,* 31–51.

The Silent Worker (1892). *5,* 4.

Simmons, A. (1962). A comparison of the type-token ratio of spoken and written language of deaf children. *Volta Review, 64,* 417–421.

Singleton, J. L., Supalla, S., Litchfield, S., & Schley, S. (1998). From sign to word: Considering modality constraints in ASL/English bilingual education. *Topics in Language Disorders, 18(4),* 16–29.

Siple, P. (1997). Universals, generalizability, in the acquisition of signed language. In M. Marschark, M., Siple, P., Lillo-Martin, D., Campbell, R. & Everhart, V. S., *Relations of language and thought: The view from sign language and deaf children* (pp. 24–61). New York: Oxford University Press.

Sisco, F. H., & Anderson, R. J. (1980). Deaf children's performance on the WISC-R relative to hearing status of parents and child-rearing experiences. *American Annals of the Deaf, 125,* 923–930.

Smith, C. R. (1901). The first two years' work in geography. *American Annals of the Deaf, 46,* 395–409.

Snitzer Reilly, J., & Bellugi, U. (1996). Competition on the face: Affect and language in ASL motherese. *Journal of Child Language, 23,* 219–239.

Spencer, L., Tye-Murray, N., & Tomblin, J. B. (1998). The production of English inflectional morphology, speech production and listening performance in children with cochlear implants. *Ear and Hearing, 19,* 310–318.

Spencer, P. E. (1993a). Communication behaviors of infants with hearing loss and their hearing mothers. *Journal of Speech and Hearing Research, 36,* 311–321.

Spencer, P. E. (1993b). The expressive communication of hearing mothers and deaf infants. *American Annals of the Deaf, 138,* 275–283.

Spencer, P. E. (2000). Looking without listening: Is audition a prerequisite for normal development of visual attention during infancy? *Journal of Deaf Studies and Deaf Education, 5,* 291–302.

Spencer, P. E. (in press). Language development of children with cochlear implants. In J. Christiansen & I. Leigh (Eds.), *Cochlear implants: The dilemma.* Washington, DC: Gallaudet University Press.

Spencer, P. E., Bodner-Johnson, B. A., & Gutfreund, M. K. (1992). Interacting with infants with a hearing loss: What can we learn from mothers who are deaf? *Journal of Early Intervention, 16,* 64–78.

Spencer, P. E., & Deyo, D. A. (1993). Cognitive and social aspects of deaf children's play . In M. Marschark & D. Clark (Eds.), *Psychological perspectives on deafness* (pp. 65–92). Hillsdale, NJ: Lawrence Erlbaum Associates.

Spencer, P. E. & Hafer, J. C. (1998). Play as "window" and "room": Assessing and supporting the cognitive and linguistic development of deaf infants and young children. In M. Marschark & M. D. Clark, (Eds.), *Psychological perspectives on deafness, Volume 2* (pp. 131–152). Hillsdale, NJ: Lawrence Eaulbaum Associates.

Steinberg, A. G., Sullivan, V. J., & Montoya, L. A. (1999). Loneliness and social isolation in the work place for deaf individuals during the transition years: A preliminary investigation. *Journal of Applied Rehabilitation Counseling, 30,* 22–30.

Stedman, L. C. (1994). Incomplete explanations: The case of U.S. performance in the international assessments of education. *Educational Researcher, 23,* 24–32.

Stern, V. W., & Summers, L. (Eds.) (1995). *Resource directory of scientists and engineers with disabilities.* Washington, DC: American Association for the Advancement of Science.

Stewart, D. A. & Kluwin, T. N. (2001). *Teaching deaf and hard of hearing students: content, strategies, and curriculum.* Boston: Allyn and Bacon.

Stinson, M. S., & Lang, H. G. (1994). Full inclusion: A path for integration or isolation? *American Annals of the Deaf, 139,* 156–158.

Stinson, M. S., Eisenberg, S., Horn, C., Larson, J., Levitt, J. & Stuckless, E. R. (1999). Real-time speech-to-text services. In E.R. Stuckless (Ed.), *Reports of the National Task Force on Quality Services in Postsecondary Education of Deaf and Hard of Hearing Students.* Rochester, NY: Northeast Technical Assistance Center.

Stinson, M. S. & Walter, G. (1997). Improving retention for deaf and hard of hearing students: What the research tells us. *Journal of the American Deafness and Rehabilitation Association, 30,* 14–23.

Stoefen-Fisher, J. M. (1985). Reading interests of hearing and hearing-impaired children. *American Annals of the Deaf, 130,* 291–296.

Stokoe, W. C. (1960). Sign language structure: An outline of the visual communication system of the American deaf. *Studies in Linguistics, Occasional Papers 8.* Buffalo, NY: Department of Anthropology and Linguistics, University of Buffalo.

Stokoe, W. C., & Marschark, M. (1999). Signs, gestures, and signs. In L. Messing & R. Campbell (Eds.), *Gesture, speech, and sign* (pp. 161–182). Oxford: Oxford University Press.

Strassman, B. (1997). Metacognition and reading in children who are deaf: A review of the research. *Journal of Deaf Studies and Deaf Education, 2*, 140–149.

Strong, C. J., Clark, T. C., Johnson, D., Watkins, S., Barringer, D. G., & Walden, B. E. (1994). SKI*HI home-based programming for children who are deaf or hard of hearing: Recent research findings. *Infant-Toddler Intervention: The Transdisciplinary Journal, 4*, 25–36.

Strong, M., & Prinz, P. (1997). A study of the relationship between American Sign Language and English literacy. *Journal of Deaf Studies and Deaf Education, 2*, 37–46.

Stuckless, E. R., & Marks, C. (1966). *Assessment of the written language of deaf students.* Cooperative Research Project 2544 (Contract OE-5–10–123). Pittsburgh, PA: School of Education, University of Pittsburgh.

Sunal, D. W., & Burch, D. E. (1982). School science programs for hearing-impaired students. *American Annals of the Deaf, 127*, 411–417.

Supalla, S. (1991). Manually coded English: The modality question in signed language development. In P. Siple & S. Fischer (Eds.), *Theoretical issues in sign language research, Volume 2* (pp. 85–109).Chicago: University of Chicago Press.

Suppes, P. (1974). Computer-assisted instruction for deaf students. *American Annals of the Deaf, 116*, 500–508.

Swisher, V. M. (1984). Signed input of hearing mothers to deaf children. *Language Learning, 34*, 69–85.

Tait, M., & Lutman, M. E. (1994). Comparison of early communicative behavior in deaf children with cochlear implants and was hearing aids. *Ear and Hearing, 15*, 352–361.

Thorton, W. (1793/1903). ADMUS, or a treatise on the elements of written language. *Association Review, 5*, 406–414.

Tiberius, R. (1986). Metaphors underlying the improvement of teaching and learning. *British Journal of Educational Technology, 2*, 144–156.

Tobey, E., Geers, A., & Brenner, C. (1994). Speech production results: speech feature acquisition. *Volta Review, 96*, (5), 109–129.

Todd, P. H. (1976). A case of structural interference across sensory modalities in second-language learning. *Word, 27*, 102–118.

Todman, J., & Cowdy, N. (1993). Processing of visual-action codes by deaf and hearing children: Coding orientation or *M*-capacity? *Intelligence, 17*, 237–250.

Todman, J., & Seedhouse , E. (1994). Visual-action code processing by deaf and hearing children. *Language and Cognitive Processes, 9*, 129–141.

Tomblin, J. B., Spencer, L., Flock, S., Tyler, R., & Gantz, B. (1999). A comparison of language achievement in children with cochlear implants and children using hearing aids. *Journal of Speech, Language, and Hearing Research, 42*, 497–511.

Tomlinson-Keasey, C., Kelly, R. R. & Burton, J. K. (1978). Hemispheric changes in information processing during development. *Developmental Psychology, 14*, 214–223.

Traxler, C. B. (2000). Measuring up to performance standards in reading and mathematics: Achievement of selected deaf and hard-of-hearing students in the national norming of the 9th Edition Stanford Achievement Test. *Journal of Deaf Studies and Deaf Education*, 5, 337–348.

Treiman & Hirsh-Pasek. (1983). Silent reading: Insights from second–generation on deaf readers. *Cognitive Psychology*, 15, 39–65.

Turner, W. W. (1851). High school for the deaf and dumb. *American Annals of the Deaf*, 4, 41–48.

Tweney, R. D., Hoemann, H. W., & Andrews, C. E. (1975). Semantic organization in deaf and hearing subjects. *Journal of Psycholinguistic Research*, 4, 61–73.

Tye-Murray, N., & Kirk. (1993). Vowel and diphthong production by young users of cochlear implants and the relationship between the Phonetic Level Evaluation and spontaneous speech. *Journal of Speech and Hearing Research*, 36, 488–502.

Ulissi, S. M., Brice, P. J., & Gibbins, S. (1990). Use of the Kaufman-Assessment Battery for Children with the hearing impaired. *American Annals of the Deaf*, 135, 283–287.

Vaccari, C., & Marschark, M. (1997). Communication between parents and deaf children: Implications for social-emotional development. *Journal of Child Psychology and Psychiatry*, 38, 793–802.

Van Cleve, J. V. (Ed.). (1993). *Deaf history unveiled: Interpretations from the new scholarship*. Washington, DC: Gallaudet University Press.

Vandell, D. L., & George, L. B. (1981). Social interaction in hearing and deaf preschoolers: Successes and failures in initiations. *Child Development*, 52, 627–635.

Vermeulen, A. M., Beijk, C. M., Brokx, J. P., van den Borne, S., & van den Broek, P. (1995). Development of speech perception abilities of profoundly deaf children: A comparison between children with cochlear implants and those with conventional hearing aids. *Annals of Otolaryngology, Rhinology, and Laryngology Supplement*, 166, 215–217.

Vernon & Andrews, (1990). *The psychology of deafness*. White Plains, NY: Longman.

Volterra, V., & Erting, C. J. (1990). *From gesture to language in hearing and deaf children*. Berlin: Springer-Verlag.

Volterra, V., & Iverson, J. (1995). When do modality factors affect the course of language acquisition? In K. Emmorey & J. Snitzer Reilly (Eds.), *Language, gesture, and space* (pp. 371–390). Hillsdale, NJ: Lawrence Erlbaum Associates.

Wahlsten, D., & Gottlieb, G. (1997). The invalid separation effects of nature and nurture: Lessons from animal experimentation. In R. Sternberg & E. Grigorenko (Eds.), *Intelligence, heredity, and environment* (pp. 163–192). New York: Cambridge University Press.

Wallis, J. (1851). Extract from Dr. Wallis. *American Annals of the Deaf*, 3, 227–233.

Walter, G. (1978). Lexical abilities of hearing and hearing-impaired children. *American Annals of the Deaf*, 123, 976–982.

Waltzman, S., Cohen, N. Gomolin, R., Green, J., Shapiro, W., Brackett, D., & Zara, C. (1997). Perception and production results in children implanted between 2 and 5 years of age. *Advances in Oto-Rhino-Laryngology*, 52, 177–180.

Waters, G. S. & Doehring, D. G. (1990). Reading acquisition in congenitally deaf children who communicate orally: Insights from an analysis of component reading, language, and memory skills In T. H. Carr & B. A. Levy (Eds.), *Reading and its development.* (pp. 323–373). San Diego, CA: Academic Press.

Weaver, C. (1990). *Understanding whole language: From principles to practice.* Portsmouth, NH: Heinemann.

Weiss, I. R. (1978). *Report of the 1977 national survey of science, mathematics, and social studies education* (National Science Foundation Report SE 78–72). Washington, DC: U.S. Government Printing Office.

Weitbrecht, W. M. (n.d.) *Making the Grade.* Unpublished essay.

Weitbrecht, R. H. Letter to Srnka, J. A. September 23, 1966.

Whitehurst, G. J., & Valdez-Menchaca, M. C. (1988). What is the role of reinforcement in early language acquisition? *Child Development, 59,* 430–440.

Wilbur, R. (1977). An explanation of deaf children's difficulty with certain syntactic structures of English. *Volta Review, 79,* 85–92.

Wilbur, R. (2000). The use of ASL to support the development of English and literacy. *Journal of Deaf Studies and Deaf Education, 5,* 81–104.

Williams, C. M., & Kubis, J. J. (1982). Concerns raised by participants in the Austin Mathematics Symposium. *Directions: Teaching Mathematics. Update on Academic, Professional, Career, and Research Activities, 3,* 46–47. Washington, DC: Gallaudet College.

Winefield, R. (1987). *Never the twain shall meet: Bell, Gallaudet, and the communications debate.* Washington, DC: Gallaudet College Press.

Winston, E. A. (1994). An interpreted education: Inclusion or exclusion? In R. C. Johnson & O. P. Cohen (Eds.), *Implications and complications for deaf students of the full inclusion movement.* (pp. 55–62). Gallaudet Research Institute Occasional Paper 94–2 Washington, DC: Gallaudet University.

Wood, D., Wood, H., Griffith, A., & Howarth, I. (1986). *Teaching and talking with deaf children.* Chichester, UK: Wiley.

Yager, R. E. (1997). Science teacher preparation as a part of systemic reform in the United States. In J. Rhoton & P. Bowers (Eds.), *Issues in science education* (pp. 24–33). Arlington, VA: National Science Teachers Association.

Yore, L. (2000). Enhancing science literacy for all students with embedded reading instruction and writing-to-learn activities. *Journal of Deaf Studies and Deaf Education, 5,* 105–122.

Yore, L. D., Holliday, W. G., & Alvermann, D. E. (Eds.). (1994). The reading–learning–writing connection. *Journal of Research in Science Teaching, 31* (Special Issue).

Yoshinaga-Itano, C. & Snyder, L. (1985). Form and meaning in the written language of hearing-impaired children. *Volta Review, 87,* 75–90.

Yoshinaga-Itano, C., & Stredler-Brown, A. (1992). Learning to communicate: Babies with hearing impairments make their needs known. *Volta Review, 95,* 107–129.

Zweibel, A. (1987). More on the effects of early manual communication on the cognitive development of deaf children. *American Annals of the Deaf, 132,* 16–20.

Author Index

Subject Index